TAIWAN

Taiwan: Manipulation of Ideology and Struggle for Identity chronicles the turbulent relationship between Taiwan and China. This collection of essays aims to provide a critical analysis of the discourses surrounding the identity of Taiwan, its relationship with China, and global debates about Taiwan's situation. Each chapter explores a unique aspect of Taiwan's situation, fundamentally exploring how identity is framed in not only Taiwanese ideology, but in relation to the rest of the world. Focusing on how language is a means to maintaining a discourse of control, *Taiwan: Manipulation of Ideology and Struggle for Identity* delves into how Taiwan is determining its own sense of identity and language in the 21st century.

This book targets researchers and students in discourse analysis, Taiwan studies, Chinese studies, and other subjects in social sciences and political science, as well as intellectuals in the public sphere all over the globe who are interested in the Taiwan issue.

Chris Shei was educated in Taiwan and studied at the Universities of Cambridge and Edinburgh, UK. He has worked at Swansea University, UK, since 2003. He teaches and researches in linguistics and translation and also edits books and online publications across the broad spectrum of Chinese studies, including Chinese politics and governance, Chinese sociology, Chinese history and cultural studies, and so on. He is the General Editor for three Routledge book series: Routledge Studies in Chinese Discourse Analysis, Routledge Studies in Chinese Translation, and Routledge Studies in Chinese Language Teaching (with Der-lin Chao).

Routledge Studies in Chinese Discourse Analysis
Series Editor: Chris Shei, Swansea University, UK

This series aims to examine Chinese discourse from a variety of angles, including linguistic, semiotic, philosophical, sociocultural, literary, political, technological, psychological, and neurocognitive perspectives.

News Framing through English-Chinese Translation
A Comparative Study of Chinese and English Media Discourse
Nancy Xiuzhi Liu

Taiwan
Manipulation of Ideology and Struggle for Identity
Edited by Chris Shei

For more information about this series, please visit: https://www.routledge.com/Routledge-Studies-in-Chinese-Discourse-Analysis/book-series/RSCDA

TAIWAN

Manipulation of Ideology and Struggle for Identity

Edited by Chris Shei

Routledge
Taylor & Francis Group

LONDON AND NEW YORK

First published 2021
by Routledge
2 Park Square, Milton Park, Abingdon, Oxon OX14 4RN

and by Routledge
52 Vanderbilt Avenue, New York, NY 10017

Routledge is an imprint of the Taylor & Francis Group, an informa business

British Library Cataloguing-in-Publication Data
A catalogue record for this book is available from the British Library

Library of Congress Cataloging-in-Publication Data
A catalog record has been requested for this book

ISBN: 9781138485822 (hbk)
ISBN: 9781138485860 (pbk)
ISBN: 9781351047845 (ebk)

Typeset in Times New Roman
by Deanta Global Publishing Services, Chennai, India

To (the memory of):
解鋒標 (1919–1991) 浙江臨海
解陳美玉 (1932–) 台灣高雄

CONTENTS

FIGURES

TABLES

CONTRIBUTORS

Bi-Yu Chang is Deputy Director of the Centre of Taiwan Studies at SOAS, University of London, UK. The central concern of her research is the politics of culture, focusing on the complex interplay between knowledge and power, and the relationship between culture, place, and identity. Her research interests include identity politics, nation-building, cultural governance, and education. In recent years, these research interests have extended to place identity, spatial construction, cartographic representation, and post-war tourism, unpicking the intricate relationship between identity, place, and power. Her monograph *Place, Identity and National Imagination in Postwar Taiwan* was published by Routledge in 2015. She has also co-edited a number of books, including *Positioning Taiwan in a Global Context: Being and Becoming* (with Lin Pei-yin, Routledge 2019) and *Imaging and Imagining Taiwan: Identity representation and cultural politics* (with Henning Klöter, Harrassowitz 2013). Bi-Yu Chang has also been published in a number of international peer-reviewed journals, *Cultural Geographies*; *China Perspectives*; *Studies in Ethnicity and Nationalism*; *NTU Studies in Taiwan Literature*, and in edited volumes including *Connecting Taiwan: Participation – Integration – Impacts* (Routledge 2018) and Cultural Discourse in Taiwan (National Sun Yat-sen University Press 2009).

Pin-ling Chang is Associate Professor at the Department of Applied Linguistics and Language Studies, Chung Yuan Christian University (CYCU), Taiwan. She earned her PhD in translation studies from Newcastle University, UK. Her current research interests range from identity and ideology issues in the past and present practices of translation and interpreting in the Chinese-language world to corpus-based and machine translation studies.

Isabelle Cheng is Senior Lecturer in East Asian and International Development Studies at the School of Area Studies, History, Politics, and Literature of the University of Portsmouth, UK. Her research focuses on migration in East Asia with reference to sovereignty, nation-building, reproduction, and political participation. Her other research interest is the Cold War in East Asia, with regard to necropolitics and soundscape. She is currently the Secretary-General of the European Association of Taiwan Studies.

Yvonne Foley is a Senior Lecturer at the University of Edinburgh, UK. Her research interests are language teacher education, teachers' beliefs and identities, bilingualism, literacy development for pupils learning English as an additional language (EAL), critical literacies, CLIL, and second-language learning and teaching.

Ann Heylen obtained her PhD in Chinese Studies from KU Leuven, Belgium, and is Professor at the Department of Taiwan Culture, Languages and Literature, National Taiwan Normal University (NTNU), Taiwan, and Executive Director of the International Taiwan Studies Center (ITSC), at the College of Liberal Arts, NTNU, Taiwan. She is a founding member of the European Association of Taiwan Studies (EATS) and editor-in-chief of the *East Asian Journal of Popular Culture* (EAJPC, Intellect, UK). Her doctoral dissertation was published as *Japanese Models, Chinese Culture and the Dilemma of Taiwanese Language Reform* (Harrassowitz 2012) and she has published on topics that cover the history and historiography of Taiwan, with special attention to Dutch Formosa, and the Japanese colonial period (1895–1945). She is currently working on a monograph exploring Formosa media narratives as part of a broader project on the relations between the Low Countries and East Asia. annheylen@ntnu.edu.tw

Hui-Lu Khoo, also known as Hui-ju Hsu, is Chair and Professor of the Department of Taiwan Culture, Languages, and Literature, National Taiwan Normal University, Taiwan. Hui-Lu Khoo is the Taigi Romanisation of her name, and Hui-ju Hsu the Mandarin Romanisation. Her research interests include language contact, language variation, and sociolinguistics, particularly of Taigi and Taiwanese Mandarin.

Lutgard Lams is a Professor of Language Pragmatics, Media Discourse Analysis and Intercultural Communication at the KU Leuven Campus Brussels, Belgium. Her areas of scholarly interest include political communication and the pragmatics of language and ideology in media discourse. Given her extensive teaching experience in Taiwan, she focuses on discourses in and about Taiwan and China. She has published various articles on identity politics and nationalism in China and Taiwan, Chinese official discourse, Taiwan electoral campaign discourse, and cross-Strait relations as represented in Chinese/Taiwanese media discourses.

Jill Northcott is Head of English Language for Arts, Humanities, and Social Sciences at the University of Edinburgh, UK. Her research includes language teaching, applied linguistics, discourse analysis, language for specific purposes, and legal English.

Chris Shei was educated in Taiwan and studied at the Universities of Cambridge and Edinburgh before 2000. He then worked at Swansea University, UK, from 2003 until the present. He teaches and researches in linguistics and translation and also edits books and online publications across the broad spectrum of Chinese studies, including Chinese politics and governance, Chinese sociology, Chinese history and cultural studies, and so on. He is the General Editor for three Routledge book series: Routledge Studies in Chinese Discourse Analysis, Routledge Studies in Chinese Translation, and Routledge Studies in Chinese Language Teaching (with Der-lin Chao).

Elina Sinkkonen is Senior Research Fellow at the Finnish Institute of International Affairs. She received her PhD from the Department of Politics and International Relations, University of Oxford, UK. Her research interests include Chinese nationalism, public opinion issues in China, authoritarian regimes, regional security in East Asia, and domestic-foreign policy nexus in IR theory. Sinkkonen is currently conducting a multiyear project on authoritarian resilience, funded by the Kone Foundation. A list of her publications with links can be accessed at www.elinasinkkonen.com.

Edward Vickers is Professor of Comparative Education at Kyushu University, Japan, where he directs the university's inter-disciplinary Taiwan Studies Program. He has published widely on education and identity politics in Hong Kong, Taiwan, and the mainland People's Republic of China, as well as the politics of heritage and public culture across East Asia. His recent works include *Education and Society in Post-Mao China* (2017) and (with Mark Frost and Daniel Schumacher) the volume *Remembering Asia's World War Two* (2019).

Chia-Ying (Annie) Yang is a Teaching Fellow in Language Education at the University of Edinburgh, UK. Her research interest includes language maintenance and shift, language attitudes, language identity, bi-/multi-lingualism, mother tongue education, and translanguaging as pedagogy. In her PhD thesis, she investigated the role of language attitudes in Daighi maintenance in Taiwanese primary school education.

Hsin-Yi Yeh is an Assistant Professor at the Department of Sociology, National Taipei University, Taiwan. She received her PhD in Sociology from Rutgers University (New Brunswick), US. She is interested in collective memory, identity-remembering, political sociology, nationalism, cultural sociology, and cognitive sociology. Her work has been published in journals such as *Qualitative Inquiry*, *Studies in Ethnicity and Nationalism*, *Journal of Public Deliberation*, *Food, Culture, and Society*, *Symbolic Interaction*, and *Memory Studies*.

INTRODUCTION

The Truman Show continues, en masse

Chris Shei

I grew up speaking Taiwanese, a variety of Southern Min, in the 1960s. My father was a mainlander but he learned to speak our language (albeit a heavily accented one) when he migrated to Taiwan with the defeated Chiang Kai-shek army. When I started to learn Mandarin in primary school, I also learned to push my mother tongue into the background. I no longer recall when or how this process started in my school life but I remember Taiwanese being forbidden in the classroom, the speaker either chided or punished. Up to this day, I find it awkward to speak Taiwanese, my mother language, in formal settings or with anyone who did not grow up speaking Taiwanese with me (e.g. my family members) or people who mainly use Southern Min (e.g. 'Taiwanese looking' older people in traditional markets). In tandem with the privileged Mandarin language in society, I also learned about the great Chinese culture, history, geography, and our national heroes such as Sun Yat-sen and Chiang Kai-shek who were enshrined in the textbooks like deities. This continued well into my high school age. When the great 'Grandpa Chiang' died in 1975, everybody in school was given a small piece of black cloth to wear on the upper arm, as is the Chinese custom to show grief and respect at the loss of a loved one for a certain period of time. A vague but genuine feeling of sadness prevailed on campus, more, I think, associated with the death of a national icon planted in our minds over the years than out of inconsolable grief over the loss of a closely related person. Sad we were, however, no matter where that feeling came from. We were taught that Mao Zedong was a bandit and a devil, and Chiang Kai-shek was the saviour of Chinese people (including people who live on both sides of the Taiwan Strait). Only many years later did I realise they were about the same, one no better or worse than the other.

When the KMT nationalist regime started to be challenged by pro-democracy activists in the 1970s, my reaction was the same as many students who were, in school, encouraged to read a short monograph published by the KMT-owned

Central Daily News in 1972 called *The Voice of a Small Citizen*, which mainly condemned student movements and professors who incited those protests. Echoing the author's view, in my heart, I despised those people who disturbed our peace and brought chaos and confusion to society. Again, only many years later did I realise that I knew nothing while making that assumption. I was like a robot with a well-designed thinking pattern and ideology implanted into my mind since childhood. I lived reasonably well under my parents' wings (although they had worked so hard to earn a living and dedicated every cent to their children's education and wellbeing) and I accepted the simple facts stated in textbooks, the contents of which I had to remember in order to pass exams. These facts said that those of us who lived in Taiwan enjoyed a much better life than our mainland counterparts who were led by a group of bandits and suffering from extreme deprivation, waiting eagerly for rescue. When this deeply embedded ideology was challenged (by those gallant freedom fighters of Taiwan in the 1970s and 1980s who I only came to acknowledge later in my life, although, subconsciously, I still find their names and images in the media 'repelling' despite all my later-acquired intellect and better judgements), my internal machinery spontaneously rejected the challenging parties and actions. I even tried writing a letter to the newspaper reiterating the view of *The Voice of a Small Citizen*.

Today, Taiwan is a democratic entity, knowledge and information is no longer manipulated in a top-down fashion, or at least not monopolised by a single party. With a permanently impaired mind, however, I still feel uncomfortable speaking Taiwanese in public. Shame on me not to have taught my children to speak Taiwanese (as I had not consciously rid myself of the acquired impression that Taiwanese was a degraded language not only in school but also in society). I still cannot bring myself to hate Chiang Kai-shek (no more than I subconsciously hate Mao Zedong as taught by a childhood textbook to do so). As my conscious self, I don't really fancy going to the polling station and casting a vote for Taiwan president or members of the parliament/local councils. As with any democratic country, corruption is still inevitable involving both government officials and democratically elected legislators. However, information is flowing freely in Taiwan now and that makes a big difference. Journalists have nothing to fear when they expose a scandal or criticise a government policy. People can speak whatever they like within the boundary of morality and the law (and we are not talking about the 'law' dedicated to protecting the political interests and monopoly of a single party). Today, information is available to everyone in Taiwan in the media and the internet just like any democratic country in the world. Everyone who has a mobile phone or computer can access all sorts of information directly from the source and judge their authenticity and value. This is so different from people who still live in Truman's world and receive mind-engineering education and well-prepared knowledge from schools and society.

Most of my students in the UK pursuing an MA degree in Chinese translation are from China (every now and then there is one from Hong Kong or Taiwan). One of the source texts I used this year for students to translate into English was an excerpt from Gideon Rachman's article *Chinese censorship is spreading beyond its borders*, published in the Financial Times on 14 October 2019. I asked students to write a commentary to accompany the target text which discussed translation problems and strategies and share their thoughts about the content of the text. This year two students surprised me by revealing their disgust in the commentary about the control of speech they were subject to in China's social media and the suppression of oppositions they were aware of. One even felt ashamed about their compatriots' antagonism towards the democratic activities in Hong Kong and their support of one-party rule as a whole. However, these two are very rare exceptions. Over the many years I have worked in the UK, most students from China repeat the same ideology taught in textbooks as a child or absorbed from the heavily censored media as adults, such as Taiwan being a part of China, the KMT (and now DPP) are betrayers of the motherland, the United States is an evil imperialist, China had suffered great humiliations in the past and it was the Party which has lifted the country out of shame and poverty, and anyone challenging the rule of the Party is committing treason against the country. In their commentary, most of my students are proud of their country, approve the governance of the Party, condemn the West (the United States in particular) for not wanting to see a strong China, and echo the official view on social activism and other domestic and international policies. Their unanimous view reminds me of how our minds were conditioned by Chiang Kai-shek's regime after it fled to Taiwan and assumed control. I am awakened now, what with the change of political atmosphere and the transformation of my own mind. But elsewhere *The Truman Show* continues, and Truman's current reincarnations still live in their prefabricated world with a well-designed set and props, well-trained actors, and well-prepared scripts.

This book is a collection of essays concentrating on the issue of Taiwan identity including its political complication and implication, its permeation into language, culture, and ideology, and its involvement in various intellectual and sociopolitical battlegrounds. In Chapter 1, Elina Sinkkonen explains why the issue of Taiwan identity is intrinsically linked to China's identity built on the so-called 'national humiliation narrative' and bolstered by Chinese patriotism and nationalism. Alarmingly, but not at all surprising to me, she found in two surveys that 40% in a first survey and 30% in a second survey of China's top university students were *strongly in favour of* the use of armed force against Taiwan (while 35% in the first survey and 30% in the second *agreed* on the use of force) if it declares independence. In Chapter 2, Hsin-Yi Yeh analyses in great detail the methods used by the KMT government to inculcate a Chinese identity into the young mind of a child after the regime relocated to Taiwan, and how that pre-engineered identity changed over time in three stages corresponding to the change in political environment and aspiration. Following this fascinating account of particular relevance to me, Bi-Yu Chang in Chapter 3 examines the same tools provided by education for 'manufacturing of national identity and citizenship', by comparing several Chinese terms used in Social Studies textbooks, such as *Zhong Guo* and *Zhong Hua, Zhong Hua Min Guo* and *Taiwan*, and *woguo* ('our country'), and so on. She also analyses the change of strategies in imbuing ideology as political climate changes over time. Chapter 4, written by Hui-Lu Khoo, directs the focus towards language as a symbol of national identity where *Taigi* is the preferred Romanised form for Khoo to represent the word 'Taiwanese' alphabetically. In this chapter, Khoo retraces the application of *Taigi* to the creation of a Taiwanese identity throughout the Japanese colonial period, the KMT administration, and the DDP era. Amazingly (and unexpectedly), the new generation of Taiwanese do not favour *Taigi* as a primary tool to express Taiwanese identity (perhaps due to the lamentable fact that many of them were not taught *Taigi* as a mother tongue by parents like myself who were taught to despise *Taigi*); instead, they introduce various Taiwanese elements into their mother tongue, now Mandarin, to create the special flavour of 'Taiwan Mandarin' to assert their Taiwanese identity. Ann Heylen investigates the same issue of language and identity in Chapter 5, using a sociolinguistic approach to assess the situation of standardising *Taiyu* (her preferred Romanised expression, as opposed to Khoo's *Taigi* for the same word and meaning) to support the formation of Taiwanese identity. The model Ann adopts consists of four steps in language standardisation: The selection of norm, its codification, the elaboration of its function, and its acceptance by the community. For each step, she painstakingly explains what Taiwanese intellectuals and organisations have done to facilitate the standardisation of *Taiyu* orthography as part of the endeavour to develop a unique Taiwanese identity. Finally in this thread, in Chapter 6 Chia-Ying Yang and her colleagues explore how *Daighi* (their use for the same word previously appearing as *Taigi* or *Taiyu* in this introduction) has become a marker for Taiwanese identity and how *Daighi* teachers they interviewed connect the language to Taiwan's cultural heritage and ethnic and national identity.

In Chapter 7, with Lutgard Lams, we begin the next leg of our journey where a divided Taiwan comes into view as ideological clashes broke out between the pro-unification (KMT) and the pro-independence (DDP) parties on Taiwan's English-language newspapers. Apart from finding Taiwan to be a mature democracy where government policy is openly debated in the press, Lutgard Lams presents her 'partisan press landscape in Taiwan' where the KMT-owned English-language newspaper highlights the advantages of cooperating with China in economic and cultural aspects; while the DPP-oriented newspapers are more concerned about Taiwanese identity and sovereignty. Next, in Chapter 8, Pin-ling Chang uncovers another ideological clash erupting on the translation battlefield. Specifically, she analyses two translations of Peter Hessler's *River Town*, one from China and the other from a Taiwanese translator. The perception of political and social realities is shown to be strikingly different across the Strait, and the discursive strategies used in translation to foreground national identity are clearly presented by the author. Penultimately, Edward Vickers in Chapter 9 recounts the epic tale of Koxinga (aka Zheng Cheng Gong, or 'the general who received his surname from the emperor'), who led the final resistance army against the Manchu invasion of China's Ming Dynasty. Posthumously, over the generations and across the three regions of China, Taiwan, and Japan, Koxinga's spirit and legacy has been continually celebrated as a national hero, ancestral deity, or a tourist attraction. In Japan, the birthplace of Koxinga at Hirado became an arena for commemorative efforts from both Taiwan and China. In China, he is officially commended for liberating Taiwan from Dutch occupation and returning the island to the bosom of the motherland. In Taiwan, Koxinga's celebration is more multifaceted and can change over time as Taiwan's identity and mainstream ideology change. A likely current interpretation is the potential links he provides to connect Taiwan to the wider world. This takes us to the final chapter of the book, where Isabelle Cheng, in Chapter 10, presents a globalised and multi-ethnic Taiwan, where migrant women from Vietnam, Indonesia, and the Philippines do their best in the so-called 'linguistic borderland', utilising every linguistic resource they have access to, to perform their public and private duties for the benefits of themselves, the community, their families, and, in particular, their children. This chapter shows, among other things, how Taiwan has become a cosmopolitan polity to incorporate and integrate multiple ethnicities from neighbouring countries into its ever vibrant and tolerant new identity.

It is not the intention or capacity of this book to offer a comprehensive review of Taiwan's political circumstances, past or present. Instead, the editor and the authors are keen to present the complicated nature of Taiwan's identity and the ideological imposition Taiwanese folks had been subject to as a result of political ambitions and military aggressions from home and abroad. The reason Taiwan's quest for identity is an important one is that people in Taiwan are now able to do so (i.e. to figure out their own identity), rather than passively assume an identity defined by a ruling ideology. Like Truman, Taiwanese people were brave enough to break away from the insidious design of the show and venture into the unknown world. Come what may, they are now free men and women, enjoying democracy and freedom of speech. Hopefully, *The Truman Show* will end for all people in the world one day. To contribute to that vision, this book brings together ten essays that, together, explain how an autocracy can supress opposition both by force and by mind control, how Taiwan's democratic transition has enabled its quest for a more dignified and cosmopolitan identity, and how this vibrant new entity is still in danger of being subjugated by a regional hegemon.

1

THE ROLE OF THE TAIWAN QUESTION IN CHINESE NATIONAL IDENTITY CONSTRUCTION

Elina Sinkkonen

In the 1990s and 2000s, China's national identity discourse revolved around the themes of national humiliation and China's rise. For many Chinese, national division from Taiwan is the last symbol of national humiliation. The domestic discourses of China's rise and its victim mentality are essential in understanding China's complicated relationship with the outside world. They also bear relevance with regards to the Taiwan issue. If China could unify with Taiwan, it would finally get rid of its divided country syndrome, which would improve its status and increase legitimacy of the Chinese Communist Party (CCP).

This chapter analyses Taiwan's role in Chinese national identity by examining the dynamic relationship of territory and national identity and the ways in which the emotional connection to territory is constructed. After presenting theoretical premises on national identity construction, the chapter looks at the evolving meaning of Taiwan's separation in China's wider domestic and international political contexts and ends with a section on what elite university survey data reveals on perceptions of the Taiwan issue in mainland China.

On national identity and territoriality

National identities are social and shared identities among those who feel they belong to the same nation. Identity defines the relationship between entities in a manner that asserts a certain degree of sameness (Wodak et al. 2009: 11). The idea of 'community of sentiment' or 'imagined community' is central in the definition of national identity, thus the first part of the definition of national identity utilised emphasises the belief of belonging to the same group (Anderson 1991). Montserrat Guibernau (2007: 11) defines national identity as 'a collective sentiment based upon the belief of belonging to the same nation and sharing most of the attributes that make it distinct from other nations'. The second part of the definition links nation and state. National identity is the relationship between nation and state that obtains when the people of that nation identify with the state (Dittmer and Kim 1993: 13). This identification to state is socially constructed. To create the nexus between the nation with which people identify, and the state, politics often play an important role. The way the content of national identity is presented in the official sphere including the education system and the media frames people's perceptions.

In addition to in-group coherence, national identity construction includes border drawing in the form of 'othering'. National identity defines the limits of in-group and out-group and thus, includes relational comparisons. Identities are ontologically dependent on the existence of other identities and identity involves the creation of boundaries that separate the self from the other (Abdelal et al. 2009: 19, 23–24; Billig 1995: 61; Citrin and Sears 2009; Guibernau 2007: 11; Neumann 1996; Wodak et al. 2009: 2; Woodwell 2007: 13). This boundary drawing brings in the international perspective, as national identities are not pre-social but constructed in the international reality in relation to other national identities, and the international system of nation-states is the precondition of the existence of any national identity (Giddens 1987: 171; Wendt 1999). In national identity formation there are necessarily multiple 'others' with which the 'self' or 'selves' are in constant interaction. Some 'others' may be more important at times, and their importance may vary according to the issue area. As a certain amount of in-group cohesion is necessary for a functioning society and especially for social mobilisation, slandering out-groups can be used as a strategy in order to increase in-group cohesion when it is otherwise hard to acquire. According to David Campbell (1998: 70), the intensity of discourses on danger and threats increases when the cohesion and clarity of identity decreases.

In more practical terms, factors increasing in-group identification include cultural and historical issues, shared values and norms, as well as territorial space. Cultural factors such as common myths play an important role in national identity (Smith 1998, 2009). Constitutive norms refer to the formal and informal rules that define group membership. Identities also have a temporal aspect to them. The emergence of national identities is a historically located phenomenon, thus the contemporary forms of national identities should not be treated without acknowledging their historical roots. The temporal aspect of national identity highlights its changing character and continuity over time, as well as the importance of historical roots (Guibernau 1996: 131, 2007: 10). National identity also has a future orientation, so it does not only refer to the past (Guibernau 2007: 10; Wodak et al. 2009: 26). Members of a nation are connected by common goals such as increasing national wealth, obtaining symbolic recognition, or increasing influence in the international community.

Territorial space or homeland is a crucial part of national identity construction as national identity cannot be conceived without a territorial ideology (Kaplan and Herb 2011). Territory is a basic requirement in organising other attributes that form a specific identity (Greenfield 1992). It marks the differentiation between internal and external. David Kaplan and Guntram Herb (1999: 10) argue that bounded space or territory make visible tensions between power and identity and territoriality has become increasingly important due to the modern international system of nation-states. Sovereign political power in the post-Westphalian world of nation-states is almost exclusively defined and exercised territorially as there cannot be a state without a demarcated territory. Territorial sovereignty anchors the nation among other nation-states in the international system (Herb 1999).

For national identity, territory provides tangible evidence of the nation's existence and its historical roots. Yet territory's importance is not limited to the material aspect of boundary drawing. Rather, the interaction between nation and space forms a 'discursive landscape' (Häkli 1999: 123–126). Felt connection with the homeland is acquired via educational policies and in many countries, people gain knowledge on territorial issues only through media and education (Guibernau 2007: 21). When there is a strong emotional connection between the people and their national space, losing part of the national territory evokes strong reactions in the public. There are some divided nations which build their core national narratives on the trauma of being divided and the common goal of reuniting the motherland. China and the two Koreas are East Asian examples of such divided countries.

Territorial disputes, loss aversion, and war proneness

Maintaining the territory controlled by the nation 'is the goal of the nationalist mission' (Kaplan and Herb 1999: 2). There is ample research on nationalism and how nationalist discourses tend to frame questions related to territory. Framing is essential in shaping people's perceptions: Prospect theory holds that the majority of people will choose the risky option when it is framed in terms of avoiding losses, whereas they would be risk-averse if the options are framed in terms of gaining. Fear of losing or ending up in a worse situation in comparison to the status quo evokes higher activity levels than possible gains. Unfortunately, greater efforts to avoid losses often lead to even greater losses (Tversky and Kahneman 1986). Robert Jervis (1992) has analysed the political implications of loss aversion and found that wars are triggered by the fear of losing because leaders are risk-acceptant for losses rather than gains. This is not only because leaders themselves may suffer from loss aversion fallacy, but rather that they will have to deal with publics that suffer from it.

Loss aversion could also partly explain why rivalries caused by a territorial dispute increase war proneness more than other types of rivalries (Vasquez and Leskiw 2001): Territory and national borders are so concrete that if borders move in a way that diminishes a national area, it is very hard for policymakers to frame things as anything other than a loss. Still, territorial disputes can be on different levels of severity: A link between domestic politics and territorial dispute tends to signify increased tensions (Nakano 2016: 167) and political leaders can often influence at least to a degree how the connection between domestic politics and territorial dispute is built. In analysing the practical implications of loss aversion in the context of territorial disputes and national identity construction, it is essential to understand the benchmark from which gains or losses will be evaluated. What is the 'status quo' in the eyes of the different parties of the dispute? Where and when did it emerge on all parties involved?

The People's Republic of China (PRC), the United States, and Japan have all directly or indirectly expressed that they would be prepared to use force in the Taiwan issue if deemed necessary. Taiwan was separated from China and ceded to Japan by the Treaty of Shimonoseki, which concluded the First Sino-Japanese War in 1895. From 1895 Taiwan was under Japanese rule until the Kuomintang came in 1945. After the Chinese Civil War, which ended in 1949, the Kuomintang stayed in Taiwan and Taiwan represented 'China' in the UN until 1971. While Taipei has ceased to state that its government represents the whole of China, the PRC has not given up its claim. Currently Taiwan is one of the few locations in the world most likely to be involved in a major power armed conflict (You 2008: 81). During the Taiwan Strait crisis in 1995–1996 China and the United States were on the verge of military escalation, after which the United States enhanced its military alliance with Japan.

In 2005 China ratified the Anti-Secession Law, which states that China shall use 'non-peaceful means' if Taiwan declares independence (Xinhua 2005). The US support for Taiwan includes military backing and repeated arms sales (Kan 2013). To make matters even more complicated, Japan as a US ally in Asia is also involved in the Taiwan problem due to its geographical proximity to the island and alliance agreement with the United States. Japan's involvement in the Taiwan issue deepened after 1997 because the concept of 'situation in areas surrounding Japan' was added to Japan's security agreement with the United States, officially called the Guidelines for Japan–US Defense Cooperation (Ajemian 1998). In 2015 the security guidelines were further modified increasing the geographical scope of US–Japan security cooperation and making it more likely for Japan's involvement in case of conflict escalation between China and the United States on Taiwan. Chinese leadership tends to perceive that the United States and Japan try to contain China's rise by keeping it divided (Zhao 2004: 282).

In the spring of 2018, the sharp deterioration of US relations with China increased tensions in the Taiwan Strait. In January 2018, the United States passed the Taiwan Travel Act aiming to enhance high-level visits between the United States and Taiwan. Beijing applied stronger language on Taiwan, stating that the US travel bill risks war (Xinhua 2018). Oral statements were backed with military showoffs when China's aircraft carrier Liaoning passed the Taiwan Strait accompanied by some 40 ships and submarines in March 2018 (Grossman 2018). In April 2018, the United States agreed to sell Taiwan necessary technologies for building its own submarines (Zheng 2018). On 1 January 2019, in his first speech on Taiwan as president, Xi Jinping reiterated that unification must be the ultimate goal of cross-Strait relations. In April 2019, the People's Liberation Army (PLA)

Air Force conducted drills involving fighters, bombers, and reconnaissance planes to threaten Taiwan (Lin 2019).

Evolution of Chinese national identity

From the establishment of the People's Republic of China, national unification has been its foreign policy aim. While China's goal can thus be regarded as stable, the relative weight given to accomplishing it has evolved greatly over the years. The Taiwan issue is a concrete reminder of the past issues that have not been resolved and plays an important role in Chinese national identity.

According to Frank Hsiao and Lawrence Sullivan (1979: 464), China's earliest known claim to recover Taiwan came on 6 October 1942, when Chiang Kai-shek met US Presidential Representative Wendell Willkie (Hsiao and Sullivan 1979: 464). Yet Taiwan has not always been a central part of China's national identity construction; rather, its relative importance has evolved along with changes in Chinese domestic dynamics and its relations with the outside world. According to Christopher Hughes (1997: 15–16), events such as the PRC–US rapprochement taking place in the 1970s significantly influenced China's approach and made Taiwan gradually more important. Mentions of Taiwan's 'liberation' in the PRC constitution support this interpretation as the first mention was in the preamble to the March 1978 version (Hughes 1997: 15–16). The latest edition of the 1982 constitution (Chinese Government 1982/2018) states in its preamble: 'Taiwan is part of the sacred territory of the People's Republic of China. It is the inviolable duty of all Chinese people, including our compatriots in Taiwan, to accomplish the great task of reunifying the motherland'.

The Taiwan question grew in importance due to China's emerging national identity crisis. In the late 1970s China's reform and opening up policies dramatically changed the official approach to the outside world and created a need for redefinition of China's identity. Years of radical Maoism were in the past, but there was uncertainty about the alternative. China's adaptation to the post-Mao era in the late 1970s and early 1980s has sometimes been described as a national identity crisis (Brady 2012: 58). When Deng Xiaoping made reunification with Taiwan one of the main tasks for the CCP in the 1980s, he linked the issue with the integrity of the PRC's own international status and the stability of CCP rule, considerably raising the stakes in the Taiwan issue (Hughes 1997: 15–16).

The collapse of the Cold War system and the end of the Soviet Union, the Tiananmen massacre, huge economic growth in the 1990s, and the decreasing ideological value of communism as the legitimisation of the Communist Party's leadership all affected Chinese people and made them rethink their national identity. Some locate the main identity crisis to the early 1990s, arguing that the economic transition towards a capitalist economy generated a pair of identity crises in the PRC: A national identity crisis, caused by being one of the few remaining socialist countries in the world, and a Party identity crisis, due to the weakening public support (Law 2006: 607). Since the early 1990s there has been a strong need to find something to bind Chinese society together and it is often thought that a unified national identity could serve that purpose.

One reaction to the national identity crisis in the 1990s was the rise of the so-called national humiliation narrative, which also contributed to repositioning the Taiwan issue. The so-called 'century of national humiliation' period (*bainian guochi*, 百年国耻) refers to a period from the Opium Wars in 1840 to the establishment of the People's Republic of China in 1949, during which China's position in the international system was weak and it was forced to open up to the outside world causing a strong feeling of victimhood (Mitter 2003: 211–213; Wang 2012: 7–8). While the so-called humiliation narrative has long roots – in the early 20th century the Chinese adopted a carnivalesque stance to national humiliation and celebrated it – a discursive shift in the 1990s indicated changes in national identity dynamics (Callahan 2004, 2010).

Taiwan is linked to the humiliation narrative as its separation from the mainland happened during the century of national humiliation. In the narrative promoted by the CCP, China was able to overcome the century of national humiliation because of the Party, who should also be thanked for the long economic boom which started after the reform and opening up period (1978) and transformed the way of living for most Chinese (Chinese Government 2011). Furthermore, traumatic experiences resulting from Japan's invasion in the 1930s help in highlighting China's moral legitimacy within international society, as China has suffered from its portrayal as an outlier in the Western dominated international system (Suzuki 2007).

A shift in national identity discourse in the 1990s resulted in a nationwide patriotic education campaign, which utilised China's humiliating experiences in the hands of foreign powers, offered one CCP-dictated version for how to love China, and tended to stir up anti-Japanese sentiments. Educating Chinese schoolchildren from kindergartens to universities on national unity and Taiwan is also part of the patriotic education. The 2019 Outline for Implementing Patriotic Education in the New Era mentions strengthening practical education on the 'one country, two systems' as one of the goals of patriotic education and continues that this thinking should be applied to people living in Hong Kong, Macao, or Taiwan (Central Committee of the Communist Party of China 2019). Through patriotic education and other political campaigns, the CCP further links its own legitimacy with the reunification goal.

The rise of the humiliation discourse has not been the only change in China's national identity dynamics. Along with China's economic growth, discourse on its rise became more prominent leading to further soul searching with strong links to China's international position. China has a history of being an ancient civilisation, and the early advances of this civilisation form a source of pride. In the Chinese discussion, China's rise is often referred to by the terms 'revitalisation' (*fuxing*, 复兴) or 'rejuvenation' (*zhenxing*, 振兴), which emphasise the perspective that China's position as a great power is nothing new and the current rise is actually more of a return. This brings a degree of entitlement to the current circumstances (Medeiros 2009: 7–9). In China's 2015 Military Strategy, unification with Taiwan was clearly linked with Xi Jinping's regime's goal of national rejuvenation, which the regime aims to reach by 2049. The paper states that Taiwan's reunification with China is 'inevitable in the course of national rejuvenation'.

Keeping Taiwan within China continues to be seen as crucial for the CCP's legitimacy from various perspectives (Zheng 2008). In December 2010 Dai Bingguo, the then state councillor for external relations, stated that China's core interests (*hexin liyi*, 核心利益) were first, stability of the political system and socialism with Chinese characteristics; second, sovereign security, territorial integrity, and national unification; and third, China's sustainable economic and social development (Dai 2010). The Taiwan issue is relevant with regards to all of these core interests. Although Taiwan's road to democracy has been far from easy (Mattlin 2011), Taiwan's democratic political system undermines the CCP's claim that democracy suits only Western countries whereas the Chinese system is suitable for Chinese conditions (Brady 2015), endangering the stability of China's political system. Furthermore, China's view is that the United States interferes in China's internal affairs by supporting democratic Taiwan against socialist PRC. America's democracy promotion agenda, to which Taiwan belongs, is understood in China as designed to sabotage the Communist Party's leadership (Lieberthal and Wang 2012). Regarding the second core interest, territorial integrity and national unification, Taiwan is not relevant only because of reunification. Taiwan matters also as part of China's wider policy towards autonomous regions. If Taiwan is not unified with the mainland, it could further provoke separatist claims in Tibet, Xinjiang, and possibly elsewhere (Yahuda 2004: 307). Hong Kong's demonstrations in 2019 and 2020 have probably accented these considerations. Such conflict scenarios are not something that would support China's economic development, the third listed core interest.

Surveys

From a Chinese domestic perspective, the Taiwan issue is one of the few topics that unite the Chinese in the post-1989 era (Brady 2008: 102). Unifying the Chinese domestically has been the goal of political communication on the subject. While there are few studies done on the success of these measures or Chinese views on the Taiwan issue in general, based on what we know so far it seems that Chinese views on Taiwan tend to follow the official line (Pan et al. 2017; Sinkkonen 2013; Zheng 1999: 100).

The reason why this is the case is actually more puzzling than one might first think. At least before the Xi Jinping era, while not by any means easy, it was still possible to collect public opinion survey data from China despite the authoritarian political context. Daniela Stockmann et al. (2018) demonstrate that surveys on political trust in China show no significant respondent bias; in other words, respondents have not been afraid to respond truthfully. Earlier research shows that Chinese respondents differ a great deal in their views on, for example, protectionist economic policies, the role of international organisations, or preferred foreign policy on the United States and Japan (Gries et al. 2011; Sinkkonen 2013, 2014). When we have evidence that Chinese respondents differ in other politically controversial topics, their unanimous views on the Taiwan issue can be seen from a different angle: Fear of expressing one's true views is not likely the defining factor explaining these views.

An established way to contextualise a specific issue attitude within the broader identity framework is to build on core values (Hurwitz and Peffley 1987, 1990). The core values approach defines a set of poles around which opinions might be based, that is, people attach importance to certain issue-specific attitudes because of the links these issues have with their core values. The list of potential core values is enormous, which is why in studies linking core values and specific attitudes, it is necessary to define which core values matter most in the issue area under scrutiny (Alvarez and Brehm 2002: 1–12). There also needs to be a certain level of issue-specific knowledge to make links with values in the first place. People can gain issue-specific knowledge via many means, perhaps the most important sources being educational institutions and the media. In some issues such as threat perceptions, media content has been found to be a decisive factor in differentiating Chinese respondents' views on the United States and Japan (Sinkkonen and Elovainio 2020). China's patriotic education policy, discussed above, has made sure that no Chinese person can be ignorant of the Taiwan issue and we can expect Chinese respondents to be familiar with this topic.

Nationalism and patriotism as part of Chinese national identity represent core values most relevant regarding the Taiwan issue. This chapter treats 'nationalism' and 'patriotism' as attitudinal clusters following Rick Kosterman and Seymour Fechbach (1989). In the survey research presented below, 'nationalism' is defined as a view that one's country is superior to other countries and that provides for uncritical support of the home country's actions; 'patriotism', on the other hand, is defined as a feeling of pride and emotional attachment to one's country. The key difference between the concepts is that nationalism compares one nation's qualities with those of other nations, whereas patriotism relates only to internal qualities. Earlier research in China has shown that these core values are separate concepts in the Chinese context and differently associated with issue attitudes. Moreover, nationalism tends to have a stronger association with foreign policy linked statements in comparison to patriotism (Gries at al. 2011; Sinkkonen 2013, 2014).

Core values and their association with views on Taiwanese independence presented below are based on two elite university student surveys conducted in China. The first survey was collected together with Julie Tomaszewski in Renmin University of China, Peking University, and Tsinghua University between April and June 2007 (N = 1346). I conducted the second sample (N = 771) in Shanghai Jiaotong University, Fudan University, Nanjing University, and Zhejiang University in November and December 2011, and in Renmin University of China, Peking University, and Tsinghua University in March 2012. Except for Renmin University of China, these universities belong to the C9 league (*jiuxiao lianmeng*, 九校联盟) of Chinese top universities. These universities were chosen because of their prestige and the likelihood that the students would assume leading roles in society after graduating. Other scholars have selected these same universities as sampling sites for similar reasons (Chen 2011; Zhao 2003: 11). As the samples were taken from elite universities, the results cannot be directly generalised to all Chinese students, not to mention the general population compared to which the participants were much more educated and younger.

The questionnaire used in the research was a modified version of the ISSP (International Social Survey Program) National Identity II questionnaire, which is an international standardised questionnaire used in 34 countries in 2003. As National Identity II questionnaires had not previously been used in China, some cultural adjustments were needed. The Taiwanese ISSP 2003 National Identity questionnaire was an important reference in making the adjustments. For the second sample, the questionnaire was changed to include elements from questionnaires used by Peter Gries et al. (2011) and Gregory Fairbrother (2008).

Owing to the political sensitivity of the research topic, both surveys were conducted as convenience samples in the university lecture halls used for studying when no teaching is going on.[1] To see whether the 2007 student sample resembled the entire student population in the selected universities, we need to compare the student profile of the sample with that of the student body at the three universities. Based on a *China Daily* article, we know that, in 2006, 20% of Tsinghua University's undergraduates were Party members, as were half of the graduate students (China Daily 2006). In our Tsinghua sample approximately 17% of undergraduates and 51% of graduate students were Party members. The 2007 edition of Tsinghua University's yearbook shows that in 2006, 6.5% of all students belonged to one of the ethnic minorities (Tsinghua University 2008: 536). In our sample the percentage of students from ethnic minorities was 5.5%. Also, in 2005, the percentage of female students at Beijing University was 45.2%; in our Beijing University sample, the percentage of female students was 47.3% (Liu and Wang 2009: 37). Based on this information, the make-up of the sampled students resembled that of the entire student population at Tsinghua University and at Beijing University. The 2011–2012 sample was collected from seven different universities, which makes it harder to compare the samples with the student populations in the respective institutions as each sample is smaller. However, the 2011–2012 samples cover a wider range of universities and are not only limited to Beijing, which is also valuable.

Sample characteristics of the first sample

In the 2007 data, the response rate was approximately 95% and we obtained 1346 valid responses. Of these 1270 (94.4%) were collected by Julie Tomaszewski and the author and 76 (5.6%) by Chinese students. The possible effect of who collected the questionnaire was examined with linear regression models, which showed that who collected the data (ourselves or Chinese students) was not statistically significant regarding any of the statements, which is why no further data is presented here. This indicates that our foreign background did not influence students' responses.

The participants' gender ratio was approximately 50:50 (692 men and 641 women), 21% were from Tsinghua University (N = 275), 32% from Peking University (N = 419), 38% from Renmin University of China (N = 507), and 9% from other universities (N = 129).[2] The respondents had studied on average for 3 years (ranging from 1 to 7 years), 270 (21%) of them were members of the CCP, 34% had applied or were planning to apply for membership, and 590 (45%) were not members. Most of the students were studying technology-related majors (N = 522, 39%) and economics (22.5%). Of the participants 233 (18%) had grown up in the countryside, 515 (39%) in a town or small city, 279 (21%) in a medium-sized city, and the rest (N = 282, 21.5%) had had an urban upbringing. 577 respondents (44%) reported that at least one of their parents had higher education (*gaodeng jiaoyu*, 高等教育) and they classified their own social status as, on average, 5.8 on a ten-point scale (from 10 low to 1 high). Their ethnic background was most often Han Chinese (N = 1231, 93%), whereas 91 respondents (7%) classified themselves as belonging to an ethnic minority.

Sample characteristics of the second sample

For the 2011–2012 sample the possible effect of the collector's foreign background was not tested, as I assume the conditions were similar enough to those in 2007. The response rate of the latter sample was approximately 93% and we obtained 771 valid responses. The participants' gender ratio was approximately 56:44 (416 men and 325 women); 14% were from Fudan University (N = 94), 14% from Shanghai Jiaotong University (N = 94), 15% from Nanjing University (N = 104), 21% from Zhejiang University (N = 142), 8% were from Tsinghua University (N = 76), 11% from Peking University (N = 76), 9% from Renmin University of China (N = 63), and 8% from other universities (N = 51).[3] Twelve per cent of respondents refused to report their home institution (N = 96). The respondents were on average 21 years old (ranging from 17 to 34 years), 182 (25%) of them were members of the CCP or probationary members, 205 (28%) had applied or were planning to apply for membership, and 347 (47%) were not members. Most of the students were studying engineering (N = 140, 19%) and economics (N = 101, 14%). Of the participants 131 (18%) had grown up in the countryside, 306 (42%) in a town or small city, 150 (20%) in a medium-sized city, and the rest (N = 151, 21%) had had an urban upbringing. 269 respondents (37%) reported that their father had university education and 212 (29%) that their mother had university education. Respondents classified their own social status on average 5.7 on a ten-point scale (from 10 low to 1 high). Their ethnic background was most often Han Chinese (N = 695, 93%), whereas 48 respondents (7%) classified themselves as belonging to an ethnic minority.

Measures: Nationalism and patriotism

In the 2007 survey nationalism and patriotism were both measured using three items and participants responded to these items on a five-point Likert scale from

5 ('strongly agree') to 1 ('strongly disagree'). Statement two on the patriotism scale was measured on a scale in which 4 indicated 'very close' and 1 'not close at all'. Statement 3 on the patriotism scale also had a four-item scale from 4 ('very proud') to 1 ('not proud at all'). All of these statements are modifications of the Taiwanese version of the 2003 ISSP National Identity II questionnaire. Eldad Davidov (2009), Kosterman and Feshbach (1989: 263–264), Gries et al. (2011), Fairbrother (2008), and Wenfang Tang and Benjamin Darr (2012) have used similar statements to measure nationalism and patriotism.

The items in the 2007 nationalism scale were:

1. The world would be a better place if people from other countries were more like the Chinese.
2. Generally speaking, China is a better country than most other countries.
3. People should support their country even if the country is in the wrong.

The items in the 2007 patriotism scale were:

1. How proud are you of being Chinese?
2. How close do you feel with China?
3. I am often less proud of China than I would like to be. (Reverse coded.)

The items in the 2011–2012 nationalism scale were:

1. China's policy decisions are almost always right.
2. China is the best country in the world.
3. The world would be a better place if people from other countries were more like the Chinese.
4. I support my country whether its policies are right or wrong.
5. I think that the Chinese people are the finest people in the world.
6. Chinese foreign policies are almost always morally correct.
7. Generally speaking, China is a better country compared to most other countries.

The items in the 2011–2012 patriotism scale were:

1. I am glad to be Chinese.
2. I am very proud to be Chinese.
3. I love my country.
4. I often regret that I am Chinese. (Reverse coded.)
5. Being Chinese is an important reflection of who I am.
6. I would like personally to help my country attain its goals.
7. How close do you feel to the following? – China.

Analysis

The associations of nationalism and patriotism on foreign policy attitudes, and the contribution of potential other explanatory factors to the relationship between

TABLE 1.1 The associations of nationalism and patriotism with Taiwanese independence*

	If the province of Taiwan declares independence, China should use military force against Taiwan. (Both datasets)					
	STD-Beta		t-value		p-value	
Adjusted for						
1. None						
Nationalism	0.14	0.15	4.73	3.73	<0.001	<0.001
Patriotism	0.16	0.11	5.44	2.72	<0.001	0.01
2. Gender						
Nationalism	0.12	0.14	4.35	3.15	<0.001	0.002
Patriotism	0.17	0.11	5.88	2.60	<0.001	0.01
3. Gender and all other potential explanatory factors						
Nationalism	0.12	0.14	4.14	3.06	<0.001	0.002
Patriotism	0.17	0.11	5.88	2.56	<0.001	0.01
R2	0.08	0.07				

*Adjusted for gender as well as gender and all other potential explanatory factors: University in which the respondent was studying, field of study, years studied, parents' educational background, self-assessed societal ranking, place of origin (rural/urban), membership in the Communist Party, and ethnic background. In addition to these background factors, age was also included in the analysis of the 2011–2012 data. The figures are standardised regression coefficients, t-values and p-values. Results from the 2007 data are presented in the left-hand column and figures in italics concern results from the 2011–2012 data.

nationalism, patriotism, and policy attitudes were explored with linear regression models. First, nationalism and patriotism were included; second, gender; and third, gender and all the rest of the potential explanatory factors. The regression analyses for the 2007 data were performed using SAS 9.2 and for the 2011–2012 data SAS 9.3.

In both surveys, nationalism and patriotism were statistically significantly and positively associated with views on Taiwanese independence. These associations were also quite robust to adjustments for all covariates considered. None of the covariates, or their combination, accounted for more than a small portion of the relationship. The linear regression model tested explained a relatively small amount of the variance regarding attitudes on Taiwanese independence (8% in the 2007 sample and 7% in the 2011–2012 sample). These outcomes are complex and multifactorial and it is not expected that these two variables would explain much of their variance.

The Taiwan question unites people who otherwise respond differently from each other. Chinese university students agree with the government that Taiwan should not be allowed to become independent, and these results are consistent with other survey results on the Taiwan issue. In the 2007 data, only 6.8% of respondents were against or strongly against the use of force if Taiwan declared independence.[4] In the 2011–2012 data the percentage of those who were against or strongly against the use of force rose to 16.0%.[5]

There is little other research available to contextualise these results. I have reported the broader findings of the 2007 survey elsewhere and there nationalism had stronger links with foreign policy preferences than patriotism, and 'patriots' and 'nationalists' differed in their views in all other foreign policy statements except for the statement concerning Taiwan. Compared to nationalism, patriotism was associated with more cooperative and internationalist attitudes, whereas nationalistic Chinese supported economic protectionism and a more prominent international stance (Sinkkonen 2013).

According to a telephone survey conducted in ten major cities in China in 2013, respondents' understanding of their regions' economic status influenced their views on preferred Taiwan policy. When Chinese respondents thought the city in which they live is economically more advanced than Taipei City, they tended to support a faster process towards a resolution of the Taiwan issue and the use of military force to resolve cross-Strait confrontations. In other words, the feeling of economic superiority increases willingness to proceed faster and to use military force in solving the situation (Pan et al. 2017: 617). Discourse on China's rise and its great power identity may also be loosely linked with attitudes on Taiwan policy.

Concluding remarks

Over the years, the CCP's legitimacy has been increasingly connected to the Taiwan issue, which has at least in part been a conscious decision. During the past decade, China's great power ambitions and its problematic relations with the United States have tied the issue more to China's great power identity. Furthermore, young Taiwanese people have a strong Taiwanese identity making it increasingly difficult to unify the two Chinas without opposition (Lin 2019). China's harsh actions against demonstrations in Hong Kong or ethnic minorities in Xinjiang do not indicate that its policies on autonomous regions are loosening. While the Covid-19 crisis and economic recession following on from it may delay some policies, it will not bury them forever. If economic recession increases domestic dissatisfaction, there may even be an increased need for using the Taiwan issue to increase domestic unity.

Notes

1 Almost all Chinese university students live in the campus area in dormitories, where four to eight people generally share a room. This makes it almost impossible to study in the dormitory, so the great majority of students study and do their homework in the empty lecture halls between lectures.
2 These students from other universities happened to be at one of the three selected universities when the sampling was done.
3 These students from other universities happened to be at one of the three selected universities when the sampling was done.
4 If Taiwan were to declare independence, 41.2% were strongly in favour of the use of armed force, 35.2% agreed on the use of the army, 16.7% could not decide whether

to use armed force or not, 5.3% were against the use of the military and 1.5% were strongly against the use of armed force in 2007.

5 If Taiwan were to declare independence, 31.3% were strongly in favour of the use of armed force, 29.2% agreed on the use of the army, 23.5% could not decide whether to use the armed force or not, 13.9% were against the use of the military, and 2.1% were strongly against the use of armed force in 2011–2012.

References

English references

Abdelal, R., Herrera, Y.M., Johnston, A.I. and McDermott, R. (2009) 'Identity as a variable', in R. Abdelal, Y.M. Herrera, A.I. Johnston and R. McDermott (eds.) *Measuring Identity: A Guide for Social Scientists*. Cambridge: Cambridge University Press, 17–32.

Ajemian, C. (1998) 'The 1997 U.S.–Japan defense guidelines under the Japanese constitution and their implications for U.S. foreign policy', *The Pacific Rim Law and Policy Journal*, 7(2): 323–350.

Alvarez, M. and Brehm, J. (2002) *Hard Choices, Easy Answers. Values, Information, and American Public Opinion*. Princeton: Princeton University Press.

Anderson, B. (1991) *Imagined Communities: Reflections on the Origins and Spread of Nationalism*. London: Verso.

Billig, M. (1995) *Banal Nationalism*. London: Sage Publications.

Brady, A.-M. (2008) *Marketing Dictatorship: Propaganda and Thought Work in Contemporary China*. Lanham: Rowman and Littlefield Publishers.

Brady, A.-M. (2012) 'The velvet fist in a velvet glove: Political and social control in contemporary China', in A.-M. Brady (ed.) *China's Thought Management*. New York: Routledge.

Brady, A.-M. (2015) 'Unifying the ancestral land: The CCP's 'Taiwan' frames', *The China Quarterly*, 223: 787–806.

Callahan, W. (2004) 'National insecurities: Humiliation, salvation, and Chinese nationalism', *Alternatives*, 29(2): 199–218.

Callahan, W. (2010) *China: The Pessoptimist Nation*. Oxford: Oxford University Press.

Campbell, D. (1998) *Writing Security: United States Foreign Policy and the Politics of Identity*. Minneapolis: University of Minneapolis Press.

Chen, S. (2011) 'Survey study on Chinese university students' perceptions of the political systems of China and the United States', *Chinese Education and Society*, 44(2–3): 13–57.

China Daily (2006) 'Party now has 70.8 members', 1 July 2006. Retrieved from http://www.chinadaily.com.cn/china/2006-07/01/content_630773.htm.

China's Military Strategy (2015). Retrieved from http://english.www.gov.cn/archive/white_paper/2015/05/27/content_281475115610833.htm.

Chinese Government (1982) The Constitution of the People's Republic of China (adopted on December 4, 1982, full text after amendment on March 11, 2018). Retrieved from http://en.pkulaw.cn/display.aspx?cgid=311950&lib=law.

Chinese Government (2011) 'China's peaceful development white paper', September 2011. Retrieved from http://english.gov.cn/official/2011-09/06/content_1941354.htm.

Citrin, J. and Sears, D.O. (2009) 'Balancing national and ethnic identities', in R. Abdelal, Y.M. Herrera, A.I. Johnston and R. McDermott (eds.) *Measuring Identity: A Guide for Social Scientists*. Cambridge: Cambridge University Press, 147–150.

Davidov, E. (2009) 'Measurement equivalence of nationalism and constructive patriotism in the ISSP: 34 countries in a comparative perspective', *Political Analysis*, 17(1): 1–19.

Dittmer, L. and Kim, S.S. (1993) 'In the search of a theory of national identity', in L. Dittmer and S.S. Kim (eds.) *China's Quest for National Identity*. Ithaca: Cornell University Press, 1–31.

Fairbrother, G. (2008) 'Rethinking hegemony and resistance to political education in Mainland China and Hong Kong', *Comparative Education Review*, 52(3): 381–412.

Giddens, A. (1987) *Social Theory and Modern Sociology*. Cambridge: Polity Press.

Greenfeld, L. (1992) *Five Roads to Modernity*. Cambridge: Harvard University Press.

Gries, P., Zhang, Q., Crowson, M. and Cai, H. (2011) 'Patriotism, nationalism, and China's U.S. policy: Structures and consequences of Chinese national identity', *The China Quarterly*, 205: 1–17.

Grossman, D. (2018) 'Beijing's threats against Taiwan are deadly serious', Foreign Policy, 22 May 2018. Retrieved from https://foreignpolicy.com/2018/05/22/beijings-threats-a gainst-taiwan-are-deadly-serious/.

Guibernau, M. (1996) *Nationalisms: The Nation-State and Nationalism in the Twentieth Century*. Cambridge: Polity Press.

Guibernau, M. (2007) *The Identity of Nations*. Cambridge: Polity Press.

Häkli, J. (1999) 'Cultures of demarcation: Territory and national identity in Finland', in D. Kaplan and G. Herb (eds) *Nested Identities: Nationalism, Territory, and Scale*, Lanham: Rowman and Littlefield, 123–149.

Herb, G. (1999) 'National identity and territory', in D. Kaplan and G. Herb (eds.) *Nested Identities: Nationalism, Territory, and Scale*. Lanham: Rowman and Littlefield, 9–30.

Hsiao, F. S. T. and Sullivan, L. R. (1979) 'The Chinese Communist Party and status of Taiwan, 1928–1943', *Pacific Affairs*, 52(3): 446–467.

Hughes, C. (1997) *Taiwan and Chinese Nationalism: National Identity and Status in International Society*. London and New York: Routledge.

Hurwitz, J. and Peffley, M. (1987) 'How are foreign policy attitudes structured? A hierarchical model?' *The American Political Science Review*, 81(4): 1099–1120.

Hurwitz, J. and Peffley, M. (1990) 'Public Images of the Soviet Union: The Impact on Foreign Policy Attitudes', *The Journal of Politics*, 52(1), 3–18.

International Social Survey Programme Data Archive/GESIS Data Archive (2003). 'National Identity survey 2003.' Retrieved from http://www.gesis.org/en/services/data/ survey-data/issp/modules-study-overview/national-identity/2003/.

Jervis, R. (1992) 'Political implications of loss aversion', *Political Psychology* 13(2): 187–204.

Kan, S. (2013) 'Taiwan: Major U.S. arms sales since 1990', *CRS Report for Congress*: 1–58.

Kaplan, D. and Herb, G. (1999) (eds.) *Nested Identities: Nationalism, Territory, and Scale*. Lanham: Rowman and Littlefield.

Kaplan, D. and Herb, G. (2011) 'How geography shapes national identities', *National Identities*, 13(4): 349–360.

Kosterman, R. and Feshbach, S. (1989) 'Toward a measure of patriotic and nationalistic attitudes', *Political Psychology*, 10(2): 257–273.

Law, W.-W. (2006) 'Citizenship, citizenship education, and the state in China in a global age', *Cambridge Journal of Education*, 36(4): 597–628.

Lieberthal, K. and Wang, J. (2012) 'Addressing U.S.-China strategic distrust', John L. Thornton Monograph Series 4, March 2012. Washington: Brookings Institution.

Lin, S. S. (2019) 'Xi Jinping's Taiwan policy and its impact on cross-strait relations', *China Leadership Monitor*, 2 June 2019. Retrieved from https://www.prcleader.org/lin.

Liu, Y. and Wang, Z. (2009) 'Women entering the elite group: A limited progress', *Frontiers of Education in China* 4(1): 27–55.

Mattlin, M. (2011) *Politicized Society: The Long Shadow of Taiwan's One-Party Legacy.* Copenhagen: Nias Press.

Medeiros, E. (2009) *China's International Behaviour: Activism, Opportunism, and Diversification.* Santa Monica: RAND Corporation.

Mitter, R. (2003) 'An uneasy engagement: Chinese ideas of global order and justice in historical perspective', in R. Foot, J. L. Gaddis, and A. Hurrell (eds.) *Order and Justice in International Relations.* Oxford: Oxford University Press, 207–235.

Nakano, R. (2016) 'The Sino-Japanese territorial dispute and threat perception in power transition', *The Pacific Review,* 29(2): 165–186.

Neumann, I. B. (1996) 'Self and other in international relations', *European Journal of International Relations,* 2(2): 139–174.

Pan, H.-H., Wu, W.-C. and Chang, Y.-T. (2017) 'How Chinese citizens perceive cross-strait relations: Survey results from ten major cities in China', *Journal of Contemporary China,* 26(106): 616–631.

Sinkkonen, E. (2013). 'Nationalism, patriotism and foreign policy attitudes among Chinese University Students', *The China Quarterly,* 216: 1045–1063.

Sinkkonen, E. (2014). *Rethinking Chinese national identity. The wider context of foreign policy making during the era of Hu Jintao, 2002–2012.* University of Oxford, Department of Politics and International Relations, DPhil thesis.

Sinkkonen, E. and Elovainio, M. (2020). 'Chinese perceptions of threats from the United States and Japan. Analysis of an Elite University Student Survey', *Political Psychology,* 41(2): 265–282.

Smith, A. (1998) *Nationalism and Modernism: A Critical Survey of Recent Theories of Nations and Nationalism.* London: Routledge.

Smith, A. (2009) *Ethno-symbolism and Nationalism: A Cultural Approach.* London: Routledge.

Stockmann, D., Esarey, A. and Zhang, J. (2018) 'Who is afraid of the Chinese state? Evidence calling into question political fear as an explanation for overreporting of political trust', *Political Psychology,* 39(5): 1105–1121.

Suzuki, S. (2007) 'The importance of 'othering' in China's national identity: Sino-Japanese relations as a stage of identity conflicts', *The Pacific Review,* 20(1): 23–47.

Tang, W. and Darr, B. (2012) 'Chinese nationalism and its political and social origins', *Journal of Contemporary China,* 21(77): 811–826.

Tversky, A. and Kahneman, D. (1986) 'The behavioral foundations of economic theory', *The Journal of Business,* 59(4): 251–278.

Vasquez, J. and Leskiw, C. (2001) 'The origins and war proneness of interstate rivalries', *Annual Review of Political Science,* 4: 295–316.

Wang, Z. (2012) *Never Forget National Humiliation: Historical Memory in Chinese Politics and Foreign Relations.* New York: Columbia University Press.

Wendt, A. (1999) *Social Theory of International Politics.* Cambridge: Cambridge University Press.

Wodak, R., de Cillia, R., Reisigl, M. and Liebhart, K. (2009) *The Discursive Construction of National Identity.* Edinburgh: Edinburgh University Press.

Woodwell, D. (2007) *Nationalism in International Relations.* New York: Palgrave Macmillan.

Xinhua (2018) 'Chinese mainland opposes U.S.–Taiwan travel bill: Spokesperson', 2 March 2018. Retrieved from http://www.xinhuanet.com/english/2018-03/02/c_1370 10759.htm.

Yahuda, M. (2004) *The International Politics of the Asia Pacific*. London: Routledge.

You, J. (2008) 'China's 'new' diplomacy, foreign policy, and defense strategy', in P. Kerr, S. Harris and Y. Qin (eds.) *China's 'New' Diplomacy: Tactical or Fundamental Change?* New York: Palgrave MacMillan, 77–106.

Zhao, D. (2003) 'Nationalism and authoritarianism: Student–government conflicts during the 1999 Beijing student protests', *Asian Perspective*, 27(1): 5–34.

Zhao, S. (2004) *A Nation-State by Construction: Dynamics of Modern Chinese Nationalism.* Stanford: Stanford University Press.

Zheng, S. (2018) 'We need more subs, says Taiwan, as it aims to bolster its naval defences in face of Beijing's increasing belligerence', *South China Morning Post*, 14 July 2018. Retrieved from https://www.scmp.com/news/china/diplomacy-defence/article/21 55280/we-need-more-subs-says-taiwan-it-aims-bolster-its-naval.

Zheng, Y. (1999) *Discovering Chinese Nationalism in China. Modernization, Identity and International Relations*. Cambridge: Cambridge University Press.

Zheng, Y. (2008) 'Anticipating China's future diplomacy: History, theory, and social practice', in P. Kerr, S. Harris, and Y. Qin (eds.) *China's 'New' Diplomacy. Tactical or Fundamental Change?* New York: Palgrave MacMillan, 131–149.

Chinese references

Central Committee of the Communist Party of China 中共中央　国务院印发 (2019) 新时代爱国主义教育实施纲要 (Outline for Implementing Patriotic Education in the New Era). Retrieved from http://www.gov.cn/zhengce/2019-11/12/content_5451352.htm.

Dai, Bingguo 戴秉国 (2010) 坚持走和平发展道路 (Adhering to the road of peaceful development), 7 December 2010. Retrieved from http://www.chinanews.com/gn/2010 /12-07/2704984.shtml.

Tsinghua University 清华大学 (2008) 清华大学年鉴 2007 (2007 Yearbook of Tsinghua University). Beijing: Tsinghua University Press.

Xinhua 新华 (2005) 反分裂国家法 (Anti-Secession Law), 14 March 2005. Retrieved from http://news.xinhuanet.com/newscenter/2005-03/14/content_2694168.htm.

2

REMEMBERED CHINESE-NESS AND ITS DYNAMICS

Analysing the national-remembering in Taiwan after 1949

Hsin-Yi Yeh

Unveiling the bridging techniques employed for inventing a '5,000-year Chinese history' after the 1949 retreat

This chapter examines the Kuomintang (KMT) government's *mnemonic engineering* for the invention of a 5,000-year Chinese national history after the 1949 retreat to Taiwan (Yeh 2015, 2018a,b). I suggest that the KMT's effort is the first wave of nation-building in official nationalism in Taiwan after 1949. However, due to historical particularity, Taiwan has repeated the invention of nation-ness via official nationalism, and each wave of nation-building has tried to lead people to remember a different state of nation-ness (Halbwachs 1992[1925]; Gillis 1994). Since 1949, Taiwan has seen three waves of nation-building (Yeh 2014). The first wave was from 1949 to 1988 (narrating a 5,000-year Chinese history with Taiwan Island playing the part of a 'sacred bastion' to rescue 'Great China' from the 'evil' Chinese Communists); the second wave ran from 1989 to 2008 (narrating a 400-year Taiwanese history with Taiwan as a valid nation in itself); and the third wave started from 2008 (attempting to 'braid' both Chinese and Taiwanese elements into the national history).[1] Each wave of nation-building narrates a distinct national history for people in Taiwan and facilitates a different imagination of nationhood (or, say, 'we-ness').

This chapter mainly focuses on the first wave of nation-building by the KMT government and deals with the second and third waves of nation-building briefly for three reasons.[2] First, the first wave of official nationalism in Taiwan left mnemonic imprints around people's everyday lives in Taiwan; second, since the narration of the national past in the first wave of nation-building is highly institutionalised, the following waves of nation-building treat the first wave as the reference point to compete with and to eradicate and/or reduce its vestiges; third, even today, it is common for the narration of the 5,000-year Chinese history to still exert great influence on people's commemorations in Taiwan.

Based on rich materials derived from various data sources – such as research on memory studies, Taiwanese history and nationality, and related newspaper articles and observations – this chapter has two primary goals. One is to advance understanding of bridging techniques in inventing a historical continuum by illuminating the '5,000-year Chinese history', which is still significant – albeit with various meanings – in today's Taiwan.[3] The other is to validate the constructiveness and selectiveness of collective memories by investigating the case of the KMT after the 1949 retreat.

The 'authentic' descendants of a 5,000-year Chinese history

After being defeated by the Chinese Communists in the Chinese Civil War and retreating from mainland China to Taiwan Island in 1949 with 2 million mainlanders, the KMT government began a wave of nation-building in Taiwan (Fell 2012; Dittmer 2004; Lynch 2004; Rigger 1999; Roy 2003; Rubinstein 2006). By narrating a unilinear historical development, during its initial decades the KMT government aimed at convincing the people of Taiwan in general, and 6 million Islanders (who had lived in Taiwan before 1949) in particular, that they had 'a shared past': The 5,000-year Chinese history. This shared past not only facilitated the imagination of a connected community but also fostered people's vision of a common present and future (Yeh 2018a). By diminishing the moral standing of the Chinese Communists, the unilinear 5,000-year dynasty-succession national history that the KMT government described claimed that, on the one hand, it was the only legitimate ruling party of mainland China and that it was an 'abnormal' and 'temporary' situation that the People's Republic of China (PRC) government had 'stolen' mainland China; on the other hand, people in Taiwan were the 'authentic' descendants of the Great China history, and recovering mainland China was their common and desperate goal. Put simply, the KMT government narrated a 5,000-year Chinese national history for people in Taiwan to weave them into a single commemorative schema and to urge them to envision a shared (bright) future (Zerubavel 1995; Olick 1999; Mische 2009).

The narration of a 5,000-year national history involves a subtle and active sociomental process that engages not only the construction of a 'unilinear' historical development but also the creation of historical continuity which connects what happens on Taiwan Island after 1949 to the unilinear Chinese history. Whereas a unilinear historical development is derived from selecting in certain events and selecting out other events, a collective sense of 'continuity' comes from bridging techniques (Zerubavel 2003). Although all national histories are constructed (Hobsbawm 2009[1990]: 9–13; Anderson 2006[1983]: 141–154), the KMT government nevertheless confronted an extraordinarily tricky situation in retreating to Taiwan in 1949. On the one hand, the KMT government had to make people in Taiwan 'remember' that while more than half of them had never been to mainland China, they were the 'authentic' descendants of Great China and their goal was to 'continue' the 'sacred' 5,000-year Chinese history. On the other hand, the KMT government not only had to 'select out' almost all events – for instance, the repeated colonisation by Spain, Holland, and Japan – which happened on Taiwan Island before 1949, but also had to ignore the fact that the Chinese Communists had already established the PRC government and ruled mainland China after 1949. In short, bridging a unilinear Chinese history required a twin mnemonic process: The creation of both historical continuity and historical discontinuity (Zerubavel 2003; Berger 2006).

Under the narration of a 5,000-year Chinese history, people in Taiwan are expected not only to be proud of their 'superior' (or, say, 'pedigree') status as the 'descendants' of a long-term national history (which can easily 'outpast' most other nations), but also to remember the 'unusual' situation in which the 'evil' PRC government occupied mainland China. In addition, making people in Taiwan become mnemonic members of the 5,000-year Chinese history worked to reduce the collective identity crisis that the KMT government and the 2 million mainlanders faced in 1949: By narrating a shared national history to people in Taiwan, Chinese nationalism led people to remember their 'nostalgia' for mainland China (even when they were born in Taiwan and had never set foot in mainland China).

I suggest that, to enhance the premises of Chinese-centred ideology, the KMT government, as the ruling party in Taiwan for decades after the 1949 retreat, employed various 'bridging' and 'dis-bridging' techniques to connect people in Taiwan and to commemorate that they were 'unmistakably' the 'authentic' descendants of Chinese history.

Various techniques of 'bridging' according to tangibility

As Zerubavel points out (2003), the mnemonic illusion of continuity facilitates our imagination of a 'same' entity (in this case, a Chinese nation) and social actors use various mental bridging techniques to produce the 'connecting historical tissue' that helps us fill any historical gaps between the past and the present. These techniques typically involve some mental editing to produce an illusory quasi-contiguity that can help offset the actual temporal gaps between noncontiguous points in history.

That is, through 'mnemonic pasting', noncontiguous points in time are transformed into an unbroken historical continuum. Following the same logic, during the initial decades after retreating to Taiwan Island, the KMT government employed different 'bridging' techniques to sociomentally 'edit' a 'continuous' Chinese history. While different bridging techniques exist, the techniques that the Chinese Nationalists employ to 'edit' a continuous Chinese history are articulated from the most tangible (place) to the most abstract (narrative and language).[4]

All these mentioned bridging techniques indeed work together to redundantly and repetitively guide people to remember a shared national history of 'us'.

The 'same' place: Bridging noncontiguous points in time by bridging noncontiguous points in place

Whereas constancy of place is a formidable basis for establishing a strong sense of sameness, being defeated in the Chinese Civil War and retreating to Taiwan Island in 1949 resulted in an especially disadvantageous situation for the KMT government; the lack of constancy of place made it difficult to bridge people in Taiwan to the 5,000-year Chinese history. While most national history only has to bridge noncontiguous points in time, due to the retreat, the KMT government had to accomplish one more task: Bridging noncontiguous points (Taiwan Island and mainland China) of place.

The KMT government employed various methods to strategically 'bridge' the two noncontiguous places (Taiwan Island and mainland China). First, by officially renaming streets and roads with the names of Chinese provinces and famous places, Taiwan Island (especially Taipei City) was turned into a miniature of mainland China. Hence, it is intriguing to know that, even if people live on Nanjing Road, they can arrive at their office in Tianjin Street within minutes. To some extent, through 'copying' the places of mainland China and 'pasting' them on Taiwan Island, people in Taiwan can more easily commemorate their 'Chinese' national history. Second, the coastal areas of mainland China are liminal areas that 'bridge' mainland China and Taiwan Island. For instance, Chinese Nationalists argue that most people in Taiwan are immigrants from the coastal areas of mainland China. Moreover, although Taiwanese Islanders lived in Taiwan before 1949, they should nevertheless remember that mainland China is 'unmistakably' their 'motherland'. Third, the KMT government maintained that Taiwan Island is and always has been only one part of mainland China (hence the commemorative, collective goal of people in Taiwan is to recover mainland China, and Taiwan Island is only a bastion). However, to some degree, by claiming that people in Taiwan are the 'authentic' descendants of Great China and that the KMT government is the only legitimate ruling party, Chinese Nationalists ironically employed synecdoche to use Taiwan Island to represent all of mainland China and the 5,000-year Chinese history. Fourth, whereas places in Taiwan Island that are related to mainland China are foregrounded and marked to provide people in Taiwan with 'convincing' evidence that they are connected to the Chinese history, places in Taiwan Island that are related to events before 1949 are backgrounded and unmarked. Places where Chinese officers and heroes have been marked include, for example, Sword Lake, which is where the Chinese hero Cheng dropped his sword, and the places where Chiang Kai-shek (the political leader of the KMT) lived, which are all established as conservation areas for people to commemorate. Last but not least, all of mainland China has been transformed into a sacred place for people in Taiwan. People in Taiwan not only remember that mainland China should be recovered in the future, but also commemorate mainland China as the sacred place of their roots.

By propagandising mainland China as 'the' motherland, Chinese Nationalists skillfully 'bridge' people in Taiwan to mainland China and urge them to collectively remember their nostalgia. Several examples can prove that under this wave of nation-building, mainland China has been turned into a sacred place. First, during this period, on the official national map, not only is mainland China located in the centre and Taiwan Island situated in the marginal corner, but also the shape of mainland China's territory has not been changed to reflect the independence of Mongolia. Two reasons can explain why the KMT government refused to change the shape of mainland China's territory: On the one hand, the independence of Outer Mongolia occurred after 1949, and the KMT government actively selected out those events that happened in mainland China under the 'illegitimate' rule of the PRC government; on the other hand, the shape of mainland China had been turned into a sacred symbol (it was symbolised as a leaf of the Chinese flowering crab apple) and any change to its shape could create problems for the collective memory. Second, for decades after 1949, in the standardised geography textbooks, students were required to memorise every detail of mainland China, such as the distribution of rivers and the specific production of each province.[5] However, the information regarding Taiwan's geographic characteristics was ignored. Third, the representatives of the KMT government would face the orientation of mainland China during national ceremonies and thereby remotely worship the Yan Emperor and Yellow Emperor (the shared ancient ancestors of the 5,000-year Chinese lineage) in Taiwan.

In short, by strategically bridging these noncontiguous points of place, the KMT government overcame its disadvantage of lacking constancy of place. Through the bridging of place, Chinese Nationalism not only provided people in Taiwan with a strong sense of 'sameness' as a Chinese nation, but also went one step further to claim that what happened in mainland China after 1949 was 'invalid' and could not be included in Chinese national history: Only the events that happened in Taiwan Island should be included in the 5,000-year Chinese history (narrated by the KMT government).

Relics and memorabilia: Bridging Chinese history through portable objects

The KMT carried a great number of relics when retreating from mainland China to Taiwan in 1949, and the National Palace Museum (NPM) was established in Taipei in 1961 to exhibit the cultural artefacts of different Chinese dynasties, such as the Sung, Yuan, Ming, and Qing dynasties. These cultural artefacts, as the portable relics of the 5,000-year Chinese history, play a role in 'bridging' people in Taiwan to their national history. Visitors to the NPM may feel that they are entering a time machine and their collective memory of their Chinese national history is being refreshed. What is more intriguing is that the NPM in

Taiwan is not an original; it is claimed to be a 'rebirth' of the Beijing NPM which was established in 1921. In other words, under the logic of Chinese Nationalism, even the Beijing NPM became an illegitimate 'national' museum. The KMT government thus claimed that the Taipei NPM should not be viewed as a reproduction or copycat of the Beijing NPM; rather, it should be considered 'the' NPM after 1949.

Furthermore, the KMT moved precious artefacts from the Beijing NPM to Taiwan in 1949, and the Cultural Revolution in mainland China during the 1960s and 1970s destroyed almost all the cultural artefacts of previous dynasties. Therefore, after Chinese travellers were officially allowed to visit Taiwan in 2008, many Chinese people have eagerly gone to the Taipei NPM to refresh their memory of Chinese history. That is, the extra-economic functions of antiques that Shils mentions in his investigation (1981: 62–73) play a crucial role in bridging people to their national history. Moreover, in Taiwan's case, because the Beijing NPM was emptied, the Taipei NPM became the only place that stores the 5,000-year Chinese history. Hence, Chinese Nationalists find this (that the antiques of previous dynasties can only be found in the Taipei NPM) is another powerful reason to maintain that the people in Taiwan are the 'authentic' descendants of Great China.

Imitation and replication: Bridging Chinese history through repetition and exaggeration

Aside from trying to bridge the past and the present through tangible contact, the KMT government also attempted to use iconic representation to resemble the past. The imitation and replication of the past all too often facilitate an illusory conflation of the present and the past. Therefore, to bridge a 5,000-year Chinese history, it is not surprising to know that Chinese Nationalists insisted on maintaining and replicating certain behaviours and concepts for decades after they retreated to Taiwan. For instance, while they no longer live in mainland China, representatives of the KMT government remotely worship the shared Chinese ancestors. Confucianism is kept intact and people in Taiwan, by and large, still behave according to its precepts. Chinese traditional attire is promoted as an elegant clothing style and even today, people in Taiwan wear traditional clothing on special occasions to show their respect. Most Chinese customs are deemed crucial and non-negotiable and many customs are even officially followed by the government; for instance, the Chinese New Year is one of the most important festivals and many specific, detailed customs should be obeyed. Although mainlanders have lived in Taiwan for decades, they are still proud of the food of their homeland and consume their 'hometown' food regularly. Finally, people in Taiwan write using 'traditional' Chinese instead of simplified Chinese. To put it simply, all Chinese elements were in 'revival' in Taiwan to bring the effect of 'iconic connectedness' once the KMT government was determined to 'temporarily' settle down, and people in Taiwan derived a sense of past-present conflation by repetitively being immersed in Chinese culture and being required to follow it.

It is intriguing to know that when Chinese Nationalists were trying to 'transplant' and 'replicate' Chinese elements in Taiwan, they not only aimed at muting and marginalising the Taiwanese elements (and even the Japanese elements that were left by colonisation) to bridge a 'pure' and 'unilinear' Chinese national history for people in Taiwan, but they also attempted to prove that people in Taiwan were '120% Chinese' by exaggeratedly sticking to traditional and antiquated Chinese customs, behaviours, and concepts.[6] Therefore, while mainland China went through the Cultural Revolution during the 1960s and 1970s and used simplified Chinese in place of traditional Chinese, Chinese Nationalists in Taiwan refused to make any significant adjustments to antiquated customs, behaviours, and concepts. For Chinese Nationalists, after the 1949 retreat, people in China are 'less Chinese' than people in Taiwan and one can only find '120% Chinese' culture and people in Taiwan, not in mainland China.

'Same' time: Creating 'periodic fusion with the past' by establishing an annual cycle of commemorative holidays

Establishing an annual cycle of commemorative holidays is the main function of the calendar that facilitates periodic fusion with the past (Zerubavel 2003: 46). This indicates that historical time is transformed into narrative time, and there is nothing absolutely neutral about the calendrical representation (Bodnar 1992). As Yael Zerubavel puts it, 'The holiday circle determines which aspects of the past become more central to collective memory and which are assigned to oblivion' (1995: 216), and she suggests that the observation of holidays can reveal what aspects of the past are regarded as more crucial and should therefore be commemorated. Also, she goes further to argue that the celebration of holidays all too often facilitates the illusion of historical continuity and 'Their [holidays] celebration thus allows the society to replenish and reshape its memory of the past, while preserving an overall sense of continuity' (1995: 216).

Following the same logic, the KMT government also uses the commemoration of holidays to narrate a 5,000-year Chinese national history and 'bridge' the people in Taiwan to it. Thus, it is hardly surprising to find that each year people in Taiwan celebrate 10 October – which is the date that the founding father of the KMT, Sun Yat-sen, successfully launched a revolution to overthrow the Qing government – as the National Day; moreover, people in Taiwan observe the birth dates and death dates of several 'crucial' Chinese figures and heroes, such as Confucius, Chiang Kai-shek, and Sun Yat-sen. On the contrary, there is no single Taiwanese event or observance of a birth date or death date of Taiwanese figures collectively commemorated under the first wave of national-remembering after 1949. In short, Chinese Nationalism foregrounds and marks the Chinese aspects and events of the development of the KMT (the high commemorative density of the KMT's past); meanwhile, the Taiwanese aspects and events are backgrounded and left unmarked.

Historical analogy: Bridging by finding parallel situations in the past

The 'unfortunate' present, wherein the 'legitimate' ruling party KMT was forced to flee to Taiwan Island and the 'authentic' descendants of Great China must 'temporarily' stay in Taiwan, is linked to the past by historical analogies. The analogies can be with figures, events, and moments. For instance, the revolutions that were launched by the KMT to overthrow the corrupt Qing Dynasty are viewed as similar to the ancient Shangtang Revolution which overthrew the Shia Dynasty around 1600 BC. The spirit of the KMT's founding fathers is viewed as the reappearance of several ancient Chinese figures of nobility such as Guojian, who successfully defeated his immoral enemy after numerous bitter trials. Moreover, the defeated KMT government is generally regarded as the 'new edition' of the Shaokang resurgence (which happened around 1700 BC; although Shaokang was forced to leave his territory and lost his regime, he eventually recovered the Shia Dynasty) and Tiandan Fukuo (which happened around 300 BC and describes Tiandan's strategies to retake his country). Moreover, the decades after the 1949 retreat were analogised to be just as salient as the 'decisive moment' right before the establishment of the Republic Era in 1912. Hence, people in Taiwan were seen as important agents that would bring the 'inevitable' change needed, in this case, to recover mainland China.

Through historical analogies, the thousand-year temporal distance between the present and the past is 'offset' and the historical specificity of events is transcended. These historical analogies not only facilitate the bridging of a 5,000-year national history (the past is invoked by these ancient figures and events), but also express the message that the Chinese Nationalists selectively analogise the present with certain past signifiers: Only the (constructed) positive past events and figures are chosen to be the signifiers of the KMT government's present situation (and the expected bright future).

Discursive continuity: Bridging Chinese history by nominal continuity

The mnemonic significance of nominal continuity (and its effect of bridging the historical gaps) helps explain why the KMT government stubbornly insists on using 'Republic of China' as the official national name, with the words 'Taiwan' and 'Formosa' forbidden to appear in any official document or at any official occasion for an extended period after the 1949 retreat. It is worth noting that for the Chinese Nationalists, the nominal discontinuity was equivalent to announcing the 'end' of the Republic Era, and the implication of the end of the Republic Era meant that the bridged 5,000-year Chinese national history also came to an end. After considering the crucial role that nominal continuity plays in maintaining the 'sameness' of the Chinese nationhood and the continuity of its national history, it seems reasonable to suggest that using 'Republic of China' as the official name actually brought Taiwan to a decades-long stalemate in terms of its diplomatic relations (Fell 2012; Stockton 2008; Wu 2002). Only in recent decades, when the government reluctantly accepted 'Chinese Taipei' as the compromised official name, have international associations allowed Taiwanese representatives to participate in sports competitions and certain apolitical conferences and meetings.

When the Taiwanese Nationalists attempted to challenge the 5,000-year Chinese national history that is narrated by the Chinese Nationalists, their first step was to start the 'Rectification Campaign' in the late 1990s, which claimed to not only reconfigure spaces by renaming streets and parks, but also replaced 'China', 'Republic of China', and 'Taipei' with 'Taiwan' on official documents and in the names of Taiwan-registered organisations, companies, and public enterprises. The aim of the 'Rectification Campaign', which was launched by the Taiwanese Nationalists, is to strategically employ a 'nominal discontinuity' to create the discontinuity of the Chinese national history. Interestingly enough, knowing full well the importance of nominal continuity, the very first thing that the Chinese Nationalists did when the KMT's presidential candidate, Ma Jing-jeou, was elected as the president in 2008 (before that, the KMT had been the opposition party for eight years from 2000 to 2008) and assumed office was to raise a 'New Rectification Campaign'. The main purpose was to replace the term 'Taiwan' with terms such as 'China', 'Republic of China', and 'Taipei' on official documents as well as the names of public enterprises. In short, the official name, 'Republic of China', is regarded by the KMT as an 'unmistakably essential' aspect of maintaining a Chinese national identity and bridging people in Taiwan to the 5,000-year national history.

Another vivid example of how discursive continuity helps to bridge the historical gaps is that when the KMT retreated to Taiwan Island in 1949, the 'year' of the Republic Era was used continuously without any interruption. Therefore, while 1948 is the 37th year of the Republic Era, 1949 is the 38th year and 1950 is the 39th year. In other words, although being defeated by the Chinese Communists in the Chinese Civil War was a great transition (or, say, 'turning point') for the KMT (and the Republic Era), it didn't reflect on the continuous timeline for chronological dating. The 'continuity' of the Republic Era which was established by the KMT through its overthrow of the corrupt Qing government in 1912 is not influenced by the retreat; this implies that the Chinese dynasty succession was not interrupted as a result of the Chinese Civil War. Hence, the continuity in the KMT government's counting of the years of the Republic Era helps to 'bridge' people in Taiwan to the succession of Chinese dynasties.[7]

Two other bridging techniques: 'human bridges' and 'dis-bridging'

Two other bridging techniques mentioned in the previous sections should be briefly discussed here. On the one hand, by employing the 'ethnic myths of descent' to facilitate nation-building, the Chinese Nationalists indeed maintained that people in Taiwan are all descendants of a 5,000-year Chinese bloodline (and the shared ancestors of all Chinese are the Yan Emperor and the Yellow Emperor) and they can, without exception, find their Chinese ancestors by stretching their lineage back. Thus, according to Chinese Nationalism, people in Taiwan can be seen as 'human bridges' who not only 'bridge' their own genealogy but also foster the continuity of the 5,000-year Chinese national history. To put it simply, by narrating Chinese national history as a 5,000-year ancestral line, people in Taiwan are transformed into 'human bridges'; they themselves become the 'bridges' that connect their Chinese national history.

On the other hand, since it is an inevitably twin mnemonic process, when trying to 'bridge' a 5,000-year Chinese national history, people in Taiwan also experienced 'dis-bridging'. Following this logic, 'dis-bridging' can be regarded as one of the 'bridging' techniques. In this case, first, to narrate a 'Chinese' national history, the KMT government had to employ mnemonic decapitation to 'dis-bridge' people in Taiwan from a 'Taiwanese national history': Almost all the Taiwanese events that happened before 1949 are selected out of the narration of the past. Hence, Chinese Nationalism urges people in Taiwan to collectively remember their Chinese nationhood and the linear succession of dynasties and to collectively obliterate the history of Taiwan itself, such as its repeated colonisation. All things about Taiwanese history are downplayed and backgrounded; for example, while the Taipei National Palace Museum exhibits 'an enormous treasure trove of objects inherited from the previous Sung, Yuan, Ming, and Ching dynasties', no single cultural artefact of Taiwan Island was displayed there for a long time after the 1949 retreat. Another striking example of the 'dis-bridging' from Taiwanese history is that not until recently did the annual cycle of commemorative holidays include holidays that commemorate events concerning Taiwan. It wasn't until the second wave of nation-building that national members were encouraged to memorialise elements of Taiwan more; for example, the 228 Incident is now observed annually to commemorate a series of intense conflicts between mainlanders and Islanders from February to May of 1947 (Fleischauer 2007).

Second, to narrate 'a' Chinese national history requires a mnemonic myopia on the part of the Chinese Nationalists to remember a unilinear Chinese national history: Certain past events are deemed 'irrelevant' and are selected out to 'dis-bridge' people in Taiwan from the multi-linear Chinese history. A vivid example is that while the KMT was defeated in the Chinese Civil War and the Chinese Communists occupied mainland China and established the PRC government in 1949, according to the Chinese national history which is narrated by the KMT government in the first wave of nation-building, the PRC government is only an immoral rebellious force and it is just an 'abnormal' and 'temporary' situation that causes the legitimate ruling party of mainland China and the '120% descendants' of Great China to stay on Taiwan Island. That is, the PRC government is marginalised and ignored in the KMT's version of Chinese national history to avoid multiple historical developments. Thus, people in Taiwan collectively remember a unilinear succession of Chinese dynasties that doesn't include the era of the

People's Republic of China (because the latest dynasty is still the 'Republic Era', which was established by the KMT in 1912). That is, the unmistakably multilinear Chinese national history is manipulated into a unilinear history.

Beginning(s), turning points, and the politics behind the process of periodisation

There are many 'small beginnings' in the 5,000-year Chinese history; after all, each Chinese dynasty has a beginning. However, there is only one 'big beginning': The very beginning of Chinese national history starts from the war between the Yellow Emperor (who is then regarded as the shared ancestor of all Chinese people) and Chiyou in about 2696 BC in the 'Legendary Era'. During the war, the Yellow Emperor defeated Chiyou by summoning the Fire Goddess, and the victory of the Yellow Emperor is seen as the triumph of 'Han' ethnicity and the beginning of Chinese history. Although the 'big beginning' indicates a 5,000-year Chinese national history and provides a long-term national history that can easily 'outpast' most other nations, events that happened before 2696 BC are left unmentioned in Chinese history. In other words, by collectively remembering the war between the Yellow Emperor and Chiyou as the beginning of national history, events that occurred before it are not only deemed to be 'irrelevant' but are also seen as 'prehistory', having nothing to do with the national history (Zerubavel 1997: 314–328). Therefore, as Zerubavel puts it, people are inclined to remember 'the beginning as preceded by actual void', and it is the assumed 'prehistorical void' which facilitates the mnemonic decapitation (2003: 93). It is the collective amnesia that leads people in Taiwan to 'bracket' events that happened before 2696 BC, and it is social convention that causes people in Taiwan to commemorate 2696 BC as the big beginning of Chinese national history without feeling it is arbitrary. Figure 2.1 shows the sociomental effect of the narrated big beginning.

In terms of the 'small beginning' of each Chinese dynasty, it seems that we need no less mnemonic manipulation to sociomentally find a 'neat' temporal point to anchor the 'dynastic beginning'. Thus, the dynastic beginnings are actually no less 'arbitrary' than the big beginning of Chinese national history. Taking the Republic Era, for example, while people in Taiwan are inclined to 'remember' the first year of the Republic Era (which is 1912) as the 'beginning', it is not

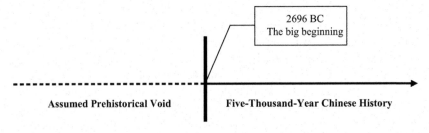

FIGURE 2.1   The mnemonic decapitation of 'prehistory'.

unreasonable to treat the 11th revolution (the Wu Chang Revolution) launched by Sun Yat-sen and his force, which successfully overthrew the Qing government on 10 October 1911, as the 'beginning'. Additionally, it is also possible and reasonable to regard 1928 as the 'beginning' as it was in this year that the KMT eventually ruled over mainland China by defeating all the rebellious forces (Chou 2009): Nevertheless, 1928 is never a candidate for the small beginning.

Whereas the 5,000-year Chinese history has many 'turning points', according to the national history, which is mainly narrated by the KMT government, three turning points are the most important in the national history mnemonic engineering: The beginning of the Republic Era, the retreat to Taiwan Island, and the (expected) recovery of mainland China. In terms of the Republic Era, for Chinese Nationalism, the deeper implication is the beginning of 'modern' Chinese history and the end of the 'pre-modern' Chinese history. The reason that 'the retreat to Taiwan Island' in 1949 is regarded as a crucial turning point in Chinese history is that it represents the concept that Chinese history entered into a 'temporarily' 'abnormal' situation: While it is still the Republic Era, the 'rebellious force' (the Chinese Communists) 'stole' mainland China and the 'legitimate' ruling party, the KMT, had to stay on Taiwan Island. Furthermore, the recovery of mainland China, which is expected, implies that the 'abnormal' situation of Chinese history will end soon and that there is still a bright future in which the '120% Chinese' people can return to their 'motherland' (and Chinese national history can return to its 'normal' condition).

Both the beginning(s) and turning point(s) help to facilitate the sociomental process of periodisation. Therefore, only by collectively commemorating the war between the Yellow Emperor and Chiyou as the starting point of Chinese history can people in Taiwan 'remember' the 'history' and 'prehistory' as two discrete chunks. Also, only by identifying several dynastic beginnings can people in Taiwan commemorate Chinese national history as having different social partitions, such as the Tang Dynasty, Sung Dynasty, Yuan Dynasty, Ming Dynasty, Qing Dynasty, and the Republic Era; these dynasties are remembered to not be 'overlapped' and, thus, there is an 'unmistakably' unilinear dynastic succession in Chinese history. Likewise, without remembering the beginning of the Republic Era in 1912 as one of the turning points in the 5,000-year Chinese national history, people in Taiwan cannot sociomentally compartmentalise the pre-Republic Era as the 'pre-modern' period, and the beginning of the Republic Era implies that Chinese history stepped into the 'modern' time period. Moreover, without identifying the retreat to Taiwan Island in 1949 and the expected recovery of mainland China in the future as two turning points, people in Taiwan cannot regard their 'present' as an 'abnormal' and 'temporary' time period.

The sociomental logic and process behind the periodisation leads us to assign different social meanings to distinct historical periods (Zerubavel 2003; Berger 2006). For instance, it is not uncommon for people in Taiwan to collectively remember the Tang Dynasty as a bellicose dynasty, the Sung Dynasty as a literary dynasty, and the Qing Dynasty as a corrupt dynasty. It is not only the 'interperiodic splitting' but also the 'intraperiodic lumping' that urges people in Taiwan to remember the time periods (e.g. before 2696 BC and after 2696 BC, the pre-Republic Era and after the establishment of the Republic Era, distinct dynasties, before 1949 and after 1949) in the 5,000-year Chinese national history as discrete compartments coloured in different hues. The politics behind the socio-mental process of periodisation works to transform historical time into narrative time, and while the narrative plot seems to divide the national history into chunks, it indeed creates a unilinear national past for people to memorise (and hence to facilitate the national solidarity).

The alternatives: Remembered Taiwan-ness and the braided ones

After close examination, it becomes apparent that we should avoid essentialising the 5,000-year Chinese national history as something 'neutral' or 'inevitable'. Indeed, two alternative national histories of Taiwan exist and each narrates a distinct national history for people in Taiwan (Chou 2009; Chiu 2007).[8] On the one hand, after the first wave of official (Chinese) nationalism which was propagandised by the KMT government and the Chinese Nationalists from 1949 to 1988 came the second wave of official (Taiwanese) nationalism; it was propagandised by the Taiwanese Nationalists from 1989 to 2008 (Chou 2009; Manthorpe 2008). To crack the 'illusion' of a (continuous and unilinear) 5,000-year Chinese national history, the Taiwanese Nationalists narrate a 400-year Taiwanese history as the national history for people in Taiwan (Shi 2005[1962]). Instead of bridging people in Taiwan to selective past events that happened almost exclusively in mainland China before 1949 and regarding what happened on Taiwan Island before 1949 as 'irrelevant', the 400-year Taiwanese history employs ways to 'bridge' people in Taiwan to selective past events that happened exclusively on Taiwan Island and downplays the relation and interactions between mainland China and Taiwan Island. This includes foregrounding the repeated colonisation experiences, encouraging people to speak Taiwanese in public, and promoting the local Taiwanese culture. Therefore, it is not surprising that the 400-year Taiwanese national history employs a distinct 'beginning', different turning points, and an alternative periodisation for the 'Taiwanese' national history.[9]

On the other hand, after 2008, the official nation-building entered a 'braiding' period in mnemonic engineering. No matter whether the Chinese Nationalists controlled the central government (2008–2016) or the Taiwanese Nationalists owned more power by taking the presidential office (since 2016), they knew full well that it is highly improbable (if not impossible) to exclusively narrate a 'pure' Chinese national history or a 'pure' Taiwanese national history due to the specific contexts of Taiwan. The third wave of official nationalism started in May 2008 (when the candidate of the KMT, Ma Ying-jeou, won the presidential election), and it began to narrate an alternative national history which attempts to 'braid' both the Chinese and Taiwanese elements into it. Therefore, Ma's government not only commemorates the 5,000-year Chinese history but to some extent also regards events which happened on Taiwan Island before 1949 as 'relevant'. The reason that some Chinese Nationalists try to narrate an alternative national history which 'braids' the 5,000-year Chinese national history and the 400-year Taiwanese national history is that more and more people in Taiwan have found that a 'pure', 'unilinear' Chinese national history is less and less reasonable for them to memorise collectively. This partially accounted for the KMT's failure in the presidential elections and becoming the opposition party for eight years (2000–2008) (Fell 2012). Therefore, rather than letting people in Taiwan become loyal mnemonic members of the 400-year Taiwanese national history who regard the 5,000-year Chinese national history as irrelevant and treat the recovering of mainland China as questionable and unfulfillable, some Chinese Nationalists prefer to 'braid' the two histories.

Intriguingly, whereas starting from the third wave of nation-building we see mnemonic organisers begin to 'braid' different elements in their mnemonic engineering, they nevertheless downplayed (and even rejected) some facets and layers of the past advocated by the oppositional party. For instance, Ma's government marginalised the establishment of the PRC government after 1949 and the Japanese rule of Taiwan from 1895 to 1945 and, needless to say, put much more emphasis on the Chinese elements instead of other counterparts. Under the same logic, when Taiwanese Nationalists returned to govern the central government (when the candidate of the Democratic Progressive Party (DPP), Tsai Ying-wen, won the presidential election), while they tolerated alternatives and braided elements in their mnemonic engineering, they favoured Taiwanese elements much more. Yet, whereas Tsai's government undoubtedly preferred 'the 400-year Taiwanese history' and wanted to highlight the Taiwanese elements, we still observe braiding in the mnemonic work to be more inclusive with the aim of earning more supporters. For example, the date of the National Day, the nominal continuity of the Republic Era, and even the official name of the country on government-issued passports remain intact.

The mnemonic braiding in both camps caused upset and provoked anger among the hawks in recent decades. Consequently, the extremists in the Taiwanese Nationalism camp left and established their own political parties, and the fundamentalists of Chinese Nationalism quit the party. After all, for the hawks in both camps, on the one hand, tolerating the alternative commemorative narrative and allowing its elements to mix with their own national-remembering equalled acknowledging the alternative identification; on the other hand, the braiding process may have jeopardised the mnemonic engineering. Even though we can observe that the pro-Taiwanese Nationalism forces still cooperate during elections and in specific policy decision-making occasions, and the pro-Chinese Nationalism forces collaborate in these situations also, the disputes and critiques evolving from the mnemonic braiding are evident.

Then, why mnemonic braiding? First, the mnemonic styles influence the tendency to conduct mnemonic braiding. Differing from the first wave's official nationalism (1949 through to 1987), which adopted a zero-tolerance attitude towards any mnemonic alternative, the second wave of official nationalism employed a rather reformative (instead of revolutionary) mnemonic style. Since Taiwanese nationalism experienced suppression for decades, it tends to be habitual to allow blending. Hence, when the Taiwanese nationalists held the central government, they tended to tolerate alternatives while promoting Taiwanese Nationalism mnemonic engineering. Second, to respond to the transformations of societal contexts, the mnemonic engineering had to adjust the mnemonic style and content of master commemorative narratives. Confronting the continuous social changes, the Chinese Nationalists had to include elements that it never mentioned and even alternative narratives. Although, during the first decades after the 1949 retreat, the Chinese nationalists claimed the 5,000-year Chinese history and eliminated the Taiwan elements, with decades of transformations in various levels, the credibility of phrases like 'the present is merely a temporary and abnormal situation', 'the PRC government is a bad branch of Chinese history and will be trimmed in no time', and 'we will recover the mainland China very soon' seems questionable. Facing the challenges from mnemonic enemies, mnemonic braiding maintains its own legitimacy and earns voters' support. Third, with the developmental trajectory of national-remembering in Taiwan and the effects of path-dependency, it is difficult (if not impossible) for the 'returned' Chinese nationalists in 2008 to once again completely deny the Taiwanese elements, and it is difficult for the returning Taiwanese Nationalists in 2016 to totally clean out the Chinese elements as well.[10]

As with all mnemonic engineering, heterogeneous motivations behind mnemonic braiding include rational calculation, identification-maintenance, and habitual-inclination. Of note is that the coexistence of inconsistent (and even contradictory) national-remembering elements has frequently caused ambiguities and disputes have evolved over numerous issues in Taiwan. While these can be regarded as the representations of mnemonic battles between distinct mnemonic engineering, the style of mnemonic braiding may stretch the engineering. Taking the Covid-19 pandemic as an example, whether Taiwan should donate masks to mainland China evoked heated debate. Because of the ambiguous remembered relationship between Taiwan and mainland China, the pro-Taiwan camp suggested that we should save the masks to protect 'our own members', while the pro-Chinese camp called the previous standpoint 'selfish' and said we should lend a hand to whoever needs help. Even though the Chinese Nationalists can no longer formally claim that we should help people in mainland China because 'they are also our national members' or 'the mainland is also our territory', an ambivalent (but rather positive) attitude towards the mainland remains. On the contrary, Taiwanese Nationalists remember a 400-year Taiwanese history which is discontinuous from the Chinese history, so they draw a mnemonic boundary line between Taiwan and the mainland.

In brief, the mnemonic battles on national-remembering continue in Taiwan, and the developmental trajectory of mnemonic engineering after 1949 resulted in coexisting inconsistent and even contradictory elements. As a consequence, people in Taiwan experience ambivalent struggles and sometimes fierce contention between and even within camps.

Concluding remarks

Due to its history, Taiwan is 'an identity laboratory' (Corcuff 2002: 249). Even in today's Taiwan, national identifications cause disputes among people from time to time. Adopting a memory perspective, this article suggests that a memory studies approach can greatly facilitate our understanding of the struggles with Taiwan's national identities. The delineations of national-remembering after 1949 in general and remembered Chinese-ness in particular illuminate how mnemonic engineering guided the people of Taiwan to remember their nation-ness. Focusing more on the mnemonic techniques of bridging, the chapter reveals that the KMT government employed mnemonic work to invent continuity with the preferred lineage and to maintain its own legitimacy.

Nevertheless, the transformation of social contexts caused the dynamics of national-remembering and the contentious mnemonic battles in Taiwan. Whereas the mnemonic braiding seems to be more 'inclusive' and allows the coexistence of heterogeneous elements, the consequence of maintaining the internal consistency of a given mnemonic engineering may ironically cause internal inconsistencies, uncertainties, and discords. Mnemonic battles are no less furious than 'conventional' battles and wars, and the consequences are substantial and influential. For instance, the pro-Taiwan camp and pro-China camp still constitute the two most significant sides in election campaigns and heavily influence people's political stances and decisions in Taiwan. More empirical observations on the national-remembering in Taiwan within and among camps may refine our understandings of this very issue.

Notes

1 The third wave of nation-building should be further divided into two periods. One is from 2008 through to 2016, when Chinese Nationalists regained the central government and, whereas the mnemonic engineering emphasised braiding both Chinese and Taiwanese elements, it nevertheless foregrounded the Chinese elements. The second period began in 2016, when the Taiwanese Nationalists took the office of president once again: While it still works on braiding collective memories, it highlights the Taiwanese element much more than the Chinese element. Only after the second wave of national-remembering do we witness the arrival of braided memories: Because of the developmental trajectory of national-remembering, central governments tend to adopt an ambivalent attitude towards different national remembrances to attract more voters' support.
2 However, it is worth noting that while this article mainly focuses on the first wave of nation-building after 1949, it by no means indicates that the second and third waves of nation formation in Taiwan are any less 'constructive' or employed any fewer mnemonic techniques than the first wave.
3 Admittedly, with waves of nation-building in Taiwan and with the drastic transformations in contexts, people's attitudes towards the '5,000-year Chinese history' changed

and varied in Taiwan. However, it is still worth providing a detailed description of the bridging techniques employed in it.

4 Although it is impossible to exhaust the bridging techniques employed to bridge a 5,000-year Chinese history during this wave of nation-building, this chapter aims to point out significant aspects and provide typical examples.

5 Efforts paid to the de-Sinofication of standardised textbooks can be observed during the second wave of nation-building.

6 Just as Agnes has to act like a '120% female' to prove her gender (Garfinkel 1967: 128–131).

7 According to official Chinese nationalism, the dynastic succession of the 5,000-year Chinese history is the Yellow Emperor, Tang Yu, Xia Dynasty, Shang Dynasty, Zhou Dynasty, Spring and Autumn Period, Warring States Period, Qin Dynasty, Han Dynasty, Three Kingdoms, Wei and Jin Period, Southern and Northern Dynasties, Sui Dynasty, Tang Dynasty, Five Dynasties and Ten Kingdoms, Song Dynasty, Yuan Dynasty, Ming Dynasty, Qing Dynasty, and Republic of China.

8 These two types of alternative national histories are indeed no less 'selective' than the 5,000-year Chinese history: It is the (dis)bridging techniques that lead people to select specific past events into their version of national history and essentialise certain historical developments as 'inevitable' and 'neutral'. The heated mnemonic battles in Taiwan simply come from each of the different parties tending to regard its own historical narrative, which is normally based on its own typically one-sided 'time map', as the only correct one (Zerubavel 2003: 109).

9 The 'beginning' of the 400-year Taiwanese national history is 1624 AD, and before 1624 AD is the 'prehistory' period (thus, events happening before 1624 AD are deemed 'irrelevant'). The 400-year Taiwanese national history is periodised into several time periods: Dutch Formosa (1624–1662), Kingdom of Tungning (1662–1683), Qing Dynasty Rule (1683–1895), Republic of Taiwan (1895), Japanese Rule (1895–1945), and Republic Era (Post-War Taiwan, 1945–present). For Taiwanese Nationalists, the Qing Dynasty rule should be regarded as another experience of being colonised.

10 Although scholars have noticed that more and more people in Taiwan claim to be 'Taiwanese', under the logic of election competition, this is safer to earn more people's support. Internal inconsistency within mnemonic engineering can be found in both Chinese Nationalism's camp and Taiwanese Nationalism's camp.

References

Anderson, Benedict. (2006 [1983]). *Imagined Communities*. London and New York: Verso.

Berger, Stefan (ed.). (2006). *Narrating the Nation*. New York: Berghahn.

Bodnar, John. (1992). *Remaking America: Public Memory, Commemoration, and Patriotism in the Twentieth Century*. Princeton, NJ: Princeton University Press.

Chiu, Kuo-Zhen. (2007). *The Miserable Modern History of Taiwan*. Taipei: Avanguard Press (In Chinese).

Chou, Wan-Yao. (2009). *A Taiwan History*. Taipei: UDN Press (In Chinese).

Corcuff, Stephane (ed.). (2002). *Memories of the Future: National Identity Issues and the Search for a New Taiwan*. New York: M.E. Sharpe.

Dittmer, Lowell. (2004). 'Taiwan and the Issue of National Identity.' *Asian Survey* 44(4): 475–483.

Fell, Dafydd. (2012). *Government and Politics in Taiwan*. London: Routledge.

Fleischauer, Stefan. (2007). 'The 228 Incident and the Taiwan independence movement's construction of a Taiwanese identity'. *China Information*, 21(3): 373–401.

Garfinkel, Harold. (1967). *What is Ethnomethodology? Studies in Ethnomethodology*. Malden: Blackwell Publishers Inc.

Gillis, John R. (1994). 'Memory and identity: The history of a relationship'. In John R. Gillis (ed.) *Commemorations: The Politics of National Identity*. Princeton, NJ: Princeton University Press, pp. 3–26.

Halbwachs, Maurice. (1992 [1925]). *On Collective Memory*. Chicago: University of Chicago Press.

Hobsbawm, Eric J. (2009 [1990]). *Nations and Nationalism Since 1780: Programme, Myth, Reality*. Cambridge: Cambridge University Press.

Lynch, Daniel C. (2004). 'Taiwan's self-conscious nation-building project'. *Asian Survey*, 44(4): 513–533.

Manthorpe, Jonathan. (2008). *Forbidden Nation: A History of Taiwan*. London: Palgrave Macmillan.

Mische, Ann. (2009). 'Projects and possibilities: Researching futures in action'. *Sociological Forum*, 24: 694–704.

Olick, Jeffrey K. (1999). 'Collective memory: The two cultures'. *Sociological Theory*, 17(3): 333–348.

Rigger, Shelley. (1999). *Politics in Taiwan: Voting for Democracy*. London and New York: Routledge.

Roy, Denny. (2003). *Taiwan: A Political History*. Ithaca and London: Cornell University Press.

Rubinstein, Murray A. (2006). *Taiwan: A New History (East Gate Books)*. New York: M.E. Sharpe.

Shi, Ming. (2005 [1962]). *The 400-Year Taiwanese History*. Taipei: Hong Ju Tang Book Co., Ltd. (In Chinese).

Shils, Edward. (1981). *Tradition*. Chicago: The University of Chicago Press.

Stockton, Hans. (2008). 'National identity, international image, and a security dilemma: The case of Taiwan'. In Peter C.Y. Chow (ed.) *The 'One China' Dilemma*, New York: Palgrave Macmillan.

Wu, Rwei-Ren. (2002). 'Toward a pragmatic nationalism: Democratization and Taiwan's passive revolution'. In Stéphane Corcuff (ed.) *Memories of the Future: National Identity Issues and the Search for a New Taiwan*. Armonk, NY: M.E. Sharpe.

Yeh, Hsin-Yi. (2014). 'A sacred bastion? A nation for itself? Or an economic partner of rising china? — Three waves of nation-building in Taiwan (1949–2012)', *Studies in Ethnicity and Nationalism*, (14)1: 207–228.

———. (2015). 'Maintaining and strengthening a shaky regime with mnemonic work: Inventing a Chinese national day from 1949 through 1987 in Taiwan', *Symbolic Interaction*, 38(1): 22–41.

———. (2018a). 'Telling a shared past, present, and future to invent nationality: The commemorative narrative of Chinese-ness from 1949 through 1987 in Taiwan', *Memory Studies*, 11(2): 172–190.

———. (2018b). 'Towards a conceptual framework of identity-remembering: The construction of identification with mnemonic engineering', *Identity: An International Journal of Theory and Research* 18(3): 218–231.

Zerubavel, Eviatar. (1997). *Social Mindscapes: An Invitation to Cognitive Sociology*. Cambridge, MA, London, England: Harvard University Press.

———. (2003). *Time Maps: Collective Memory and the Social Shape of the Past*. Chicago and London: The University of Chicago Press.

Zerubavel, Yael. (1995). *Recovered Roots: Collective Memory and the Making of Israeli National Tradition*. Chicago and London: The University of Chicago Press.

3

RECENTRING THE NATIONAL SELF

The trajectory of national selfhood in *Social Studies* education

Bi-Yu Chang

The national self in textbooks

If affection for and loyalty to one's country are generally taught in childhood, how is a sense of self beyond a child's immediate environment and experience encouraged and guided? It has been widely acknowledged that primary education in particular is crucial in forming national identity and fostering nationalism (Tuan 1977: 158–160; Mohammad-Arif 2005; Lind 2011; Chang 2015). What better tool is there than education to construct an ideal national identity for the next generation methodically and efficiently? Patriotism in education takes many forms – romanticising and inventing the past, glorifying the uniqueness of the people, celebrating the political achievements of the ruling regime, as well as distancing or demonising the enemy. Not only do educational institutions become the primary agents of official knowledge, reproducing dominant values, but they also systematically and effectively consolidate the national self. Within education, textbooks are regarded as particularly powerful 'vehicles through which a government transmits national identity to a country's young people' (Lind 2011: 15). By constructing and extolling the idea of '*my* country', the self-image of the nation is embedded in the knowledge that shapes children's worldviews. This kind of 'banal nationalism' becomes second nature, maintained and practised unconsciously (Billig 1995: 42).

To explore how the national self is portrayed and perceived in Taiwan's primary education, this chapter presents a study of the textbooks used in social studies education, one of the most important instruments of childhood socialisation. Social studies is recognised as the most comprehensive subject in primary education and the key to providing young people with 'the knowledge, skills, and values necessary for active participation in society' (Ross 2006: 17–18). Through a systematic and consistent process, children learn social norms and values, take on social roles, and develop a sense of self, both as an individual and collectively. The study examines 72 volumes of post-war social studies textbooks in order to trace the genealogy of the idea of the national self-image and reveals how social studies education presents a particular vision of the collective 'we'. The investigation concludes with an exploration of the ways in which the collective 'we' has been imagined, represented, and re-centred over the period in question.

The study finds that the change in official national self-image is not just a revisionist move from China to Taiwan. Rather, the changing meaning of 'we' is best understood as a repositioning process, the usage and meanings of various self-references are fluid and contingent. The decentring of China started as early as the late 1960s, triggered by the Cultural Revolution on the mainland and strengthened by growing international isolation. An earlier emphasis on 'where we came from' is replaced, as early as the 1968 curriculum, by a shifting focus, first to 'what we have achieved' and then to 'what we have become', highlighting modernity and liberal-democratic values. In other words, over the period studied, the self-image projected in primary education moves away from the 'historical we' to construct a 'contemporary we' with a different value system and worldview.

Methodology: What to look out for

Students are seldom aware of the linkage between power and knowledge and most children cannot see beyond the official knowledge they are taught. Little wonder then that Althusser (1971: 153–155) calls education the 'number-one' ideological state apparatus (ISA) in his discussion of the reproduction of capitalist relations of exploitation and dominant values. He cautions that the power of education is usually invisible and that dominant values are disseminated discursively and silently. Because education selects and presents certain knowledge before transmission in schools, such selective partial truth appears to the students as the only reality. As Apple points out, schools process people as well as knowledge (2004: 5). Extended and systematic inculcation through compulsory education[1] is particularly influential within an environment that values academic achievement highly and in a period during which education is almost the only opportunity for upward social mobility (except for the privileged). Thus, education provides the perfect platform for the 'manufacturing of national identity and citizenship', guiding the young to form an officially sanctioned worldview and selfhood (Mohammad-Arif 2005).

In understanding how a rooted sense of national identity is fostered from childhood, social studies textbooks are particularly illuminating. As a powerful and silent ISA, the design and content of social studies education is a crucial battleground in the fight for ideological hegemony and political loyalty. Worldwide, social studies were only introduced as a formal subject in the school curriculum in 1916, with an emphasis on the development of citizenship. Since then, the goals, nature, and content of social studies have been contested, with a debate between a social-issue approach that treats the subject as one comprehensive field of study and a more discipline-based approach that combines a cluster of separate disciplines (Ross 2006: 2, 7). The origin and development of social studies education in post-war Taiwan has followed a similar trajectory. The subject, social studies, was first introduced into the Republic of China's (ROC) 1923 curriculum (Sheng 1934: 125).[2] The discipline-based approach was adopted during the early post-war period in Taiwan, dividing social studies into individual subjects such as history and geography for the higher year-group (Year 5 and Year 6). Starting from the 1968 curriculum, the discipline-based approach started to lose ground. It was not until the 1975 curriculum that the social-issue approach became the norm, and all related content merged into one single subject: Social studies. Since then, social studies has been an all-encompassing subject covering everything the state deems children need to be considered good citizens.

Over the years, the content of *Social Studies* was arranged concentrically – teaching children to understand their family, their immediate environment, and basic daily norms in the lower year-group (Years 1 and 2, age 7–8),[3] broadening to understand wider society in the middle year-group (Years 3 and 4, age 9–10), and transmitting more abstract concepts about the nation, history, and geographical knowledge in the higher year-group (Years 5 and 6, age 11–12). Although older children were taught about the country's history and geography, the construction of a sense of we-ness started much earlier than in the explicit patriotic education that older year-groups received. Rather, the idea of a national self and collective we-ness could be inculcated much earlier through different topics and a hidden curriculum.[4]

This chapter examines 72 social studies textbooks published by the semi-official National Institute for Compilation and Translation (NICT)[5] between 1945 and 2000.[6] The list of textbooks examined here includes 12 volumes of *General Studies* (*changshi*)[7] and 60 of *Social Studies* (*shehui*):

Post-1945 version
    Chinese and General Studies (*Guoyu Changshi*). Taipei: NICT. [8 volumes; Year 1–Year 4]
1952 version
    General Studies (*Changshi*). Taipei: NICT. [4 volumes; Year 3–Year 4]
1962 version
    Social Studies (*Shehui*). Taipei: NICT. [4 volumes; Year 3–Year 4]
1968 version
    Social Studies. Taipei: NICT. [8 volumes; Year 3–Year 6]
1975 version
    Social Studies (1st ed.). Taipei: NICT. [12 volumes; Year 1–Year 6]
    Social Studies (2nd ed.). Taipei: NICT. [12 volumes; Year 1–Year 6]
    Social Studies (3rd ed.). Taipei: NICT. [12 volumes; Year 1–Year 6]
1993 version
    Social Studies. Taipei: NICT. [12 volumes; Year 1–Year 6]

To reveal the sometimes ambiguous and contradictory nature and implications of the national self, the study selects five keywords commonly used to index or point to an image of the national self in post-war Taiwan's social studies textbooks. The five self-references are: *Zhongguo* (China), *Zhonghua* (Chinese or China), *Zhonghua minguo* (Republic of China, ROC), *Taiwan* (Taiwan), and *woguo* (my/our country). The study also considers a few related alternatives – such as *dalu* (the mainland), *jiaxian* (hometown), and *baodao* (precious island) to see which other options might describe similar ideas. Combing through the 72 textbooks and mapping out their usages, this chapter explores the ways in which these terms are employed to construct a national narrative and reveals the changing trajectory of the national self-projection.

Another important factor to consider is the curriculum version, because curriculum revisions are often part of educational transformations, which are both a result and symptom of social change (Durkheim 2006: 166). There were seven (i.e. the two post-1945 versions,[8] 1952, 1962, 1968, 1975, and 1993) curricula during this period. Thus, the frequency and the scale of Taiwan's curriculum revisions have reflected the drastic political and social changes closely. For example, the 1975 curriculum went through two revisions, first in 1985 and again in 1989,[9] in order to respond to the major political and social transformation.

A sense of 'we-ness' in textbooks

An examination of the terms that index the national self throughout the textbooks reveals that these keywords are used strategically and in specific ways with varying frequencies during different periods. They are used in conjunction to construct a clear image of an ideal national self and to contrast between 'superior we' and 'inferior they'. In deploying various self-referencing terms, the ROC national rhetoric is written and rewritten, while a very different 'we-ness' emerges during different periods.

Before delving into the textbooks, it is important to sketch out the ways in which these keywords are employed. Without doubt, both *Zhonghua minguo* and *Taiwan* are the least ambiguous terms. The former is the name of a state that was established in 1911. It is used in the textbooks as an official self-reference, and sometimes taken as synonymous with the Kuomintang (KMT) regime; the latter literally refers to the geographical region of Taiwan. The mention of Taiwan in the early textbooks is often associated with its history (from a Han Chinese perspective), its geographical characteristics, and its status as a Chinese province. Taiwan becomes important after the 1968 curriculum when a more superior sense of 'we' emerges in contrast to the inferior other, or the 'contaminated mainland'. During the mid- to late 1980s, the once marginalised Taiwan subjectivity shifts to the centre. Taking Taiwan as the core of national self, *Zhongguo* is shifted to the periphery.

The term *Zhongguo* is similar to but different from the term *Zhonghua*. Literally, *Zhongguo* means 'the middle kingdom' or 'central state' emphasising its pivotal position and importance, while *Zhonghua* suggests 'the magnificence in the centre', extolling the brilliance of Chinese culture and the Han Chinese. In Taiwan's textbooks, the term *Zhongguo* represents many aspects of China – the various states and dynasties throughout its history, the geographical region, a generic idea, and a political entity. In comparison, the term *Zhonghua* carries a broader and more general association of China and is often used as an adjective to describe its people (*Zhonghua minzu*)[10] and culture (*zhonghua wenhua*). In other words, *Zhongguo* indexes history and geography, while *Zhonghua* indexes cultural heritage. The most versatile term is *woguo*, or sometimes simply *women de* (our/ours). This self-referencing term could easily replace other keywords under all political climates. Consequently, it is the most useful and used phrase throughout the period examined.

The following sections explore the different functions and characteristics of the terms in pairs.

Zhongguo *and* Zhonghua

Although similar, the two terms *Zhongguo* and *Zhonghua* have different implications. The former is mostly used in lessons about Chinese history and geography, while the latter is associated with cultural excellence and Han superiority. They are both important self-references, especially in early curricula, for students to identify with and be proud of.

One of the most common usages of *Zhongguo* in the earlier textbooks is to celebrate the 'greatness of China', for instance, '*Zhongguo* is a great country…and the No. 1 most populous country in the world' (*SS* 1968 VI: 63).[11] The concentration of such an approach in the early post-war years reflects an official suspicion towards the Taiwanese about their supposed ideological enslavement by the Japanese. Post-war education, therefore, aimed to indoctrinate a Chinese national awareness and educate the Taiwanese to 'become' Chinese again (Chen and Chen 1989: 93–98, 221–231). Little wonder then that China's brief emergence from the ashes onto the world stage to become one of the victorious Big Four (Kimball 1991) after WWII is constantly emphasised and reiterated. Such lessons proudly announce that China was 'the first democratic republic in Asia' (*SS* 1968 VII: 37, 44), and 'one of the four superpowers in the world after winning the anti-Japanese war, on a par with the US, the UK and Russia' (*SS* 1968 VII: 67). Being one of the 'world's four great powers' (*GS* post-1945 VII: 27; *SS* 1968 IV: 57), China is then described as the 'leading hegemon in East Asia' (*GS* post-1945 VII: 17, 27). By extolling a powerful China, social studies education in the early post-war years prepared Taiwanese children to get to know their 'motherland', to develop pride in being part of China after the Japanese surrender, and to learn to be Chinese.

This term also plays an important role in constructing a narrative of national suffering to arouse patriotic fervour and indignation. In a lesson entitled 'National Trauma', children learn about imperialist aggression against China, the destruction and humiliation of China's ancient civilisation, and the ensuing Communist upheaval in modern Chinese history. Many lessons describe ceaseless assaults by the British, the French, and the Russians. Facing invasion and attack from all sides, *Zhongguo* becomes a victim 'besieged and encroached on…[suffering from] unrelenting imperialist offensive' (*SS* 1968 VII: 19). Foreign encroachment on territory and sovereignty is compared to a massive pair of pliers squeezing the country and 'forcing all doors into *Zhongguo* open…the international status of *Zhongguo* collapsed as a result' (*SS* 1968 VII: 22–26; *SS* 1975 [2nd ed.] XI: 16–23).[12] To lament the trauma and learn lessons from the century-old disgrace, the textbooks teach students about the shame and humiliation of colonial invasion. A stark contrast is made between the old fallen empire, humiliated for centuries, and the powerful new republic that rose from the ashes to win international respect. Both emphases are designed to stir up patriotic feeling and indignation against external aggressors such as Taiwan's previous occupier, Japan, and also to encourage students to be proud of a rising [Nationalist] China, accept their ROC identity, and strive to build a 'new China' (*xin Zhongguo*) free from colonial invasion (*GS* 1952 III: 33; *SS* 1962 I: 58; ibid. II: 70; ibid. IV: 76; *SS* 1968 IV: 55, 69; ibid. XI: 71; *SS* 1975 [2nd ed.] VIII: 140).

Since the ROC authorities had always insisted on their political legitimacy to represent the whole of China, one would expect to see the term *Zhongguo* more widely used to stake ownership. Yet surprisingly, the term does not appear as frequently as one might expect. After the initial tribute to a glorious Chinese past and its greatness in the world, the use of this term soon becomes problematic. The trouble seems to stem from its ambiguity. The political separation and ensuing discursive struggle between the two Chinese regimes after 1949 make any reference to *Zhongguo* confusing. For example, to which *Zhongguo* does this refer? Does it mean the Chinese government, and if so, is it the ROC or the PRC (People's Republic of China)?[13] Does it mean 'the whole of China' or the 'Chinese mainland'? Does it mean a general idea about 'China' or communist-controlled China today? The ambiguity of the term and the impossibility of removing any association with the PRC makes it difficult to avoid confusion and risks attaching positive associations to the enemy.[14]

Maps, for instance, are also an obvious source of such confusion. In the early post-war textbooks, maps often have *Zhongguo* in their titles, such as 'Map of *Zhongguo*', 'Political Regions and Important Cities in *Zhongguo*', 'Topographic map of *Zhongguo*', and 'The [central] position of *Zhongguo* in the world' (*GS* post-1945 VII: 28; ibid. VI: 50). Their titles are later replaced with *Zhonghua minguo* or *woguo* – for instance, 'Topographic map of *Zhonghua minguo*' (*SS* 1975 [2nd ed.] X: 7) or 'The lost lands and border towns of *woguo*' (*SS* 1968 VII: 101).

To avoid misleading associations, the term *Zhongguo* is soon replaced by other alternatives, such as *woguo*, *dalu*, and *guxiang*. Such replacements are convenient ways to reduce confusion and avoid the embarrassment of claiming to represent the whole of China. For example, in a four-lesson 24-page unit entitled '*Zhongguo* geographical foundations', the term *Zhongguo* is used only once (*SS* 1968 VI: 24). Throughout the text, it is referred to as *woguo*, 'our ROC', or 'we *Zhonghua minzu*' (ibid.: 1, 5, 19, 21). Similar cases are common. For example, the condemnation of the Chinese Communist regime in the lesson 'Rescue *Zhongguo* and Save the World' uses the two alternatives *woguo* and *dalu* to replace *Zhongguo* (*SS* 1968 VIII: 99–102). Its ambiguity combined with ROC expulsion from the United Nations in 1971 leads to a decline in occurrences of *Zhongguo*. This reflects the awkwardness of its claim to be the legitimate representative of the whole of China. The limited presence of *Zhongguo* also demonstrates the editors' dilemma in presenting a desirable image of China (ancestral homeland, splendour of its culture, and Confucian heritage) while condemning the PRC. One major strategy is to avoid *Zhongguo* altogether and discredit the PRC by hurling insults at the Chinese Communist Party (CCP) as the 'Communist bandits' (*gongfei*) (e.g. *GS* post-1945 V: 17; *SS* 1962 IV: 59, 72; *SS* 1968 IV: 55).

In contrast to the ambiguous *Zhongguo*, the implication of *Zhonghua* is broader and more positive, extolling the glorious and superior national self, especially relating to 'our' culture and 'we' as a nation. *Zhonghua* is much more widely used and less controversial for the ROC. In many instances, it replaces the more politically contentious *Zhongguo* to stress we-ness and evoke national sentiment. In early curricula, this term is often used with a highly nationalistic tone – for instance, 'I love *Zhonghua*' (*GS* post-1945 V: 17); '*Zhonghua*! *Zhonghua*! The great *Zhonghua*!' (*SS* 1962 I: 52). It is particularly useful after the ROC's 1967 launch of the Cultural Renaissance movement to highlight its own legitimacy as the true heir of Chinese tradition and cultural orthodoxy.[15]

The two extended phrases *Zhonghua minzu* (Chinese nation) and *Zhonghua wenhua* (Chinese culture) are widely used throughout the period examined. These related terms are employed to index national sentiment and cultural achievement and act as the adhesive cementing and glorifying a collective self. *Zhonghua minzu* is celebrated as 'the largest', 'the oldest', and 'the most superior nation in the world' (*GS* post-1945 VII: 23–24; *SS* 1962 I: 44; *GS* 1952 III: 1), and *Zhonghua wenhua* is described as the rightful heir to a '5,000-year civilization' combining tradition, morality, kinship, ethics, and arts (*SS* 1968 VIII: 77). By reminding students that they are all 'descendants of Huangdi'[16] and members of this *Zhonghua minzu* 'big family' (*GS* post-1945 VII: 23–24; *SS* 1968 V: 20–23), the discourse of national self embedded in social studies textbooks also echoes a dominant late-Qing rhetoric around the Chinese nation (Shen 1997). In other words, the century-old Chinese myth of national origin casts its long shadow over post-war education in Taiwan, framing and shaping a sense of we-ness and connecting Taiwanese to the Huangdi bloodline.

An extended term *Zhongguoren* (Chinese people) is another convenient way to imply a collective 'we' and consolidate students' Chinese identity with less connection to any political regime. In the early curricula, students were encouraged to be 'decent Chinese' (*tangtang zhengzheng de Zhongguoren*)[17] and to contribute to the building of a 'new China'. In the earlier curricula, *Zhongguoren* mainly indexes the collective self and an aspiration to construct a new China. The focus of *Zhongguoren* begins to change from the mid-1980s when cross-Strait relations started to thaw and unification seemed possible. Lessons begin to emphasise shared cultural and ethnic roots and insist that '*Zhongguoren* in Taiwan were all from the mainland [at different periods of time]' (*SS* 1975 [1st & 2nd ed.] VII: 55). The lesson 'Wishes of *Zhongguoren*' compares the civil war to a family row in which both sides insisted on 'conflicting views about how to make China great' (*SS* 1975 [2nd ed.] VIII: 136–144).

While constructing the national 'we', it is also crucial to connect this identity to the more intimate 'I'. To encourage students to identify with and learn from characters in textbooks, many lessons (for the lower and middle year-groups) are written from the children's perspective and experience after the 1968 curriculum. The names given to them are highly significant, such as Hsin-min, or 'new citizens', and Chien-kuo, or 'building the country'. Among the main characters, the most common name used throughout the decades was Hsiao-hua, or 'little *hua*'.[18] The word *hua* can mean many things, including 'flowers', 'splendour', and 'essence', and often refers to the Han Chinese (Brown 2004: 22–25, 255n28). Thus, the conscious and consistent naming of the main character Hsiao-hua, as the representation of all students, seems to suggest a young Chinese identity, and encourages a Chinese cultural belonging.

Zhonghua minguo *and Taiwan*

In contrast to the wistful and nostalgic *Zhonghua* and politically suspect *Zhongguo*, the meanings of both *Zhonghua minguo* and *Taiwan* are much more straightforward. *Zhonghua minguo* is usually used in the materials researched to emphasise the ROC's political legitimacy and an ROC vision of China. In the earlier curricula, the term is less frequent than *Zhongguo* because it is taken for granted that the two are the same. *Taiwan*, however, is used at first purely as a geographical region and later as a general expression about an environment in which the state resides and of which students have direct experience. In other words, *Zhonghua minguo* is a political term presenting an officially defined 'we', while the latter gradually comes to replace the identity centre, and represents a pragmatic approach to indicate 'where we are' and 'who we have become' over time.

After retrocession, it was paramount for the education authorities to teach Taiwanese children to become Chinese and get to know their motherland. The specific reference to the ROC is thus connected to the Republic's history and political legitimacy, its leading role during and after the Sino-Japanese War, and modernisation in Taiwan.

As the post-1945 version shows, basic knowledge about the ROC is high on textbook editors' agendas. For instance, a lesson entitled '*Zhonghua minguo*' extols the greatness of the ROC, its superior political structure, administrative divisions, and its status as the leading country in Asia (*GS* post-1945 VII: 27). However, the most striking example is an illustration of the ROC national flag in the first volume of an early general studies textbook. This image occupies half a page, and the accompanying text claims, '[h]ere is our national flag…National flag! National flag! I love you, and I respect you' (*GS* post-1945 I: 7). While most textbooks in the 1950s were printed in black and white, the image of the ROC national flag is the only coloured picture in all eight volumes. This prominence is designed to make Taiwanese children recognise 'our' national flag and draw it correctly. Similarly, National Day celebrations are another important topic, requiring students to not only memorise ROC history, but also perform a collective identity through direct participation in schoolyard decoration, celebrations, ceremonies, and parades. 'National Day' presents the establishment of the Republic (e.g. *GS* post-1945 V: 17) and develops into a depiction of children's National Day celebrations and extracurricular activities (*GS* 1968 III: 28–30; *SS* 1975 [1st & 2nd ed.] I: 23–28, 32).

To create a unified 'we', early textbooks reiterate connections between the nation and the students. For example, lessons often use the possessive pronouns 'my' or 'our' to associate the self positively with the ROC. For example, sentences state, '[t]his is our ROC map' (*GS* post-1945 VI: 51) with the shape of a 'beautiful *qiuhaitang* [begonia] leaf'[19] (*SS* 1968 I: 4; *SS* 1975 [2nd ed.] X: 10); or emphasise pride in being part of a great country in 'this is our *Zhonghua minguo*, the No.1 country in Asia' (*SS* 1962 IV: 70), or declare 'our country, *Zhonghua minguo*, was the first democratic republic in Asia' (*SS* 1968 VII: 37, 44).

As a rule, national history and (pre-1949) ROC geography are formally taught in the higher year-group materials. Yet, a simple introduction to the ROC can be found as early as Year 1 textbooks ('I love the national flag' [*GS* post-1945 I: 7] or 'Double Tenth…is the national day of the ROC' [*GS* post-1945 V: 17]). An official version of national history and geography, especially regarding the legitimacy of the ROC, is taught and reiterated as facts. In order to disguise the KMT defeat in the civil war and the successor government, as well as the PRC having territorial control over the Chinese mainland, content about post-1949 China is deliberately omitted, except for condemnation of Chinese Communist atrocities against their own people. Moreover, the PRC is never named in these textbooks. One strategy to account for the ROC's retreat to Taiwan is to demonise the CCP as 'evil' and 'usurpers' (*SS* 1962 IV: 62, 72; *SS* 1968 VIII: 101–102). Many lessons describe the CCP regime as 'rebels' and 'Communist bandits' (*gongfei*), and assert that this 'pseudo regime' has 'usurped the mainland', 'imposed tyranny enslaving the people', and is 'the root of Chinese turmoil' (*SS* 1962 IV: 62; *SS* 1968 IV: 55, 57; ibid. VII: 67–69; ibid. VIII: 99; *SS* 1975 [2nd ed.] VIII: 130; ibid. XI: 67). It is only after the late 1980s, 40 years later, that the name *gongfei* is replaced by the less derogatory expression *Zhonggong* (Chinese Communist Party) (*SS* 1975 [2nd ed.] VIII: 137).

In order to support the ROC's claim to be the only legitimate Chinese government, social studies textbooks present a geography and history of pre-1949 China. In the materials examined, Taiwanese children are taught to accept pre-PRC history and ROC territory as real. This includes the rightful place of the ROC in Chinese history; ROC administrative divisions (different from those of the PRC), and the ubiquity of ROC national symbols such as the national flag, national leaders, and the ROC map both in textbooks and in school. For example, the administrative divisions are an important indicator of territorial control. Thus, one of the most important tasks in social studies education is to instil knowledge about ROC administrative divisions in China. These consist of 35 provinces, 12 municipalities, two *difang* (literally 'places', Mongolia and Tibet), one Special Administrative Region (Hainan), and the national capital in Nanjing. Even though these are defunct, the materials require students to remember and recite them.

In the early textbooks, content about Taiwan is disproportionately absent because the island is seen simply as a reference point for ROC legitimacy (Chang 2011). Any mention of Taiwan is limited to its historical relationship with China, its geography and rich natural resources, and its status as an ROC province. To bolster the greatness of China, descriptions of the island are sometimes disparaging. For instance, in materials from the 1960s, it is described as a 'desert island' (*SS* 1968 IV: 1) that originally consisted of undeveloped wildness (*Manhuang wei pi*), covered in forest with no farmland or dwellings (*SS* 1962 IV: 12). After the launch of the Cultural Renaissance Movement, a significant repositioning can be seen. The post-1968 textbooks swiftly shift from asserting the ROC's political legitimacy to emphasising its Chinese cultural authenticity.

Two identities are also attached to Taiwan – first, as a 'base for retaking the mainland' and, second, as the *baodao* (literally precious island) in the anti-Communist battle. These portrayals speak volumes about how social studies construct the collective 'we'. Being the ROC's final foothold from which it might retake the mainland, Taiwan's anti-Communist role is reiterated in all curricula before 2000. For example, Taiwan is described as an 'anti-Communist fortress' (*fangong baolei*) (*SS* 1968 III: 3), 'the operational base for launching the anti-Communist war' (*fangong fuguo de jidi*) (*GS* 1952 I: 2; *SS* 1962 IV: 29, 69, 73–75; *SS* 1968 IV: 20, 38), and 'the lighthouse of world freedom' (*ziyou de dengta*) (*SS* 1975 [1st ed.] VII: 30). The text urges students to fulfil the mission to recapture the mainland and rescue all Chinese compatriots (ibid. III: 33).

The term *baodao* is used as a synonym with another phrase, 'beautiful island' (*meilidao*, or *meili de baodao*) (e.g. *SS* 1962 IV: 11, 28; *SS* 1968 IV: 4–5, 19–20, 59; *SS* 1975 [2nd ed.] VII: 4, 6, 16, 20, 82; ibid. VIII: 45; *SS* 1993 VII: 101). Although the term *baodao* is a positive expression that highlights the preciousness and irreplaceability of the island, the implication is ambiguous. It implies Taiwan's abundant resources and geopolitical importance in the anti-Communist struggle (*SS* 1968 IV: 19–20; *SS* 1975 [1st & 2nd ed.] VII: 4–6; ibid. [3rd ed.] VII: 6). Yet, the hierarchical relationship between Taiwan and China is clear: Taiwan's importance rests solely on its strategic role in retaking the mainland and is thus subordinate to *Zhongguo*. Despite being celebrated as 'precious' and 'beautiful', Taiwan's subjectivity is always secondary to that of China in the materials. The term also seems to imply something exotic, foreign, and different from *Zhongguo*. For example, the ROC national territory is compared to a perfect 'begonia (*qiuhaitang*) leaf' (*SS* 1968 I: 4), suggesting a complete and inseparable Chinese territory (Wang 2003; Chang 2015: 171–173). In this *qiuhaitang* analogy, Taiwan has no place. Rather, the shape of Taiwan is more often compared to a 'banana leaf' in the textbooks (*GS* post-1945 VII: 7; *SS* 1968 IV: 19) and Taiwan-related content is always separated from discussion of China. Such exclusion from *Zhongguo* and the ambiguity attached to *baodao* fundamentally reflects a clear categorical distinction between the inside and the outside, placing Taiwan at the margin of the imagined political centre (Chang 2015).

After its expulsion from the UN in 1971, the ROC's claim to represent the whole of China becomes increasingly unsustainable and the national narrative has to be drastically reinvented. The focus of the ROC thus moves to Taiwan. Although this decentring process is carried out reluctantly and is purely a survival tactic, separating 'Free China' from the fallen area constructs Taiwan as the 'hometown' (*jiaxiang*), the place where students 'were born and bred', and a 'happy land of freedom' that they 'adore and would protect' (*SS* 1968 IV: 55–57; *SS* 1975 [3rd ed.] VI; *SS* 1993 VI: 6–17).

In the wake of increasing international isolation, the initial glorification of China is reduced, and the hierarchical position of Taiwan is reversed in the materials. The images of two Chinas are juxtaposed, contrasting 'paradise in Taiwan' under the KMT with hell on the mainland under the CCP. In a lesson entitled 'Life in Taiwan Today' (*SS* 1962 IV: 58–59), Taiwan is praised for having become a prosperous, modern, happy society with the benefits of traditional culture and family values, whose people live in 'a democratic society, leading a life of freedom and equality'. At the end of the lesson, this harmonious picture is deployed in contrast to alleged devastation and misery on the mainland, characterised by enslavement, poverty, and ruin of family life. The illustrations in the lesson accentuate this contrast. Images of broken homes, barren land, and hungry masses in the People's Communes on one side clash with shopping districts, roads, cars, comfortable apartments, and happy three-generation families on the other. The disparity between the mainland's backwardness and Taiwan's 'perfect marriage' of modernity and tradition is described as the difference between 'living in heaven and hell' (*SS* 1968 IV: 59). This is the starting point at which the collective self began to split into two – Taiwan became practically synonymous with the ROC, while China exclusively related to the mainland. Although labelled 'a Chinese province' until the 1990s, previously backward Taiwan seems to replace the originally superior Chinese 'centre of splendour' in the textbooks as a better, more modern version of the here and now, from as early as 1968. Between the two, Taiwan becomes the standard bearer – first as the 'Model Province of the Three Principles of the People' (*sanminzhuyi mofan sheng*) (*SS* 1968 IV: 38, 63–66; ibid. VII: 69; ibid. VIII: 104) and 'the model province of *our* country' [stress added] (*SS* 1975 [1st ed.] VII: 4), and later a 'good place' [stress added] (*SS* 1975 [2nd ed.] VIII: 104), where 'the Taiwan experience', 'the Taiwan model', and even 'the Taiwan miracle' become the envy of the mainland Chinese (*SS* 1975 [2nd ed.] VII: 20, 25; ibid. VIII: 114, 119–122, 128).

Woguo *and alternative self-references*

There are many alternatives and the term *woguo* ('my/our country', or 'my/our country's'), because of its flexibility and versatility, is the most widely used in the materials examined to refer to the national self.[20] In general, it is used in four different ways. The first three interpretations are more common and sometimes interchangeable, but the last usage only appears in the 1990s to serve a particular purpose to present a distinctive self-image.

The first usage suggests a general idea about China – for instance, 'Mongolia is *woguo*'s northern gateway' (*SS* 1968 VI: 19), 'the establishment of the ROC…is a great progress of *woguo* politics' (*SS* 1968 VII: 44), '*woguo* suffered from imperialist encroachment' (*SS* 1975 [2nd ed.] XI: 6), or '*woguo* lost territories' (*SS* 1968 VII: 100); the second is associated with Chinese culture and could also be used as a synonym for '*Zhonghua*', such as '*woguo* is an ancient civilization' (*SS* 1975 [2nd ed.] VIII: 32), '*woguo* glorious tradition' (*SS* 1968 VIII: 77), or 'Cultural Revolution fundamentally destroyed *woguo*'s inherent culture' (ibid. VII: 69); the third approach refers to the ROC – for example, '*woguo* government accepted the Japanese surrender in Taipei' (*SS* 1993 VII: 124), '*woguo* entered a new stage when the ROC Constitution was promulgated in 1947' (*SS* 1968 VII: 76), '*woguo* post-war reconstruction' was interrupted by the 'Communist bandits' with Russian support (ibid. VIII: 99), and '*woguo* has occupied an important place in the world and contributed greatly to world peace' in the discussion about global anti-communist struggles (*SS* 1968 VIII: 103); lastly, the term refers to Taiwan. Although rare, it seems to indicate that the tide of self-image has turned. In the lesson 'A Life of Security, Happiness and Abundance', the fast-growing textile and garment industries in Taiwan are described as '*woguo* excellent economic performance' (*SS* 1975 [2nd ed.] VIII: 47). Apparently, it refers to the textile industry in Taiwan alone.

There are a couple of alternatives similar to *woguo*, including: 'homeland' (*guxiang*) (*SS* 1962 IV: 3), *laojia* (old home) (ibid. I: 46, 48), and *jingxiu heshan* (splendid land) (*SS* 1962 IV: 68–72; *SS* 1968 VI: 1, 63; *SS* 1975 [2nd ed.] X: 8, 36). Most of these phrases are used to extol ancient China and its glorious past and to imply one's origin. Among these, the term *woguo* is most useful because of its flexibility and ambiguity. However, such a convenient reference also risks sending misleading or unintended messages. In order to avoid mentioning the CCP regime in China or the new PRC state, *dalu* becomes *the* synonym for Chinese territory under the Communist rule, especially in textbooks after the 1968 curriculum.

The impact of the lifting of martial law in 1987 and subsequent democratisation brought major changes to education in terms of the imagination of the national self, not only confirming the change in Taiwan's position but also adding a new dimension to its self-image. The 1975 curriculum goes through two dramatic revisions within a short period of time (1985 and 1989 respectively) in response to these significant changes. First, a new term, *Taiwan diqu*, or Taiwan area (*SS* 1975 [2nd ed.] VI: 4–8; ibid. VIII: 4, 16, 50, 81–83, 103–104, 108–122,

126, 129; ibid. XI: 75, 78, 81; *SS* 1993 VII: 6, 20, 37) emerges in the materials to replace terms like 'Chinese province' or 'Model Province of the Three Principles of the People'. This term is used in contrast to another term, *dalu diqu* (mainland area) (*SS* 1975 [2nd ed.] XI: 71; *SS* 1993 V: 8–53).[21] In 1991, the first ROC Constitutional Amendments were promulgated, formalising the two entities, Taiwan and mainland China, in legal terms (Office of the President 2020). This tactic of clearly demarcating the Taiwanese self and Chinese other demonstrates a further repositioning of the national self. This is not just a strategy to place Taiwan on an equal footing with the mainland area. Rather, this repositioning reflects an increasingly strong Taiwan subjectivity, and leads to a clear-cut division between the inside and the outside.

In addition to alternative referential names, the materials examined also attach a series of value-added attributes to Taiwan, describing it as a modern society that enjoys 'freedom', 'democracy', 'prosperity', and 'equality' (*SS* 1962 IV: 58; *SS* 1968 IV: 58; *SS* 1975 [1st ed.] VII: 15; ibid. [2nd ed.] VIII: 140). A new emphasis on environmental protection (*SS* 1975 [3rd ed.] VI; ibid. VII: 30–45) also emerges to showcase Taiwan's internationalism and progressive thinking.

Conclusion

Among various discursive strategies used to present a positive national self and negative other (Reisigl and Wodak 2001), this chapter has focused on systematic ways of employing collective self-reference in social studies textbooks in Taiwan over a 55-year period, and has examined how a shared sense of national we-ness was constructed and transformed. It is evident that the core national self first changed in the late 1960s and then accelerated after the 1980s, from a righteous ROC, representing the whole of China, to the ROC on Taiwan. This reflects not just how a glorious national self was constructed, but also how a gradual process of repositioning, de-centring, and re-centring of that national self from China to Taiwan occurred long before democratisation. It is interesting to note that different qualities or focuses were attached to different self-referential terms in different periods. By shifting perspectives, the original hierarchy of a magnificent and sophisticated *Zhongguo* and an undeveloped and backward Taiwan in early curricula was reversed. After the lifting of martial law, the subjectivity embedded in textbooks shifted decisively away from *Zhongguo* and centred around Taiwan.

By exploring seemingly banal self-referencing terms in social studies textbooks, this chapter has demonstrated how official knowledge and education constructed children's sense of 'we, the nation' before education reform in 2000, and considered how particular terms were used to construct a sense of pride, self-importance, and divine entitlement. In so doing, it reveals that over the period 1945–2000 the national self, embedded in social studies education, repositioned its we-ness in response to social change for political ends. These observations lead to the following conclusions.

Strategic ambiguity

The associated meanings of the self-referencing terms examined were always contingent and fluid. Although their usage was not homogeneous, there was a consistent trend in how they were employed. In comparison to the positive representations of *Zhonghua*, *Zhonghua minguo*, and *Taiwan*, the term *Zhongguo* was most problematic and tricky precisely because of its contentious associations. The term could not always be positive if it could also index the PRC. Yet, nor could it be negative when post-war education aimed to make Taiwan Chinese. The *Zhongguo* issue thus became the elephant in the room and was avoided at all costs. Facing problematic sovereignty and the loss of most of its territory after 1949, it was a tricky business for the ROC government-in-exile to effectively create a national self and to evoke patriotic sentiment. Strategic ambiguity became the dominant approach to these difficulties. To avoid direct association with the Chinese Communist regime, textbooks dodged the term *Zhongguo*, unless it indexed the past. Instead, the term *woguo* resolved the dilemma by constructing a strong sense of 'we, the nation' without specifying that nation. To enable transition and change, ambiguity became the key. Having replaced *Zhongguo* with *woguo*, the collective self was able to transform.

Turning points

After Taiwan's retrocession to the ROC in 1945, a China-centric discourse became omnipresent in post-war education. This discourse subsequently shifted to a Taiwan-focused one. There were two important turning points in this decentring process. The first was the restructuring of ROC national rhetoric in the 1968 curriculum. Although China was still the core of the discourse and Taiwan a subordinate reference point, the hierarchy seemed to shift. Taiwan had become the 'better half' of the collective self in contrast to the 'contaminated half' on the mainland. The second turning point occurred after the lifting of martial law and was reflected in a salient discursive change in the 1989 edition of the textbooks based on the 1975 curriculum (3rd ed.). Although the previous two editions of the 1975 curriculum had clearly placed a firm emphasis on Taiwan, it was not until the third edition in 1989 that the China-centre/Taiwan-periphery model was reversed. These two turning points clearly signal the post-war decentring of an officially sanctioned national self, first from China to the ROC and then to the ROC on Taiwan. This process laid the foundations for a further move centring around Taiwan in the education reform of the 21st century.

Strategies

Various strategies were utilised to achieve the repositioning identified, both by symbolic representation giving the national self a different identity and by exclusion establishing a dichotomy between self and other. Moreover, by exploiting the tactic of strategic ambiguity, two major strategies were used to facilitate repositioning – contrapuntal positioning and separation.

Contrapuntal positioning

In the process of decentring, the once important reference – *Zhongguo* – had to be othered. The tactic employed in social studies was to portray an undesirable China, tainted by communism, on the one hand and boost an image of a prosperous, appealing, and highly developed Taiwan under the ROC on the other. The early binary order of civilised China and barbaric Taiwan only existed briefly. By juxtaposing contrasting traits, the original China-centre/Taiwan-periphery model was reversed. This hierarchical position and their marked differences were reinforced in textbooks, an us-them dichotomy was reproduced, linking Taiwan to prosperity, modernity, and cultural orthodoxy; while associating China with poverty, ideological purges, human misery, and immorality. China was linked to history, Taiwan to geography; China represented tradition, while Taiwan represented modernity. Thus, in presenting China as the past, Taiwan became the present, the here and now.

Separation

Identity has always been constructed and strengthened by exaggerating difference. To buttress a strong sense of national self, setting symbolic boundaries and exercising exclusion are important. The materials examined suggest that it is after the 1968 curriculum that a clear division emerged between lessons about Taiwan and those about China. The two separate collective selves start to surface, Taiwan and the ROC are presented as one-and-the-same, while the mainland becomes synonymous with China. In other words, the separation of 'national self' is twofold, one content-based, the other structural. From 1945 to 2000, Taiwan-related topics were taught in the lower and middle year-groups and Chinese-related topics in the higher year-group. The former included Taiwan's history (emphasising the Chinese contribution), simple geographical facts about Taiwan, and post-war society and development, while the latter consisted of Chinese history, geography, and values, as well as an introduction to global affairs and world geography. Although this binary opposition was first devised with ease of teaching and the complexity of the subjects in mind, the separation unintentionally provided a convenient demarcation, and helped students differentiate 'we, Taiwan' from 'they, *Zhongguo*'. By the early 1990s, the othering process created another binary position into which the world was divided – the mainland area (where the regime upheld the foreign ideologies that had ruined Chinese culture) versus the Taiwan area (where the 'rightful' regime with cultural orthodoxy and political legitimacy had created an economic and political miracle). On many levels, Taiwan and *Zhongguo* had already been divided in terms of content and curriculum structure.

In other words, Taiwan had not been incorporated into the ROC national imagination in the first place.

This research shows that the decentring of China in social studies education started as early as the late 1960s, triggered by the Cultural Revolution on the mainland. The radical shift to a model Taiwan under the ROC was designed to tackle the ROC's increasingly detrimental international isolation and to justify its political legitimacy on the island. The shift from a China-centric position seems to have contributed to the emergence and the eventual consolidation of Taiwanese consciousness in the late 1980s. Instead of ascribing the rise of Taiwanese identity solely to political activism, this study reveals that the foundations had been laid early, fostering an awareness of difference and constructing, albeit unwittingly, an exclusively Taiwanese national self through social studies education. The decentring of *Zhongguo* in social studies textbooks represents a change in identity, moving Taiwan from the periphery to the centre, replacing 'where we came from' with a more down to earth 'who we have become' with an emphasis on the here and now.

Notes

1 In Taiwan's case, six-year compulsory (and free) education was implemented in 1947 and was extended to nine years in 1968.
2 Taiwan's pre-1945 situation was different. Under Japanese rule (1895–1945), the core courses that common schools (primary schools for the local Taiwanese) offered included: Japanese language, arithmetic, and some basic sciences (Tsurumi 1979: 619). There was no formal social studies during this period. A similar subject listed in Japanese curricula was '*Shushin*' (修身). Khan translated *Shushin* as 'moral education' and asserted that the Japanese aim was to 'enlighten children with the spirit of reverence for the emperor and patriotism' (1997: 76). Apparently, the emphasis was placed on loyalty to the emperor and the empire. In some ways, *Shushin* was like social studies education, in terms of fostering patriotism, loyalty, and obedience (Tsai 2009).
3 Between 1948 and 1968, *Common Sense* textbooks were only available for Years 3 and 4. There were only 'teaching guidelines' for the lower year-group teachers.
4 The term 'hidden curriculum' is used in pedagogy to refer to hidden educational intent and design of which most people are usually unaware (Vallance 1973: 4). This includes: The school routines, the marking criteria, the campus design and decoration, the way classes are conducted, and so on. For example, Taiwanese schools usually mark the beginning and the end of a school day by raising and lowering the national flag and singing the national anthem. The hidden message embedded in the daily routine echoes Billig's observation on American 'flagging the homeland daily' (1995: 93–127). By saluting the national flag, the daily routine served as a kind of a performance to pledge their allegiance to the ROC and naturalised an official sense of 'we-ness'.
5 The compilation and publication of school textbooks in Taiwan before the 1990s were under the direct control of the NICT. Between 1968 and 1996, the NICT oversaw the implementation of textbook standardisation for Taiwan's nine-year compulsory education. It was regarded one of the most important cultural ISAs in post-war Taiwan.
6 The reason for choosing 2000 as the cut-off point was because a new education structure – the 'Grade 1–9 curriculum' – was formally introduced in 2001 as the authorities' effort to reform the education system. It is considered one of the most important milestones in Taiwan's educational development (Wu and Huang 2010). To focus on the evolution of post-war changes, I focus on the pre-2000 textbooks.

7 The subject 'General Studies' was designed for younger children as part of social studies education in the early curricula. During the early post-war years, it was briefly taught with Chinese language (as *guoyu changshi*) between 1945 and 1948 and became an independent subject until it was abolished in 1968.

8 The post-war primary education was a mixture of ROC 1942 curriculum, the old Japanese textbooks, and a localised version in 1948. To simplify the comparison, I combine the early versions into one 'post-1945' category.

9 The second edition (revised edition) took effect in 1985 and the third (improved edition) in 1989. As a result, there were 36 volumes of textbooks of the 1975 curriculum.

10 For more information, see Brown (2004: 22–29, 242–245) and Harrell (1996).

11 For all direct quotes from these textbooks, I will reference them in the order of: The textbook title (*SS* for *Social Studies*, and *GS* for *General Studies*), curriculum version (e.g. 1952), volume number, and page number(s). For example: *GS* post-1945 VII: 28. One exception is the 1975 curriculum, the citation will include the edition, e.g. *SS* 1975 [2nd ed.] VIII: 136–138.

12 In the 1968 and 1975 [1st and 2nd] curricula, the content about Chinese history in the higher year-group was very similar with slightly different wordings and change in design. This is only one of many similar cases.

13 The PRC (*Zhonghua renmin gongheguo*) was established in Beijing in 1949 after winning the civil war.

14 This tendency of avoiding the term in order not to directly associate with China continues today. For example, after Taiwan's major education reform in 2000, the NICT's monopoly of compiling and editing textbooks was transferred to private publishers. In the textbooks published by the three major publishing companies (i.e. Nanyi, Hanlin, and Kangxuan), all references to the historical rules in Taiwan are now based on the regime's names, such as Qing rule, Zheng rule, Dutch rule, etc., replacing the expression 'Chinese rule'.

15 This movement was launched in 1967 to counterattack the Cultural Revolution on the mainland (Tozer 1970: 85). By condemning the devastation of Chinese culture, the Cultural Renaissance movement aimed to establish the ROC as the cultural guardian of Chinese culture and tradition, and thus holding the cultural and moral legitimacy to represent the Chinese.

16 The myth of Huangdi (aka Yellow Emperor) has long been portrayed as the originator of the central kingdom and the ancestor of the Han Chinese. The status of Huangdi as the 'shared ancestor of the Han Chinese and the links between Huangdi and Han Chinese nationalism were all constructed during the late Qing period' (Shen 1997).

17 This expression had become common since the 1968 curriculum. It appeared in many lessons. The lessons encouraged students to be patriotic, law-abiding, moral, and hardworking so as to become a 'lively good student, and decent Chinese' (*SS* 1968 VIII: 95–98; ibid. III: 55; ibid. I: 4–6). This 'principle' had also been included in the guideline for the 1968 and 1975 national curricula and appeared in the 'Editorial Guidelines' of the textbooks. In the 1993 version, however, the emphasis was modified to encourage students to be 'decent citizens'.

18 The name 'Hsiao-hua' appeared throughout all curricula (e.g. *GS* post-1945 III: 3, 10, 23; *SS* 1962 I: 2–4, 7–10, 16–17, 21–25, 38–40; ibid. II: 64–66; ibid. III: 10, 12–13; ibid. IV: 30–38; *SS* 1968 I: 3; ibid. IV: 33; *SS* 1975 [1st & 2nd ed.] IV: 4, 6–9, 17–18, 22–24, 28–30; etc.).

19 The shape of a begonia leaf (*qiuhaitang ye*) was commonly compared to an ideal contour of the Chinese territory. The analogy between a 'complete Chinese territory' and a perfect 'begonia leaf' first appeared in the 1920s. The symbolism was reinforced by the mass popularity of the novel *Qiuhaitang* published in 1941. The romantic image of China as a 'begonia leaf' was thus etched in the public imagination as the embodiment of 'the spirit of the Chinese people' and a popular 'representation of Republican China' (Wang 2003: 137, 161).

20 The phrase '*woguo*' could be a shortened expression for '*woguo de*' (of my/our country), '*women de guojia*' (our country), or was simplified from '*women de*' (ours). For example, '*woguo buliang fengsu*' (the unhealthy customs of our country) (*GS* 1952 V: 3–4).
21 The name of the PRC is never mentioned in social studies textbooks, and the ruling regime on the mainland – the CCP – only appears in the 1990s (*SS* 1975 [2nd ed.] VIII: 83, 94).

References

Althusser, Louis. (1971). 'Ideology and Ideological State Apparatuses'. In *Lenin and Philosophy and Other Essays*. London: NLB, 127–88.
Apple, Michael. (2004). *Ideology and Curriculum*. 3rd edition. New York: Routledge Falmer.
Billig, Michael. (1995). *Banal Nationalism*. London: Sage Publications.
Brown, Melissa J. (2004). *Is Taiwan Chinese? The Impact of Culture, Power, and Migration on Changing Identity*. Berkeley, LA, London: University of California Press.
Chang, Bi-yu. (2011). 'So close, yet so far away: Imaging Chinese "homeland" in Taiwan's geography education (1945–67)'. *Cultural Geographies*, 18(3): 385–412.
———. (2015). *Place, Identity, and National Imagination in Post-war Taiwan*. London and New York: Routledge.
Chen Mingzhong and Chen Xingtang (eds). (1989). *Taiwan's Recovery and Five Years of Rule* [Taiwan guangfu he guangfu hou wunian shengqing]. Nanjing: Nanjing Publisher.
Durkheim, Emile. (2006). *The Evolution of Educational Thought: Lectures on the Formation and Development of Secondary Education in France*. London: Routledge.
Harrell, Stevan. (1996). 'The nationalities question and the prmi prblem'. In Melissa J. Brown (ed.) *Negotiating Ethnicities in China and Taiwan*. Berkeley: Institute of East Asian Studies, University of California.
Khan, Yoshimitsu (1997). *Japanese Moral Education Past and Present*. Madison, NJ: Fairleigh Dickinson University Press.
Kimball, Warren F. (1991). *The Juggler: Franklin Roosevelt as Wartime Statesman*. Princeton, NJ: Princeton University Press, 83–106.
Lind, Jennifer. (2011). *Sorry States: Apologies in International Politics*. Ithaca, NY: Cornell University Press.
Mohammad-Arif, Aminah. (2005). 'Textbooks, nationalism and history writing in India and Pakistan'. In Véronique Bénéï (ed.) *Manufacturing Citizenship: Education and Nationalism in Europe, South Asia and China*. London: Routledge, 143–169.
Office of the President. (2020). 'The first amendment: Additional articles of the constitution of the Republic of China'. Office of the President. https://www.president.gov.tw/Page/322 (accessed on 2 April 2020).
Reisigl, M. and R. Wodak. (2001). *Discourse and Discrimination: Rhetorics of Racism and Anti-Semitism*. London: Routledge.
Ross, E. Wayne. (2006). 'The struggle for the social studies curriculum'. In E.W. Ross (ed.) *Social Studies Curriculum: Purposes, Problems, and Possibilities*. New York: State University of New York Press, 17–36.
Shen, Sung-Chiao (1997). 'The myth of Huang-ti (Yellow Emperor) and the construction of Chinese nationhood in late Qing' [wuo yi wuoxie jian xuanyuan: Huangdi Shenhua yu wanxing de guozu jiangou]. *Taiwan: A Radical Quarterly in Social Studies*, 28: 1–77.
Sheng, Lang-his. (1934). *The Evolution of Primary Curriculum* [Xiaoyue kecheng yange]. Shanghai: Zhonghua Books.

Tozer, Warren. (1970). 'Taiwan's "cultural renaissance": A preliminary view'. *The China Quarterly*, 43(July–Sep): 81–99.

Tsai, Chin-tan. (2009). 'The education and the influence of ko-gakko Shushin-education in Japanese Ruled Period'. *[rishi shiqi Taiwan gongxuexiao xiushen jiaoyu ji qi yingxiang]*, *Bulletin of Taiwan Historical Research*, 2: 3–32.

Tsurumi, E. Patricia. (1979). 'Education and assimilation in Taiwan under Japanese rule, 1895–1945'. *Modern Asian Studies*, 13(4): 617–641.

Tuan, Yi-fu. (1977). *Space and Place: The Perspective of Experience*. Minnesota, University of Minnesota Press.

Vallance, Elizabeth. (1973/4). 'Hiding the hidden curriculum'. *Curriculum Theory Network* 4(1): 5–21.

Wang, David Der-wei. (2003). 'Impersonating China'. *Chinese Literature: Essays, Articles, Reviews (CLEAR)*, 25(December): 133–163.

Wu, Chun-Hsien and Huang, Jenq-Jye. (2010). 'A study on curriculum reform policies of elementary and secondary school: Focusing on the grade 1–9 curriculum reform' *[zhong xiaoxue kecheng zhengce gaige zhi yanjiu: jiunian yiguan kecheng de huigu yu xianzhan]*. *Journal of Curriculum Studies*, 5(2): 47–62.

4

EMERGING TAIWANESE IDENTITY, ENDANGERED TAIWANESE LANGUAGE

The never-matched national identity and language in Taiwan

Hui-Lu Khoo

Introduction

The modern concept of Taiwanese identity emerged rather recently in history. It started after Taiwan fell under the rule of the Japanese colonial government in 1895, when the Ching Empire in China handed Taiwan over to Japan after being defeated in war. The formation of Taiwanese identity is a long and still ongoing process that has been entangled with Chinese identity, as the majority of the population in Taiwan are the offspring of Chinese migrants of different periods. In other words, the formation of Taiwanese identity has developed in a context of repeated Taiwanese-Chinese contrasts, and, during the Japanese colonial period in 1895–1945, as resistance.

Taigi, literally 'Taiwan language', to a certain degree functioned as a cohesive force of Taiwanese nationalism when confronting foreign political/ethnic powers, either China or Japan, both of which had applied language policies that suppressed Taigi.

However, the development of Taigi and Taiwanese identity do not align and have progressed in opposite directions after Taiwan began to be democratised in the late 1980s. Taigi survived the most severe periods shaping the formation of Taiwanese identity, while, ironically, it has been linguistically shifting to Mandarin since the political suppression of Taiwanese identity began to be relieved.

This chapter introduces the intricate relationship between Taigi and Taiwanese identity in Taiwan.

The formation of Taigi

Taigi, literally 'Taiwan language', is a localised variety of Southern Min, one of the Chinese dialects spoken in the southern part of Min (currently Fujian) Province in China. It was brought to Taiwan by migrants from the southern part of

Min from the late 17th century to the late 19th century, when Japanese colonial rule began in Taiwan.

The Southern Min people soon became the largest segment of the population in Taiwan; their language thus became Taiwan's most predominant language.

In 1905, ten years after the initiation of its rule, the Japanese colonial government of Taiwan conducted the first census in Taiwan.[1] The survey results indicated that more than 80% of the then-Taiwan population was Southern Min.

It is believed that this variety of Southern Min in Taiwan was first called Taiwanese, 'Taiuango' (台湾語) in Japanese, by the Japanese colonial government. In Taiwanese, this language is called 'Taigi/Taigu' (台語) or 'Taiuanue' (台灣話), all literally 'Taiwan language'. Among these, Taigi is currently the most widely used name. This study thus adopts 'Taigi' to refer to this language.[2]

The burgeoning of Taiwanese nationalism

Taigi, as the language with the largest number of native speakers in Taiwan, has been involved in and struggled for recognition in the recurrent endeavour to establish Taiwanese nationalism.

By the time Japan established colonial rule of Taiwan in 1895, Taiwan had been ruled by imperial China, the Ching Empire, for nearly 190 years. However, this rule was loosely structured, indirect, and marked by clientage (Wu 2014: 28), and thus was conducive to the burgeoning of indigenisation and autonomy of this Chinese immigrant society.

Under Japanese colonial rule, nationalism emerged in Taiwan; the idea that Taiwan belonged only to the Taiwanese began to appear (Wu 2014: 28). Before Japanese colonial rule, immigrants from China in Taiwan referred to themselves and one another based on Chinese localism (Hsiau 2000: 4). Thus, they were 'Fukienese', 'Kwantung people', 'Changchou people', and the like; all were referred to by their hometowns in China. Colonisation created the opposed status of the colonised and the coloniser, and the categories of *Tai-uan-lang*, literally 'Taiwan people', and Tai-uan-ue, literally 'Taiwan language', were thus created.

The early connection between Taigi and Taiwanese nationalism

The cultural and linguistic assimilation policy enforced by the Japanese colonial government on the Taiwanese people provoked antipathy towards the government, especially among Taiwanese intellectuals. An undercurrent of Taiwanese nationalism began to flow. Orthography was one of the widely discussed issues.

In the 1910s, numerous Chinese intellectuals, following the wave of new culture reforms at that time in China, called for the vernacularisation of written Chinese, which had been written as classical Chinese. Modern written Mandarin is the result of this orthographic reform movement.

In 1920s, inspired by this culture reform movement in China, some Taiwanese intellectuals advocated a Taiwanese New Literature Movement in contrast to traditional classical Chinese literature. As in China, the vernacularisation of written language was discussed, even arousing debate. The key issue of the debates was which vernacular language should be adopted as the basis of the written system. Some still favoured the newly written vernacular form of Chinese. However, starting from the 1930s, the adoption of the Chinese vernacular form aroused criticism, as Chinese was not the language spoken in Taiwan. Critics argued for the creation of local literature in local vernacular, i.e. Taiwanese literature written in Taigi, the so-called Tai-uan-ue-bun Un-tong (台灣話文運動), literally 'Taiwan written language movement'.

However, the issue of orthography remained debated only within the circle of certain literati. The Japanese colonial government did not actively step into this orthography debate. The first prioritised language issue to the Japanese colonial government at that time was Japanese language promotion, including the classes in school education; written Chinese or written Taiwanese was not an issue to the government. This debate lasted only for a relatively brief period. It came to an end after the Second Sino-Japanese War broke out in 1937, and the consequent escalation of the Japanese assimilation policy in Taiwan.

It is noteworthy that the key proponents of Taigi orthography by and large participated in the political anti-colonial movement. In other words, the pursuit of Taigi orthography and the localisation of Taiwanese literature was associated with the emergence of Taiwanese nationalism.

Suppressed Taigi and Taiwanese identity between 1945 and 1987

The Japanese rule of Taiwan came to an end in 1945, following the end of World War II; the Chinese KMT government immediately took power in Taiwan. The KMT government, on the one hand, imposed Chinese identity on the Taiwanese people, who had been colonised by Japan for five decades and had Japanese identity imposed on them in the final stages of colonisation, and, on the other hand, exclusively promoted Mandarin at the expense of Taigi and all other local languages in Taiwan. This government even imposed martial law, effective from December 1948 to July 1987. In the period of martial law, Taigi was prohibited in most public domains and Taiwanese nationalism was completely suppressed by the government.

In the later stages of the period of martial law, Taiwanese society began to see waves of pro-democracy and pro-social liberalisation demonstrations. This wave of demonstrations peaked in the 1990s. It is noteworthy that the language used in most of these demonstrations was Taigi, as a manifestation of the resistance towards the long-term autocracy that had intended to overwrite Taiwanese elements, including culture, identity, and language, with Chinese elements.

Taiwanese identity rose while Taigi continued losing

Martial law in Taiwan was lifted in 1987, followed by democratisation and liberalisation. Moreover, for the first time in history, Taiwan peacefully changed the ruling party in 2000; Taiwanese identity has grown since then, in contrast to the decline of the Chinese identity exclusively promoted in the past. The results of a long-term Chinese/Taiwanese identity survey[3] showed that the Chinese identity rate among the Taiwanese population has dropped from 25% in 1992, a few years after the start of political democratisation and social liberalisation, to less than 4% in 2019. On the other hand, Taiwanese identity has risen from 17% to 56%. Even Taiwanese/Chinese dual identity, considered the 'moderate' identity, has declined from 46% to 36%. Another long-term survey reported a similar trend of national identity in Taiwan.[4] That survey found Taiwanese identity to have risen from 27% in 1993 to 83% in 2020; Taiwanese/Chinese dual identity declined from its historic high of 43% in 1996 to 7% in 2020; and Chinese identity dropped from 33% in 1993 to 5% in 2020.

Taiwanese identity has risen, and, roughly at the same time, a series of Taigi revitalisation movements have been initiated at levels ranging from civil society organisations to local government, and since 2001, to the central government level. These Taigi reverse language shift (RLS) movements have achieved certain goals. At the educational level, for instance, starting from 2001, all primary school students in Taiwan must take one 40-minute Taiwanese local language course, and one of the options is Taigi. University departments focusing on Taiwanese local languages and cultures began to be established in the first decade of this century.

However, it is noteworthy that despite Taigi having been socially and politically destigmatised to a large degree, the effects of RLS on Taigi is limited since Taigi had been largely lost by the time the RLS on Taigi was initiated. Taigi seems to have lagged behind this liberalisation wave among the Taiwanese people. The language shift towards Mandarin has not only not stopped but even accelerated. Chen's (2007) language vitality survey indicated that Taiwanese local languages, including Taigi, remained shifted and that the implementation of the Taiwanese local languages courses in elementary school did not boost the stagnant intergenerational transmission of these languages, including, of course, Taigi. Yap (2017) explored the current situation of family language in Taiwan based on 2010 census data and the 2013 Taiwan Social Change Survey. The results pointed to the plight of local languages in Taiwan, including Taigi. One of the difficulties is that unlike the promotion of the use of Mandarin as part of Chinese identity, Taiwanese identity does not involve reviving the use of Taigi in Taigi ethnic groups. In other words, the alignment of Taiwanese identity and Taigi had become blurred.

In summary, the intertwined relationship between Taigi and Taiwanese identity could be depicted as follows. For at least a century, Taigi played a pioneering role in the formation of Taiwanese identity, from the confrontation with foreign ruling powers at the political level to de-Sinicisation at the cultural level, to furthering the emergence of a Taiwanese identity. However, Taigi seems to have lagged behind after Taiwanese identity began to grow steadily. In other words, Taiwanese identity continues to advance, while Taigi has failed to keep up.

Given that Taigi has not maintained the advances of Taiwanese identity and the consequent Taiwanese nationalism, and that language shift towards Mandarin continues, people may wonder which language should function as the ethnic language of Taiwanese identity: Taigi or Mandarin? In fact, Taiwanese society is in a predicament on this issue and the current situation appears chaotic.

Mandarin as the language of Taiwanese identity?

As mentioned above, Taiwanese society has undergone a language shift towards Mandarin due to the long-term Mandarin-only policy. A large portion of the Taiwanese population, particularly the young to middle-aged, speak Mandarin as (one of) their mother tongue(s). The selection of Mandarin as the ethnic language of Taiwanese identity thus seems an inevitable compromise with the linguistic *status quo*.

It is not uncommon to encounter young Mandarin speakers in Taiwan actively defending the legitimacy of Mandarin against Taigi, even criticising the appeal of Taigi revitalisation as 'Taigi hegemony'. It is noteworthy that the majority of them are by no means self-identified Chinese, despite that Mandarin was, in the 1950s, initially implemented and promoted together with the imposed Chinese identity in Taiwan.

Politically, the democratisation and social liberalisation following the lifting of martial law in 1987 have consequently been conducive to the decline of Chinese identity. However, the linguistic environment did not significantly benefit from the political reform. Consequently, these Mandarin-defending young people grew up in a (nearly) Mandarin-only environment, the consequence of the long-term Mandarin-only policy, and speaking only Mandarin as their major language; some are even Mandarin monolinguals (foreign languages not considered here).

More solid indications of such a detachment of the linguistic identity of Taigi from the national identity of Taiwanese can be observed in social media, where young people are the major users. For instance, a pro-Taiwanese-independence social media fan page that has at least 40,000 followers posted a message recommending their supporters to make the following statement in English when introducing themselves to foreigners: 'I am from Taiwan. I am Taiwanese. I speak Mandarin'.[5]

This fan page has called for the normalisation of the status of Taiwan as a country, a long-standing politically sensitive issue domestically and internationally. The first two sentences of the statement, as can be seen, highlight Taiwanese identity. The final sentence, on the other hand, reveals the linguistic status quo in Taiwan, i.e. even the Taiwanese independence activists adopt Mandarin as their language marker. The point of this quoted statement, according to the text of the post, was to advocate the adoption of the term 'Mandarin' instead of 'Chinese', so that 'we' Taiwanese can be less likely to be misunderstood as 'they', the Chinese.

In fact, Taiwanese identity could have been more straightforwardly linked to Taigi, so that the slogan could have been, 'I am from Taiwan. I am Taiwanese. I speak TAIGI'. However, the truth is that Taigi's statuses as the lingua franca and the de facto national language of Taiwan seem to have been disregarded in this case.

Taiwan Mandarin[6]: The localised standard Mandarin variety in Taiwan

The alignment of Mandarin, instead of Taigi, to Taiwanese identity may partly be attributed to the localisation of Mandarin in Taiwan. By the time the Mandarin-only policy was implemented in Taiwan by the Chinese KMT government after World War II, this language had no domains, either public or family, in Taiwan. However, under the active and ubiquitous enforcement of this language policy, particularly in the mass media, schools, and public domains, and the suppression of Taigi and other local languages in Taiwan, Taiwanese people have undergone a long-term 'group second language acquisition'. The consequences of this language policy include not only the aforementioned language shift to Mandarin, but the localisation of Mandarin in Taiwan.

Previous studies have reported the formation of this new variety of Mandarin in Taiwan. For instance, Tseng (1999), Fon and Chiang (1999), Fon et al. (2004), Fon and Hsu (2007), and Hsu and Tse (2009) all confirmed the subtle but distinctive tonal features of Taiwan Mandarin. Tung (1995) and Tseng (2003) reported phonological and syntactic features of Taiwan Mandarin, respectively.

In addition to differences at speech level, orthographic differences between Taiwan Mandarin and Chinese Mandarin are another distinguishing marker. Although both adopt Sinographs, Taiwan Mandarin uses traditional characters while Chinese Mandarin uses simplified characters. Moreover, the phonetic symbols for Mandarin used in the two countries are more distinct than the characters. Taiwan has adopted Zhuyin Fuhao, a system of Mandarin phonetic symbols, comprising characters and tone markers as the symbols to transcribe Mandarin syllables. Zhuyin Fuhao is more commonly called Bopomofo, which represents the pronunciations of the first four symbols of Zhuyin Fuhao, ㄅ, ㄆ, ㄇ, ㄈ, corresponding respectively to the sounds [p], [pʰ], [m], and [f].[7] Chinese Mandarin, on the other hand, uses the Latin alphabet as the phonetic symbols of Mandarin, also known as Hanyu Pinyin.

The systematic linguistic differences between Taiwan Mandarin and Chinese Mandarin seem to have legitimated adopting Mandarin as the ethnolinguistic identifier of Taiwan. In other words, to the pro-Mandarin self-identified Taiwanese, particularly the young, these differences in Mandarin are salient enough to distinguish Taiwan from China, despite the fact that Taiwan Mandarin and Chinese Mandarin are no more than two close varieties of Mandarin.

The localisation of Mandarin in Taiwan has transcended the linguistic level to reach the psychological level. The initial sense of foreignness and 'Chineseness' of Mandarin in the early days of Mandarin promotion have gradually faded in Taiwan; Taiwanese people began to recognise Taiwan Mandarin as one language of Taiwan. Her (2009: 419), for instance, not only linguistically but socially, demographically, and politically motivated, proposed that 'Taiwan should embrace Taiwan Mandarin as a new indigenous language, while making every effort to revitalise its original indigenous language'. Khoo (2019) studied young Taiwanese people's attitudes towards five Mandarin varieties, including Taigi-accented Mandarin, Northern Chinese Mandarin, Southern Chinese Mandarin, Taiwan Mandarin, and second-generation Waisheng Mandarin. Results showed that Taiwan Mandarin was highly valued and outperformed Chinese Mandarin varieties, the long-term promoted prestigious Mandarin varieties during the period of martial law.

It is not only Taiwan Mandarin, but also the Bopomofo Mandarin Phonetic Symbols that are currently functioning as Taiwanese identity markers. Speakers of the same language, regardless of national boundaries or any other boundaries, can communicate orally with each other. However, such communicability does not inherently exist at the literal and symbolic level. Compared to language per se, phonetic symbols, as writing systems, are more prescriptive and disciplinary. The Bopomofo Mandarin Phonetic Symbols, together with Mandarin, were introduced into Taiwan from China by the KMT government after the end of World War II and have remained systematically imposed and used only in Taiwan since then. In other words, despite Mandarin being spoken in various places around the world, the Bopomofo Mandarin Phonetic Symbols have remained in use only in Taiwan for seven decades; only Taiwanese people recognise these symbols. The Bopomofo Mandarin Phonetic Symbols have become a kind of Taiwanese identifier on the Internet, where Mandarin speakers from various regions meet to chat and sometimes argue with each other, particularly Taiwanese and Chinese people.

Meanwhile, the Bopomofo Mandarin Phonetic Symbols have evolved even further from phonetic symbols into a kind of 'vernacular' semi-characters, mainly used in unofficial occasions, such as internet messages, text messages, and some advertisements. For example, in the phrase 「ㄋ看ㄉ懂ㄇ？」, the three Bopomofo symbols 'ㄋ'、'ㄉ'、'ㄇ' respectively stand for the initial sounds of the word '你' (ㄋㄧˇ[ni], *you*), '得' (ㄉㄜˊ[t], a particle), and '嗎' (ㄇㄚˊ, [ma], a questioning particle) (Table 4.1).

TABLE 4.1 An example of Bopomofo Symbols as semi-characters

Phrase: '*ㄋ看ㄉ懂ㄇ？*'

Bopomofo Symbol words	ㄋ [n]	看	ㄉ [t]	懂	ㄇ [m]
	你 [ni]		得 [t]		嗎 [ma]
Gloss	you	see	DE (particle)	understand	Q particle
Translation	'Do you understand (the text, visual image…)?'				

In fact, it is ironic that Taiwan Mandarin and the Bopomofo Mandarin Phonetic Symbols function as Taiwanese identifiers, as they were by no means associated with Taiwanese identity when they were initially promoted. Both Mandarin and the Bopomofo Symbols were part of the major tools that the Chinese KMT government adopted to impose Chinese identity on the Taiwanese people and to suppress Taiwanese identity. Nonetheless, after decades of derivation and development in Taiwan, these two have become the salient distinguishers of Taiwanese and Chinese people.

In his sociological study of the changing status of the Bopomofo Mandarin Phonetic Symbols, Chen (2010: II) confirmed the functional shifts of these symbols. He further suggested a framework for the transformation of Bopomofo Mandarin Phonetic Symbols and claimed that the changes were 'from national tradition to popular culture, from national ethos to parodic games, from the representation of China to the practice of everyday life in Taiwan'.

Taiwan Mandarin merging with Chinese Mandarin

Given that Taiwan Mandarin borders on Chinese Mandarin across the linguistic gaps stated above and thus can serve as the linguistic identity of Taiwan, maintaining or even enlarging these linguistic gaps should be expected in Taiwan. However, the situation is not moving accordingly.

Currently, Taiwanese people appear to accept Chinese Mandarin, particularly at the lexical and phrasal levels. Since roughly the late 1990s, Chinese Mandarin terms and phrases have begun an influx into Taiwan Mandarin. This trend began to accelerate in the 2000s as the contact between Taiwanese and Chinese people through travel and business became more frequent with political deregulation. In addition, the rise of Internet activities since then, such as e-commerce, online videos, and social media, have further boosted this trend.

It is noteworthy that most of this influx of Chinese terms has counterparts in TaiwanMandarin. In other words, these incoming Chinese terms are not function-driven loanwords, but lexical replacements.[8] Table 4.2 presents some examples.

Discussions of the 'encroachment' of Chinese Mandarin sometimes arise in public opinions, including online social media. However, such 'encroachment alert' often incurs criticisms such as 'narrow-mindedness', 'political overreaction', and 'linguistics unknowledgeable of language contact'.

The Latin alphabet of Taiwan Mandarin is another identity-language contradiction. For decades, Wade-Giles had been the major and de facto standard Romanisation system of Mandarin in Taiwan, while various other systems had coexisted with it. In 2002, when the Chinese-origin Hanyu Pinyin had been the major Mandarin Romanisation system in the world for roughly a couple of decades, the Taiwanese government approved another Mandarin Romanisation system, Tongyong Pinyin, literally the 'generally-used spelling of sounds'. The symbols of Tongyong Pinyin overlap by 85% with Hanyu Pinyin, and thus are generally speaking comprehensible to Hanyu Pinyin users. The gap formed by

TABLE 4.2 Examples of replacements of Chinese terms in Taiwan Mandarin

	TaiwanMandarin	*Chinese Mandarin*	*English translation*
1.	號	碼	(size) number
2.	材質	面料	fabric material
3.	線上	在線	online
4.	影片	視頻	video
5.	水準	水平	level
6.	螢幕	屏幕	screen
7.	智慧型	智能	(electronic products) smart
8.	還可以	還行	(colloquial) 'Fine!'
9.	服務生	服務員	server
10.	早安/晚安	早上好/晚上好	Good morning!/Good evening!

the remaining 15% of different symbols can function to distinguish Taiwan and China. In addition to its function of national identifier, Tongyong Pinyin is more phonetically faithful in terms of symbols and their corresponding sounds (Table 4.3), and thus is more friendly to foreigners who do not read Sinographs, Chinese characters, and have no knowledge of any kind of Mandarin Romanisation systems.

However, Tongyong Pinyin's function as a Taiwanese identifier was not supported by Taiwanese society. A series of fierce 'Tongyong or Hanyu' debates occurred at that time. In the end, the Hanyu Pinyin system survived this Mandarin Romanisation battle in Taiwan, resulting in the virtual extermination of not only Tongyong Pinyin, but Wade-Giles, the Mandarin Romanisation system that had the longest history in Taiwan.

In fact, the Romanisation system of Mandarin had barely drawn public attention in Taiwan, where people read Sinographs, and Latin alphabets are usually oversimplified as 'English alphabet'. In other words, the debate of Mandarin Romanisation in the early 2000s was more likely politically than linguistically driven.

The phenomena of lexical replacement and Hanyu Pinyin's survival in the competition over Mandarin Romanisation in Taiwan reveal that the issue of language identity seems to be neglected.

Taigi has faded away but its 'spirit' remains active in various forms

The elaboration so far may have created the impression that Taigi has completely fallen out of use and been abandoned. In fact, in spite of its loss, Taigi is not obsolete in this wave of language-identity seeking in Taiwan; it remains functional at the psychological and pragmatic level. Previous studies of Taiwanese people's language attitudes towards Taigi have revealed this trend. Chen (2010) reported that the most frequently expressed positive attitudes towards Taigi were 'language worth transmitting' (79%) and 'marker of solidarity' (70%). The two least frequently expressed positive attitudes were 'marker of social status' (19%)

TABLE 4.3 The consonant symbols of Tongyong Pinyin and Hanyu Pinyin and the corresponding IPA (shading marks the different symbols of Tongyong Pinyin and Hanyu Pinyin)

Tongyong	b	p	m	f	d	t	n	l	g	k	h	jy	c	s	jh	ch	sh	r	z	c	s
Hanyu	b	p	m	f	d	t	n	l	g	k	h	j	q	x	zh	ch	sh	r	z	c	s
IPA	b	p	m	f	t	tʰ	n	l	k	kʰ	h	tɕ	tɕʰ	ɕ	tʂ	tʂʰ	ʂ	ʐ	ts	tsʰ	s

and 'marker of authority' (26%). Similar research findings were reported in Hsu (2018), where Taiwanese people, regardless of age, generally highly valued Taigi along and only along the sentimental dimension. The evaluations along the practical dimensions rated Taigi mid to low, and lower among the young than the old.

The emotional function of Taigi, particularly among young people, can be observed in the current Mandarin-dominant setting in Taiwan. This function is revealed in Mandarin in various forms, such as 'emotional loanwords' and 'deliberate Taiuan Guoyu', proposed by Khoo (2019). The elaboration of these two forms is provided below.

'Emotional loanword' refers to words that 'have equivalent or near equivalent Mandarin words. Such loanwords are adopted for their Taigi flavour as a type of softener to express solidarity, friendliness, humour, and sometimes, teasing' (Khoo 2019: 603) (Table 4.4). In other words, emotional loanwords are not functionally driven to fill linguistic gaps between the donor language and the recipient language. They are sociolinguistically driven to express speakers' emotions, identity, or at least, preference towards Taigi.

'Deliberate Taiuan Guoyu', on the other hand, is another type of performance of Taigi's emotional function discussed in Khoo (2019). Taiuan Guoyu, literally 'Taiwan national language', refers to Taigi-accented Mandarin. It is a typical L1 transfer in L2 acquisition since the Taiwanese people experienced a 'group second language acquisition' of Mandarin (Winford 2003), particularly in the early stages of the Mandarin-only policy. In other words, Taiuan Guoyu is an inevitable result of language contact between Mandarin and Taigi.

Taiuan Guoyu has been stigmatised in contrast to the prestigious status of Biaozhun Guoyu (標準國語), literally 'standard national language'. Eliminating Taiuan Guoyu had been a major goal of the Mandarin-only policy during the period from the 1950s to the late 1980s, roughly overlapping with the period of martial law in Taiwan. Consequently, Taiuan Guoyu nearly disappeared among young to middle-aged Taiwanese people, the generations that were raised in Mandarin-dominant environments and speak Taiwan Mandarin, the de facto standard Mandarin variety in Taiwan.

However, in recent years, Taiwan Mandarin speakers, most of whom are young to middle-aged people, began to adopt Taiuan Guoyu as a switching code, functioning to express humour or denote solidarity. Examples (1) and (2) below are two examples of code-switching between Mandarin and Taiuan Guoyu. Table 4.5 presents the interpretation.

(1) '那個工作，偶想去速速看耶。' ('As to that job, I want to give a try'.)
(2) '那家店的點心都好好粗喔。' ('The snacks in that store are all delicious'.)

Khoo (2019) named this sociolinguistically driven Taiuan Guoyu 'deliberate Taiuan Guoyu'. In other words, the original Taiuan Guoyu was an inevitable transfer of Taigi to Mandarin. The speakers were Taigi native speakers learning Mandarin as an L2 and were typically older. The deliberate adoption of Taiuan

TABLE 4.4 Some examples of emotional Taigi loanwords in Mandarin

Mandarin word	Taigi loanwords in Mandarin		Taigi		Borrowing principle		Translation
	loanword	pronunciation	word	pronunciation	phonetic	semantic	
漂亮	水	[ʃue]	媠	[sui]	1		beautiful
不良客人	奧客	[au kʰə]	澳客	[au kʰe]	1	2	a difficult customer
頑固	鐵齒	[tʰje tʂʰɿ]	鐵齒	[tʰiʔ kʰi]		1,2	stubborn
不好意思	歹勢	[tai ʂɿ]	歹勢	[pʰai se]		1,2	embarrassed; shy

TABLE 4.5 Taiuan Guoyu terms in (1) and (2) and the corresponding Mandarin terms

Taiuan Guoyu			Mandarin	
速速	[su su]	→	試試	[ʂiʂi]
偶	[ou]	→	我	[wo]
粗	[tsʰu]	→	吃	[tʂʰɨ]

Guoyu, however, is intentional. It is a sociolinguistic outcome of rising Taiwanese identity.

Deliberate Taiuan Guoyu, to a certain degree, can function as a substitute for Taigi at the emotional level; it may be considered a compromise between limited Taigi ability and rising Taiwanese identity. As stated previously, deliberate Taiuan Guoyu is adopted by young to middle-aged Taiwanese, the generations that speak Mandarin as their major/only language. Taiuan Guoyu is beneficial to these people in two ways. On the one hand, it carries some colours of Taigi and thus expresses solidarity. On the other hand, Taiuan Guoyu is a variety of Mandarin, the language they can manage best.

Taigi's function as marking the ethnolinguistic identity of Taiwanese is also revealed in written forms. Not until the first decade of the 21st century, when Taigi was officially standardised, was colloquial Taigi ever written. Even Taigi monolinguals wrote in Chinese, classic, or vernacular. The situation has begun to change recently. In addition to the orthography at the official level, written Taigi, in its standard form, non-standard form, or even idiosyncratic and arbitrary forms, has begun to be popular in various occasions and in various venues, including business signboards, advertisements, texts in social media, and even government propaganda. Such Taigi signs thus form the unique linguistic landscape of Taiwan (see Khoaⁿ Khang-pang 2019).

Meanwhile, the language usage in the Sunflower Student Movement may reveal young people's desire, or at least preference, to link Taiwanese national identity to Taigi. The Sunflower Student Movement is a large-scale civic movement that occurred in 2014. It protested a China-dependent trade agreement that was believed to leave Taiwan politically vulnerable to China. This movement was initiated mainly by a coalition of students, most of whom were in their 20s, and later supported by a large number of Taiwanese people, the majority of whom were young students.

In other words, most of the participants were from the generation of Taiwan Mandarin speakers, i.e. those who were raised after the language shift towards Mandarin was (nearly) complete. However, the theme song of this anti-China movement, Tó-sū Thinn-kng (島嶼天光, literally 'island's sunrise'), was a Taigi song, a language that was less familiar than Mandarin to most of the participants. The language selection of this song did not deter it from spreading among the supporters of the movement. This song was so popular that it was further rearranged for various types of musical performances, such as chorus.

The ethnolinguistic identity predicament of Taiwan

The above-mentioned current situation of the ethnolinguistic identity in Taiwan reveals the predicament that the Taiwanese people confront. Historically, psychologically, and linguistically, Taigi should be the most appropriate candidate for a Taiwanese ethnolinguistic identifier. However, young people's Taigi proficiency is limited.

In this regard, Taiwan Mandarin, due to its systematic linguistic differences from Chinese Mandarin, is thus considered, particularly by young Taiwanese people, as a substitute for Taigi, despite the fact that these two are merely two similar varieties of Mandarin and the gaps between them may not be salient enough to distinguish them.

However, should the features of Taiwan Mandarin be so distinctive that they could enable this variety of Mandarin to function as a Taiwanese ethnolinguistic identifier, Taiwan Mandarin speakers should actively and consciously maintain these features, even broadening the gap. Nevertheless, the fact is, Chinese Mandarin expressions and lexical items continue flowing into Taiwan Mandarin, and China-originated Hanyu Pinyin even replaced Taiwan-originated Tongyong Pinyin.

Will Taigi follow the track of Irish revitalisation?

The ongoing complicated sociolinguistic issue of Taigi in Taiwan may be compared to Irish in Ireland. The Irish experiences in terms of its loss and revival have inspired some Taigi revitalisation studies, for instance, Tiuⁿ (2008) and Li (2012).

There are, indeed, a number of similarities between these two cases. For instance, the decline of both Taigi and Irish is the consequence of foreign ruling powers and the languages they imposed; both of the introduced languages have dominant political power. Both Taigi and Irish have been struggling for revival.

There seems to be a positive trend for Irish. The number of self-claimed Irish speakers has risen from 13.3% at the turn of the 20th century (Hindley 1990, cited in Carnie 1995) to 19.3% in 1926, 21.2% in 1946, 31.6% in 1981, 43.5% in 1996, and 39.8% in 2016.[9] However, Irish revitalisation is seen by many as a failure (for instance, Hindley 1990, Carnie 1995, and Shah 2014). The above-mentioned percentages of Irish speakers were suspected to have been grossly inflated. Carnie (1995: 104), for instance, criticised the term 'Irish speaker' as not clearly defined; '[t]his could mean anything from having taken a few lessons in school to being a fluent native speaker'. In addition, the distribution of Irish speakers in Ireland was uneven; most of them live in Gaeltacht areas, the officially recognised regions where Irish is the predominant vernacular, or language of the home. The Irish 2016 census may be more reflective of the reality of Irish speaking. The 2016 census reported that 39.8% of the population self-reported as Irish speakers. However, among them, 23.8% never spoke it, 6.3% spoke it weekly, and only 4.2%, i.e. 1.7% of the population, spoke it daily. Even in Gaeltacht areas, self-reported Irish speakers accounted for only 66.3% of the Gaeltacht population.

Given that there are many similarities between the sociolinguistic histories of Irish and Taigi and that Irish revitalisation is considered unsuccessful, does the similar sociolinguistic history between Irish and Taigi predict the misfortune of Taigi?

In fact, despite several similarities between Taigi and Irish, the vitality of these two languages when language revitalisation started was not comparable. As stated above, at the beginning of Irish revitalisation, the language had been seriously lost. The revitalisation of Irish, thus, was tantamount to a rebirth of the language. The revitalisation of Taigi, on the other hand, is more like a boost, as the number of Taigi native speakers is not small.

Unlike Irish, the language shift from Taigi to Mandarin and the revitalisation of Taigi are contemporary. Chen (2007) reported the statistical data of her 2003 survey regarding the language vitality of five languages in Taiwan, including Mandarin, Taigi, Hakka, Taiwanese aboriginal languages,[10] and English, a new required subject for 1st to 6th graders in elementary school starting from 2001. It indicated that among the survey participants, those who were over 60 years old were all self-reported fluent Taigi speakers.

As to the younger participants, 93% of the 30 to 45- and 46 to 60-year-olds were self-reported fluent Taigi speakers, as well as 71% of the 19 to 29-year olds, 12% of the 13 to 18-year-olds, and 20% of the under 12-year-olds. In other words, in the 1990s, when Taigi revitalisation was initiated, over 90% of the adults in Taiwan were fluent Taigi speakers. In this regard, Taigi revival served to 'reboot' Taiwanese people's lethargic but not completely lost Taigi tongue, which had once been active while gradually declining due to the long-term Mandarin-only policy. Simply speaking, most Taiwanese people were 'Taigi-savvy' in the early 1990s, when the Taigi revival movement began. In this regard, despite the ongoing language shift towards Mandarin, the demographic advantage of Taigi, though not promising to be a success, seems to make Taigi revitalisation more blessed at this stage than Irish.

Identity with a language? The case of Singlish

It is ironic that in the early 1990s, Taiwanese identity began to burgeon while Taigi continued losing ground even more rapidly. However, as Taiwanese identity has robustly grown during the nearly three decades since then, is it possible that the strengthening Taiwanese identity, particularly among young people in recent years, can slow down Taigi decline or even accelerate Taigi revival? The status of Singlish in recent years may shed some light on Taigi.

Singlish refers to the colloquial Singaporean English that incorporates Chinese dialects (mainly Hokkien and Cantonese) and Malay lexical and grammatical elements. Singlish had been attached a negative label in contrast to standard English, one of the official languages in Singapore and the international language of prestigious status, particularly in the early days of its foundation, when this new, trade-dependent country began to show its eagerness to survive global competition.

Previous Singaporean prime ministers have issued statements expressing negative attitudes towards Singlish. For instance, the first prime minister, Lee Kuan Yew, in 1999 described Singlish as 'English corrupted by Singaporeans' and Lee's successor, Prime Minister Goh Chok Tong, stated that 'Poor English reflects badly on [Singaporeans] and makes [Singaporeans] seem less intelligent' (Lim 2009: 57). The Singaporean government even launched the Speak Good English Movement in 2000 to counter the use of Singlish.

In recent years, the stigmatisation of Singlish began to be weakened. There have been attempts to revive Singlish and further promote it 'as a culture marker of Singaporean identity' (Goh 2016: 749). It is noteworthy that these attempts have been driven mainly by the educated class, such as professionals, journalists, and writers, who are capable of code switching between Singlish and standard English. They mainly use standard English but view Singlish as a practical and valuable linguistic option (Goh 2013: 133–139).

Singlish has played a crucial role in the formation and reinforcement of Singaporean identity. Singaporean identity seems to have been intensified in the first two decades of the 21st century, the era of globalisation and migration (Goh 2016: 752). For instance, the measures that the Singaporean government adopted to respond to the 2008 global financial crisis and the immigration policy released in a government white paper in 2013 are immigrant- and foreign-worker-friendly. These immigration policies, on the one hand, have provoked popular discontent towards the government, and on the other hand accelerated the formation of Singaporean identity. In this period, Singlish 'moved subtly but noticeably from a discourse of playfulness in public culture, to an increasingly politicised discourse mobilised in angry social commentary especially in social media' (Goh 2016: 753).

As a symbol of the rising Singaporean language identity, Singlish has come 'full circle' (Lim 2015: 266) in various areas and at various levels. Lim (2015), for instance, reported a 'commodification of languages of heritage' at SG50, the year of the 50th anniversary of Singapore, in which local art and design stores released Singlish-themed products. In Singapore's 2015 National Day Parade, there were carnival floats featuring Singlish particles and terms. Such commodification of Singlish also functions outside Singapore. Many Singaporean restaurants overseas have their names in Singlish terms, in order to highlight their Singaporeaness and attract customers.

Language as a marker of ethnic identity is, of course, by no means a new perspective. What makes the rise of Singlish illuminating for Taiwan is its social background. Both Singapore and Taiwan are export-oriented economies; both are in East Asia, where globalisation, and thus English, have been recurrently emphasised at the social, political, and educational levels. Whether to adopt English as an official language has been debated in East Asian countries, such as Japan, Korea, and Taiwan, where English plays no historical or governmental role. In this regard, English advantages Singapore in various ways, particularly in the international competition in this region. Furthermore, unlike most of the former

Western-colonised nations, Singapore does not have distinct ethnic languages; ethnolinguistic identity is thus not inherent in Singaporean identity. Simply speaking, Singaporean identity can be developed as a national identity without an inherent national language. However, as stated above, Singlish gradually developed as the ethnic language of Singaporeans.

The rise of Singlish as an ethnolinguistic identity manifests the significance of a locally derived language in which national identity is rooted. What is noteworthy is that the development of Singlish from stigmatised non-standard English to the ethnic language of Singaporeans is a bottom-up long-term procedure that occurred in the 21st century, when language identity can no longer be easily advocated in the name of nationalism in a top-down manner.

The relation of Singlish to standard English may at first glance be analogised to that of Taiuan Guoyu, the Taigi-accented Mandarin, to standard Mandarin. However, such an analogy is inappropriate. It ignores Taigi's history and status as the lingua franca in Taiwan as elaborated above.

Despite the fact that both Taiuan Guoyu and Singlish are the result of 'group second language acquisition' of a politically dominant language, and both are thus the unavoidable transient varieties towards the standard varieties, i.e. Mandarin and English respectively, the status of Taiuan Guoyu and Singlish are sociolinguistically not analogisable. Taiuan Guoyu was derived from Taigi, literally Taiwan language. That is, there had been an established linguistic identity of Taiwan, which is Taigi, when the Mandarin-only policy was initiated soon after World War II. As to Singlish, although its starting point was also the local languages of Singapore, with Hokkienese as the major one, the linguistic identity of Singapore had not been well recognised when Singlish began to appear. At least, there was no language in the name of Singapore as, say, Singaporean. In this regard, it is Taigi, not Taiuan Guoyu, that functions as the sociolinguistic counterpart of Singlish in this wave of rising Singlish.

Conclusion

This chapter reviewed the relation between Taiwanese identity and Taigi. Taigi has a long history in Taiwan and has led the formation and growth of Taiwanese identity for almost a century since the late 19th century. During that period, Japanese identity and Chinese identity were successively imposed politically onto the Taiwanese people. The growth of Taiwanese identity has gradually accelerated since the 1990s, following political and social liberalisation. However, ironically, Taigi continued losing ground.

Taigi revitalisation since the 1990s did achieve certain targets at various levels, while Mandarin remained predominant. Due to the long-term exclusive Mandarin-only policy in Taiwan, most Taiwanese people are Mandarin speakers. Thus, in current Taiwan, the majority of Taigi speakers, most of whom are native, are Taigi-Mandarin bilinguals; this bilingualism as well as the trend of globalisation may hinder the progress of Taigi revitalisation, since Mandarin remains the most predominant language in Taiwan, and English functions as the lingua franca in the international community.

However, despite the predominance of Mandarin, Taigi's function in Taiwanese identity remains, even among the young people, most of whom are merely capable of limited Taigi. In this regard, various forms of 'expedient' Taigi appeared as the substitute of Taigi, in such phenomena as code switching between Mandarin and Taigi, deliberate Taigi, and so forth.

Taiwanese identity rose to an historically high level of 83% in February 2020. The relation between Taiwanese identity and Taigi became a predicament for Taiwanese society. Mandarin remains the predominant language in Taiwan. Can Mandarin become the ethnic language of Taiwan? The strong link between Mandarin and China may lead to a negative answer, not only because of the value of autonomy that Taiwanese people seek, but also China's hostility towards Taiwan as an independent state. Taigi may be the most appropriate language for Taiwanese identity, as it had been in the early stage of the pursuit of Taiwanese identity. However, Taigi has largely been lost, particularly among the young to middle-aged generations of people in Taiwan, and its revival through education and encouragement of daily use should be highly recommended.

Both the cases of Irish revitalisation and the rise of Singlish can shed light on the issue of ethnolinguistic identity in Taiwan, since each case reflects one part of the dilemma that Taiwan faces.

The Irish case displays the difficulty of language revitalisation, and the Singlish case indicates the effect of linguistic identity in the development of national identity even in a modern, globalised, and English-speaking society.

Taiwan is at a crossroads in the decision over ethnolinguistic identity. To decouple Taiwanese identity from Taigi and adopt Taiwan Mandarin as the representative language of Taiwan may be an alternative. However, this alternative neglects the inextricable link between Taigi and Taiwan. The adoption of Taigi as the linguistic identity of Taiwan, on the other hand, may be the most straightforward decision, one that most nation-states have made, while the young people, most of whom are only capable of limited Taigi, may resist this trend.

Notes

1 The Temporary Taiwan Household Investigation.
2 The name of this language has long been a complicated issue. In addition to the names mentioned above, there are many other names, each reflecting different linguistic, social, and political values. For details, see Khoo (2019).
3 Taiwanese Core Political Attitude Trend (1992–2019/06), conducted by Election Study Center, National Chengchi University, https://esc.nccu.edu.tw/app/news.php?Sn=166, visited on 27 February 2020.
4 Taiwanese National Identity Trend (1993–2020), conducted by Taiwanese Public Opinion Foundation,
    www.tpof.org/台灣政治/國家認同/台灣人的民族認同趨勢圖%ef%bc%88199120199/, visited on 29 February 2020.

5 Taiwan Passport Sticker, www.facebook.com/TaiwanPassportSticker/photos/a.14
 70612246581878/1477641505878952/?type=3andtheater, visited on 29 February
 2020.
6 It is noteworthy that the terms 'Taiwan Mandarin' and 'Taiwanese Mandarin' refer to
 different Mandarin varieties in Taiwan. Taiwan Mandarin refers to the localized standard Mandarin variety, while Taiwanese Mandarin refers to Taigi-accented Mandarin, a
 stigmatized variety.
7 For more on the introduction of Zhuyin Fuhao, see Shei (2014: 12).
8 https://oops.udn.com/oops/story/6698/2417233, visited on 17 June 2020; https://oops
 .udn.com/oops/story/6699/1641792, visited on 17 June 2020.
9 Central Statistical Office, www.cso.ie/en/census/census2006reports/census2006-
 volume9-irishlanguage/, visited on 20 February 2020.
10 The Formosan languages were not further subclassified in Chen (2007).

References

English references

Carnie, Andrew. (1995) 'Modern Irish: A case study in language revival failure', *Papers on
 Endangered Languages, MIT Working Papers in Linguistics*, 28: 99–114.
Chen, Su-chiao. (2010) 'Multilingualism in Taiwan', *International Journal of the Sociology
 of Language*, 205: 79–104.
Fon, Janice & Wen-yu Chiang. (1999) 'What does Chao have to say about tones?—A case
 study of Taiwan Mandarin', *Journal of Chinese Linguistics*, 27 (1): 13–37.
Fon, Janice & Hui-ju Hsu. (2007) 'Positional and phonotactic effects on the realization
 of dipping tones in Taiwan Mandarin'. In Gussenhoven, Carlos & Tomas Riad (eds.)
 *Phonology and Phonetics, Tones and Tunes: Vol. 2 Phonetic and Behavioural Studies
 in Word and Sentence Prosocly*. Berlin: Mouton de Gruyter.
Fon, Janice, Wen-yu Chiang & Hintat Cheung. (2004) 'Production and perception of two
 dipping tones (T2 and T3) in Taiwan mandarin', *Journal of Chinese Linguistics*, 32(2):
 249–280.
Goh, Robbie B.H. (2013) 'Uncertain locale: The dialectics of space and the cultural politics
 of English in Singapore'. In Wee, Lionel, Robbie B.H. Goh, and Lisa Lim(eds.), *The
 Politics of English: South Asia, Southeast Asia and the Asia Pacific*. Amsterdam: John
 Benjamins, pp. 125–144.
Goh, Robbie B.H. (2016) 'The anatomy of Singlish: Globalisation, multiculturalism and
 the construction of the "local" in Singapore', *Journal of Multilingual and Multicultural
 Development*, 37(8): 748–758.
Her, One-Soon. (2009) 'Language and group identity: On Taiwan Mainlanders' mother
 tongues and Taiwan Mandarin', *Language and Linguistics*, 10(2): 375–419.
Hindley, Reg. (1990) *The Death of the Irish Language*. London: Routledge.
Hsiau, A-chin. (2000) *Contemporary Taiwanese Cultural Nationalism*. New York:
 Routledge.
Hsu, Hui-ju. (2018) 'The entanglement of emotion and reality: An investigation of the
 Taiwanese people's attitudes towards Taigi', *Journal of Multilingual and Multicultural
 Development*, 39(1): 76–91.
Hsu, Hui-ju & John Kwock-ping Tse. (2009) 'Tonal leveling of Taiwan mandarin: A study
 in Taipei', *Concentric: Studies in Linguistics*, 35(2): 225–244.
Khoo, Hui-lu. (2019) 'The dynamics of Southern Min in Taiwan: From Southern Min
 dialects to Taigi'. In C. Shei (ed.), *The Routledge Handbook of Chinese Discourse
 Analysis*. London: Routledge, pp. 596–610.

Li, Khin-Huann. (2012) 'A comparative study of language movements in Taiwan and Ireland', *Taiwan in Comparative Perspective*, 4: 176–188.

Lim, Lisa. (2009) 'Beyond fear and loathing in SG: The real mother tongues and language policies in multilingual Singapore', *AILA Review*, 22: 52–71.

Lim, Lisa. (2015) 'Coming of age, coming full circle: The (re)positioning of (Singapore) English and multilingualism in Singapore at 50', *Asian Englishes*, 17(3): 261–270.

Shah, Inayat. (2014) 'Linguistic attitude and the failure of Irish language revival efforts', *International Journal of Innovation and Scientific Research*, 1(2): 67–74.

Shei, Chris. (2014) *Understanding the Chinese Language: A Comprehensive Linguistic Introduction*. London: Routledge.

Winford, Donald (2003) *An Introduction to Contact Linguistics*. Oxford: Blackwell.

Wu, Rwei-ren (2014) 'Fragment of/f empires: The peripheral formation of Taiwanese Nationalism'. In Shyu-tu Lee and Jack F. Williams (eds.), *Taiwan's Struggle: Voices of the Taiwanese*. Lanham, Maryland: Rowman & Littlefield, pp. 27–34.

Chinese references

Chen, Su-chiao. 陳淑嬌 (2007) '台灣語言活力研究' (The study of the language vitality in Taiwan). In Chin-chuan Cheng 鄭錦全etc. (eds.) 語言政策的多元 文化思考 *(The Multicultural Thinking of Language Policy)*. Taipei: Institute of Linguistics, Academia Sinica, pp. 19–39.

Khoaⁿ Khang-pang Team 看看板工作小組. (2019) 看看板: 廣告招牌的台語大學 問 *(Let's Find Taigi in Signboards)*. Taipei: Avan Guard.

Tiuⁿ, Hak-khiam. 張學謙 (2008) '國家能否挽救弱勢語言? 以愛爾蘭語言復振為例' (Can state actions save a minority language? On Ireland's language revitalization). 台灣國際研究季刊 *(Taiwan International Studies Quarterly)*, 4(4): 21–45.

Tseng, Chin-chin. 曾金金 (1999) 兩岸新聞播音員語音對比分析 (A contrastive analysis on the pronunciation between Mainland China and Taiwan: A case study of news reporters). NSC technical report: 88-2411-H-003-017.

Tseng, Hsin-yi. 曾心怡 (2003) 當代台灣國語的句法結構 *(The syntax structures of contemporary Taiwanese Mandarin)*. MA thesis, National Taiwan Normal University.

Tung, Chung-szu. 董忠司 (1995) '台灣漢語方言影響下的若干「國語」聲母變體初稿' (The varieties of some "Guoyu" initials under the influences of Chinese dialects in Taiwan, a preliminary study), 語文學報 2: 3–28.

Yap, Ko-Hua. 葉高華 (2017) '臺灣民眾的家庭語言選擇' (Family language choice in Taiwan), 台灣社會學刊 *(Taiwanese Journal of Sociology)*, 62: 59–111.

5

A SOCIOLINGUISTIC APPROACH TO THE STANDARDISATION OF *TAIYU* IN THE QUEST FOR A TAIWANESE IDENTITY

Ann Heylen

Introduction

In sociolinguistics Taiwan makes up an interesting case, being one of the multilingual nation-states where language is a politically and ideologically dividing factor in society. The focus of attention is the process of standardisation of Southern Min, one of the local languages once spoken by the majority of the island Han population migrating from two coastal provinces, Fujian and Guangdong, since the 17th century. An introduction warrants a few words about the terminology, as the naming of the language under discussion is itself contested, and significant to understand the sociolinguistic debate. From an overview perspective, terminology use is both geographically and historically delineated, and the variations in naming are in principle no more than other linguistic terms for the same language. In this chapter, I will use the Mandarin pronunciation *Taiyu* (台語), the equivalent of *Taigi* in Southern Min, also known as *Minnanyu* (閩南語), Taiwan Hokkien, *fulaohua* (福佬話), and *holo* (河洛) to denote the more general parlance Taiwanese, concurrent with Mandarin and Hakka. As for the sociolinguistic approach, this chapter adopts Einar Haugen's (1966, 1972) four-step matrix model that identifies phases in language standardisation. This model is organised on the level of the form and the function of a language and is presented as selection of norm, codification of form, elaboration of function, and acceptance by the community. In its application to language planning (LP) processes, 'Haugen's model is quite appropriate for assessing the different diachronic processes constituting the transition of a language from a domestic vernacular, still not properly codified, to a standard national language, suitable for use in all domains of modern society' (Hannesdóttir 2011: 110).[1]

Translocating to Taiwan, debates on language standardisation occurred in the wake of the project of nation-building which in the context of East Asia is characterised by the unification of the spoken and the written word. These debates were held both in Republican China at the beginning of the 20th century and Meiji Japan alike and are known as *yanwen yizhi / genbun itchi* (言文一致). At the time, Taiwan was a Japanese colony (1895–1945) and members of this new Japanese-educated class became equally susceptible to these nationalist models of language reform and standardisation. The Taiwanese-language makers of the late 1920s and early 1930s experimented with how to apply the model of language unification in creating a written Taiwanese (*taiwanhuawen* 台灣話文) based on the spoken form (*taiwanhua* 台灣話). The debate was mainly carried out in newspapers and literary magazines such as *Nanyin* (南音), but the outcome was curtailed because of Kōminka (*huangminhua* 皇民化 1937–1945). Kōminka refers to the increased Japanisation of society from the mid-1930s, which banned all Chinese-language publications and militarised Taiwan. In spite of the regime change and the imposition of a new language hegemony after 1945, the colonial efforts generated enough evidence and interest not to disappear.

A fair amount of research devoted to language problems and planning in Taiwan relates to identity (Hsiau 1997, 2000; Cheng 1994). Connotations that speaking *Taiyu* is associated with *Taidu*, an abbreviation for pro-independence activism, is reminiscent of other case studies where language standardisation processes are a central part of the political platform and perform an ideological function. For instance, the Corsican example's 'emphasis on language [that] justifies claims on cultural identity and political autonomy' (Jaffe 1999: 1). What I want to achieve in this chapter, using the Haugen model, is to show that the underpinnings of the *Taiyu* quest for a linguistic standard are rooted in the development of writing and the growth of nationalism (Haugen 1966: 97). Precisely because the model of Haugen's language standardisation is steeped in the framework of nation-building, it is extremely useful for understanding the situation of language contact and planning in Taiwan from a socio-political perspective, revealing the extent to which the association of *Taiyu* and *Taidu* exemplifies an ideology of standardisation. The idea that standardisation itself has ideological underpinnings follows Ana Deumert's (2003) work building on Haugen's 1987 expansion and is useful in illustrating the politically driven reversed language shift (RLS) or Taigi revitalisation movement, as has been documented by Hui-Iu Khoo (2019).

Conceptualising the Haugen model

The discourse on language and identity in Taiwan is often compounded by uses of 'language' and 'dialect' which mix up the structural (linguistic description) and the functional (social use) dimensions of both terms, defining *Taiyu* as a dialect in relation to Mandarin as the national language. The misconception lies in classifying *Taiyu* as a dialect of Mandarin, which it is not because Mandarin as a northern variant is not genetically related to the Southern Min language group.[2] Thus, in its linguistic definition, the usage of 'dialect' here is inaccurate. As a social norm, 'dialect' is thought of as standing outside the language, and Haugen finds it more appropriate to use the term 'vernacular' or 'un(der)developed language' (Haugen 1966: 100–101). In relation to Mandarin, the function and status of *Taiyu* in society is not considered on the same level as that of a fully-fledged language (read: standard). However, the linguistic term 'dialect' has been mistakenly used to denote the social subordinate relation to the standard, and the language in its vernacular stage was justified as a continuum for the functional superiority of Mandarin over the inferiority of *Taiyu*, mainly based on the perception that 'it was not written' (undeveloped). This brings us to the meaning of vernacularisation, whose interpretation as unification of the spoken and the written stood as the model for language development with standardisation of the national language as the result. A language that was not developed on the basis of unifying its spoken and written forms remained a *fangyan* (方言 regional speech) and became stigmatised as 'dialect' or substandard language in the name of nation-building (DeBernardi 1991). But the same factors in the development of writing and the growth of nationalism that enabled Mandarin to become the standard characterise the quest for *Taiyu* in doing the same. Haugen's four aspects of language development form a matrix within which it is possible to discuss these issues at stake in achieving the reverse language shift in the life of the Taiwanese nation.

The idea behind Haugen's model of standardisation is thus best perceived as a process in which the 'vernacular' or 'undeveloped' language *Taiyu* selects a norm (selection) to be chosen as the spoken and written standard, proceeds with making consistent the grammar and lexicon (codification) so that the language can be used in all domains of society (elaboration), and finally also is accepted in society (acceptance). In view of the social dialect stigma, this entailed a response to the stereotyped perception 'lack of a written form', and illustrates Haugen's observation on the development of writing as a crucial aspect in understanding the ideology of language standardisation in a nation-building framework. Hence, this chapter will have a major focus on the written debate/orthography and a minor focus on the spoken. On the one hand, a standardised spoken Taiwanese is not sufficient to qualify for language standard; while on the other hand, written Taiwanese is characterised by script variation (digraphia or polygraphia and poly-orthographia). Why all this complexity? Concurring with Brian Street in the New Literacy Studies (Street 1984, 1993, 2006), writing systems and orthographies are to be seen as the embodiment of practice; meaning that this practice is socially, culturally, and historically embedded. Mark Sebba's work has also shown that far from being 'neutral technologies', scripts have symbolic power which transcends language itself. Orthographies readily become symbolic of national or group identity (Sebba 2007: 119).

Each of the four steps in the Haugen matrix engages with the forms of script variation and elaborates the strengths but also the weaknesses of *Taiyu* in relation to the standard Mandarin (both on the linguistics as well as on the social level). Steps along this process involved a development in writing (script and spelling; orthography) and were motivated by the growth of nationalism, known as the ascendance of a Taiwanese identity and democratisation that challenged the political hierarchy. I shall pinpoint ideological, political, and pragmatic difficulties faced by its actors, be they cultural activists, academic linguists, teachers, and language pioneers. As will be shown, the quest for a Taiwanese linguistic standard was captured in a whirlwind of socio-political change played out against the background of a nation-building framework that opened more venues with the democratisation. Precisely the democratic transition enabled the challenging of the 'national' hierarchy with a policy making of 'multi' and generated possibilities in the long march for language equality; raising the status and promoting the language to the national level.

The selection of the norm

Selection of the norm means that one norm of the spoken and written form has preference over the others, and thus involves a process that delineates its appropriateness. In the case of Taiwanese, we are dealing with a double layer that entails a script form used for accurate pronunciation, and if that script is character-based, one must make sure which is a corresponding character selected from a variety of repositories given the contact-induced variations within the language. If the script form is alphabetic writing, one still needs to make sure of adherence to one register, but what about those who advocate combining characters (graphs) and alphabetic writing (roman script), and where is the norm for using the one over the other? Still others have invented their own script and the most recent expression is the so-called Taigi Martian script (*Taiyu huoxingwen* 台語火星文). These considerations taken together underlie the orthographic debate, and although the selection of the norm was equally couched in an ideological debate during the colonial period, in the post-war/colonial period, Sebba's observation that 'orthography readily take on symbolism which extends far beyond the mechanics of a writing system' fits the Taiwan situation best in addressing the controversies at stake (2007: 100). Briefly, the selection of the norm is conditioned by decisions regarding the phonology and the pronunciation of a word-compound combined with a particular script form, which in a context of polygraphia gives the choice between a character (graph), alphabetic letters (roman), a combination of both, and for some the insert of alternative idiosyncratic symbols, but the latter is not the focus of attention here.

Both the Chinese character script and the alphabetic writing script have developed into traditions with their own repositories and registers. The character script in the Southern Min variant includes regional traditions drawing from folk literature since the 16th century (van der Loon 1992; Schipper 1985; Lien 1995). The alphabetic writing was developed by the early 19th century missionaries and includes the mission literature in Romanisation (*peh-oe-ji* 白話字 or Romanised Taiwanese, hereafter POJ). During the Japanese colonial period, both script forms enabled the composition of a written literature; they were partially codified and functional in their own respective environments (Klöter 2005; Heylen 2012).

The retreat of the Chinese Nationalist one-party government (hereafter KMT) in 1945 imposed the newly adopted Chinese national language Mandarin Chinese (*guoyu* 國語), relegating the other spoken languages (vernaculars) to the level of dialect (*fangyan*) and discriminating against them in the public domain in line with the speak-Mandarin-only movement (*shuo guoyu yundong* 說國語運動). These circumstances entailed changes for both orthographies. In spite of the national language policy, there was no explicit ban for those who wished to keep on researching the local languages. Actually, the complex language situation required linguistic talent, even if this was limited to a few people. One of these was linguist Wu Shou-li (吳守禮, 1909–2005) for whom the folk traditions and its repository of characters were a sufficient resource to continue working on Chinese dialectology. His seminal works testify to the Chinese tradition of character writing and formation, and was in line with earlier work by Lian Yatang (連雅堂aka Lien Heng 連橫, 1878–1936). Lian Yatang is credited for his attempts to create the first etymological orthography for Taiwanese (Klöter 2005: 131). A younger generation of linguists – born in the immediate post-war years – who followed in Wu Shou-li's footsteps are Hsu Cheng-chang (許成章), Hong Wei-jen (Ang Ui-jin 洪惟仁), and Yao Rong-song (姚榮松) (Liao 2013).

At the other end of the orthography spectrum are the proponents of the Church Romanisation script (*peh-oe-ji* 白話字POJ), the mainstay of the Presbyterian Church in Taiwan (PCT). From the 1960s until the early 1990s a continued use of the POJ script was politically sanctioned by the government. Research on the role of the Presbyterian Church and its theological seminars in their relations with the KMT one-party state under martial law explain their stronghold in opposition politics, the support base for the exiled blacklisted community mainly in the United States, and the breeding ground for a (growing) number of KMT-critical research advocates and academics (Rubinstein 1991, 2006). Interest in and propagation of POJ literacy remained one of the key elements in its ecclesiastical work and social activism. Once the political sanctioning was lifted, the Tainan theological seminar needed to cultivate *Taiyu*-language teachers, who were not only proficient in speaking, but also able to master the POJ script for spreading the Gospel and doing church work. Theirs had the advantage of a codified linguistic standard based on the alphabet and the practice in the church paper that had been established in 1885. Therefore, priority was given to organising literacy campaigns to teach the alphabetic writing, and this was interpreted as a key element in the struggle for the revitalisation of the language with an ideological undertone of oppositional politics (Lin 1999). Associating with oppositional politics and often having close links with the Presbyterian Church nurtured the politically driven reversed language shift (RLS) or Taigi revitalisation movement. The *Taiyu*-language teachers have generally come to be referred to as 'mother tongue teachers', reflecting the generation for whom speaking *Taiyu* was the language used at home and in the private domain.

By the late 1980s, following the lifting of martial law and the democratisation process, calls for language planning and critique on the language policy could openly manifest itself in society. Hence, into the 1990s, we see the emergence of orthographic diversity appearing in publications. By definition, language as a socially differentiating factor became the distinguishing feature between social groups, and by linking language to ethnicity, it turned into a crucial tool for identity politics. Initial calls for language reform and Taiwanese-language planning were launched by a number of linguists and writers who lived in exile (United States, Japan) and formulated their treatises in a counter-nationalist narrative format. The impetus from the United States, and more in particular the support of the Presbyterian Church, fuelled the establishment of a Taiwanese-language movement (hereafter: *taiyuwen* movement). One strand of the Christian activities in the United States undertook the organisation of summer schools, cultural lectures, and the publication of a number of overseas magazines, of which *Tâi-bûn Thong-sin* (台文通訊 *Taiwanese writing Forum*, est. 1991) became the most influential (Liao 2013: 69–81). The purpose was to preserve the language as heritage, and at the same time act as a reservoir of KMT language policy resistance, given the political situation in Taiwan. These activities exerted a profound influence on a burgeoning radicalisation of the student movement whose activism had been confined to limited broadcasting (1992). A change came with the 1997 creation of the Lí Kang Khioh Foundation (Lí Kang Khioh Tâi-gí *Bûn-kàu Ki-kim-hōe* 李江卻台語文教基金會) taking the publication of the Taipei magazine *Tâi-bûn BONG-pò* (台文Bong 報, hereafter *Bong*, est. 1996) under its wings, and the establishment of the Taiwan Romanisation Association (Tâi-oân Lô-má-jī Hi'àp-hōe台灣羅馬字協會TWA) in 2001, announcing a new phase in the *taiyuwen* movement with the publication of their magazine *Tâi-oân-jī* in POJ and the number of activities organised under the auspices of the Association (Liao 2013: 81–93). Meanwhile, the distribution channels of the overseas journal *Tâi-bûn Thong-sin* acted as the medium of communication that enabled orthographic practice and created a network of supporters for the Romanised script while adhering to the ideology of the *taiyuwen* movement.

Within the selection of the norm, the discussion about what script to use turned more complex with the appearance of innovators on the scene. Robert L. Cheng's (鄭良偉) efforts advocating a mixture of both scripts (漢羅 *han-luo*) incubated linguistic attempts for an orthographic solution (see more in codification). Another complexity related to the issue of the selection resulted in an adaptation of the alphabetic orthography in a revised form of the POJ Church Romanisation, known as Tâi-lô (臺羅Taiwanese Romanisation System, 台灣閩南語羅馬字拼音方案 / *Tâi-ôan Lô-má-jī Peng-im Hong-àn*, TL) and which has been promoted by the Ministry of Education (MOE) since 2006. Used as a guideline and thus not binding, there are still alternative forms in the running, as well as a continued support for the POJ transcription, exemplified by the writings of Chiung Ui-bun (蔣為文). The diversity in street names in the cities throughout Taiwan testifies to today to this ongoing lack in orthographic unity. But the lack in orthographic unity is not seen as a necessary evil, rather, interviews with the main proponents show that flexibility still remains the preferred norm keeping the debate on the selection criteria process ongoing and fluid.

The debate on orthographic conventions is not only about the selection of an appropriate script that can serve as the norm for the development of a linguistic standard. The selection of characters is compounded with the influence of Mandarin in filling in the lexical gaps. Khoo (2019), among others, has adeptly demonstrated that because of the successful language shift towards Mandarin, the *Taiyu* form closer to its Mandarin counterpart, even if this is not the most authentic one, is often the preferred variant. Her research also shows that the gap in lexical forms between Taiwanese and Mandarin tends to be filled by the Mandarin forms, equally causing the decline of Japanese loanwords.[3]

In conclusion, the selection of the written norm achieved a fairly successful process towards standardisation of an orthography in character script, alphabetic writing, and a high degree of consensus on *han-luo*. If arguing over the linguistic standard remains problematic, this appears to be only for 'these users who are sensitive to extremely small and nuanced differences between elements in a system', so that these differences may become iconic of the groups of users themselves or of a particular social characteristic which is attributed to them (Irvine and Gal 2000: 37, cited in Sebba 2012: 4).[4]

Codification of the form

Codification of the form includes the standardisation procedures of graphisation, grammatication, and lexication. The process of graphisation no doubt went hand in hand with the selection of the norm whereby the missionary writings proved to be recommended reference sources, as much for those in favour of full character writing as those adhering to alphabetic writing (POJ). The advantage of the missionary dictionaries was that one could trace the development of vocabulary itemisation in terms of character selection and pronunciation, whereas the prints of the Presbyterian *Taiwan Church News Tâi-oân Kàu-hoē Kong-pò* (台灣教會公報est. 1885) in POJ entailed a codification blueprint of the language as a medium for written communication. These church writings are not the only venues that have proven indispensable to the process of codification. Liao (2013) reviews the socio-cultural involvement of writer groupings like *Taiwanese Pen* (台灣筆會), the Hakka magazine (客家風雲), and the Taiwan Indigenous Human Rights Association (台灣原住民族權利基金會) under the umbrella of the 'Give me back my mother tongue' (*huan wo muyu* 還我母語) movement since 1988. Within this general climate of post-martial law social movements, prime movers were the organisation of language training classes in Taiwanese (*taiyuban* 台語班) coupled with publishing efforts to practise the writing and develop the elaboration of function. Political liberalisation lent a helping hand. First, it became possible to interlock with the overseas independence movement in the 1990s, followed by the Democratic Progressive Party (DPP) coming into power in the 2000s, which enabled the mother tongue revival movement (*muyu fuzhan yundong*母語復振運動) to enter the educational system. The process of educational institutionalisation took place at the national level in the Ministry of Education (hereafter MOE) resulting in a webpage of an online dictionary with a wordlist that has the approved standard form.[5] But this meant only the beginning of more debate to come. To say the very least, a commencement was now made whereby speaking the language could be practised in writing the language with the goal of building the language canon.

From the start there developed three competing factions. These can be described as full character writing (*quanhan*), Romanised POJ, and a mixture of characters and POJ (*hanluo*), all three of which have been partly discussed by Henning Klöter in 'The people behind the scripts' (2003). For our immediate concern in propelling the debate in codifying, the graphisation is that the proponents for full character writing, with the support of language pioneer/linguist Ang Ui-jin, were successful in bringing in people from the literary world, but not just anyone. They were members of the literary circle predisposed to the cause of language revitalisation/preservation, but not modernisation and planning *per se*. Their goal was to practise the language. Along the scale of language development, this proved a continuation of the colonial period that had seen the first attempts in composing literary works in *Taiyu*. Researching the Japanese colonial period in the Taiwan subjectivity discourse paid a fair amount of attention to literature. Bringing visibility to Taiwan in firsts and bests, illustrating the past, giving it a voice and a vision, created a fertile breeding ground to facilitate the codification of written materials. From the 1970s onwards, the literary genre of the native soil movement (*xiangtu wenxue* 鄉土文學) inserted local dialect (read: *Taiyu*) phrases in novels and short stories, and had generated a distinct group of same-language speakers and writers who now had access and the opportunity to enrich their language potential. Another group of language lovers was the poetry reading clubs, prevalent in the 1990s, joining hands with the mother tongue teachers and cultural activists pressing for language reform by publishing the textbooks series 'Whale of Taiwanese Literature' (海翁台語文學 2000).[6]

Textbook material brought the spelling issue to the fore; calling for a codification ideally as uniform as possible (with the minimum amount of variation) in order to create a standard. Already in the 1930s, the debate between the purists and the reformers coalesced around the creation and acceptance of certain characters. It was not solved later on; rather, as Wu Shou-li wrote in the preface of his seminal works, he left room for alternative versions (Klöter 2003). At the time of Wu's writing, standardisation or not was a matter of passionate conviction, but it was not so when pushing for *Taiyu* to be instructed on the national level through the use of textbooks. Hence, the significance of the first approved lexicon by the MOE; it announced the acceptance of the codified character with its phonetic representation as standard, and created the blueprint for the MOE database dictionary. Bundling forces resulted in the adoption of the MOE spelling known as Tâi-lô in 2006. Liao (2013: 67) remarked that in so doing the mother tongue teachers avoided the ensuing internal script war and smoothly enlisted mother tongue classes into the national educational system.

One of the dominant elements in the ensuing script war concerned the reform of the POJ spelling erupting in the wake of the *tongyong pinyin* (通用拼音)-*hanyu pinyin* (漢語拼音) controversy since 2000. Although the controversy featured the transcription of Mandarin, some of the *tongyong* advocates considered it equally appropriate to transcribe all the local languages (*bentu yuyan*本土語言), and indirectly impacted the hereto standard position of the POJ Church Romanisation which came under fire for its phonological inaccuracies. In the creation of a linguistic standard, POJ Church spelling was conveniently used when characters (graphs) were lacking. In 1991, Ang Ui-jin promoted the Taiwan Language Phonetic Alphabet (台灣語言音標方案 TLPA), which throughout the rest of that decade came to be used by the MOE as a yardstick requiring minor adjustments concurrent with initiated research projects for the compilation of a *Taiyu* lexicon under the auspices of the Mandarin Promotion Council (國語推行委員會*guoyu tuixing weiyuanhui* MPC). When the codification of the alphabetic transcription came in competition with the variant *tongyong pinyin*, the most recent revision of TLPA was baptised Tâi-lô and endorsed by the MPC in an effort to make an end to the ongoing spelling war. In hindsight, this was a clever move because it integrated 'spelling' classes as a central component of the *Taiyu*-language curriculum for the mother tongue teachers enrolled in the in-service programs. They would learn how to correctly spell and transcribe the pronunciation of the characters.

How to situate the Romanisation spelling war within the totality of the *Taiyu*-language discourse? What was the motivation for making a change, to what end? A lot has to do with linguistic variety bringing us to the three competing discourses mentioned above. Among the practitioners of *Written Taiwanese*, there was a considerable overlap of mindsets of those who were the proponents for POJ, those favouring the use of full character writing (*quanhan* 全漢), and the ones practising a mixture of *han-luo*, when it came to the implementation of a character choice. The three discourses were not in competition with each other for the greater cause of Taiwanese-language revival, but to the degree in which their activities and/or individual network could potentially negatively impact the process of creating a linguistic standard. The push for language equality had to operate within a framework not to upset the dominant discourse too much. Caution was exercised by some not to align too closely with politically outspoken individuals, for fear of uprooting the status quo (or perceived as such) and be labelled as Taiwanese independence activists, or the ideological interpretive association with *Taidu*. The Huang-Chiung saga over literature illustrates this, as will be shown later on in the chapter.

But the bone of contention was not always about 'degree of opposition' politics. The advantage offered by technology, more precisely automation, highlights some of the competing issues underlying the codification process by the proponents for full character writing in interaction (both contestation and collaboration) with the POJ and *han-luo* camp for whom the language was a tool (object) rather than an end in itself (subject). The linguistic hurdle to overcome was achieving the social in-group acceptance of a language theory based on orthographic principles for lexicon selection – language modernization – that proceeded faster and took decisions when the selection proved indecisive or was still under discussion. Digital technology enabled the effective utilisation and analysis of text-populations transformed in a highly structured quantitative format. This automation process mainly regarded a Taiwanese computerised language input for which software was developed. Facilitated by electronic data input and retrieval, a number of controversies that fed into the linguistic mind were brought to the surface and kept the discussion over procedures by which to select and create characters, and for that matter also provided insights into the variation of the pronunciation over time, diachronically so, which is ongoing.

The codification of grammar and lexicon in *Taiyu* was not going very far with the array of individual attempts without state funding or any larger entity nurturing it, financially and intellectually. What made it possible was the input of a theoretical model that differed from those of traditional Chinese linguistics. This was found in Western theories of non-Sinitic language preservation and practice. Introducing this novel model of language planning seemed not to marry well with the Chinese traditional phonology in searching for the appropriate character, or at least that was the interpretation given (Liao 2013: 106–107). The work done by linguist Robert L. Cheng in the United States illustrates such achievements in language revival through technical innovation. As a proponent of the *han-luo* writing he was a regular contributor to the overseas journal *Tâi-Oân Gú-Bún Goéh-pō* (*Taiwan Linguistic & Cultural Monthly*台灣語文雙月刊) and he became creative, together with a group of IT technicians. His idea in the late 1970s to commence data processing using a software application greatly improved the means to write in *Taiyu* (Cheng 1993). Based at the University of Hawaii at the Center for Chinese Studies, Cheng established the 'Taiyu Data lab' (台語資料室 est. 1990). His contribution to the codification process in the automation of the writing script was like none before. The automation process allowed for typing in any kind of character text that converted into *Taiyu*, and meant the start of Cheng's team in building and collecting a substantial number of digital databases in the decades that followed. Precisely that technical innovation helped to bridge the initial disagreement among the *Taiyu* codifiers regarding the creation of characters and struggling over the six principles in the character formation which from the start had been a bone of contention. The advantage was that the automation singled out itemisation in character selection overlap, and in so doing greatly improved the quality of writing in *han-luo*. This gained the support of Taiwan-based writers and activists who did not feel like being slowed down or having to engage in an argument over the selection of one character with their peers. One of these was Chen Mingren (陳明仁). Iûn Ún-giân (楊允言) and his students developed the first online *Taiyu* dictionary, based on Robert Cheng's database.[7] Subsequent digitised corpus work equally acknowledges Cheng's accomplishments (Li 2003). Liao (2013: 107) credits Robert L. Cheng's role in the Taiwanese-language movement in spearheading the way for the creation of a post-colonial literature in Han-*taiyu* independent from those writing in Mandarin. The automation created a repository of Han-*taiyu* of which the institutionalisation could be on par with that of Mandarin, and thus one step ahead in language planning, or the push for language equality.

In that sense, a milestone for the codification of the orthography was the list of recommended Han characters approved by the Ministry of Education. The first 300 words were approved on 29 May 2007, followed by another 100 words on 1 May 2008 (Lua and Iûn 2010: 75). Research concerned with the implementation (elaboration) of these word lists made one of the regular research papers in the *Journal of Taiwanese Vernacular* (*Tâi-gí Gián-kiù* 台語研究 est. 2009).[8] Other factors that pleaded for a full character script regard the publication of a substantial grammar. Codification of characters has advantages over POJ Romanisation. To gather support by printing materials that explain *Taiyu* grammar in character script (could be in Mandarin or in Han-*taiyu*, whichever generated the need for a narrative and further practice of a codified character list), puts POJ at a disadvantage. It is easier to reach a wider audience literate in Chinese than one in POJ, and the script's 'foreign' stigma still lingers on (as was also mentioned in the colonial period). These issues will come to the fore in the elaboration section, next.

In concluding this section, the current issue in codification concerns distinguishing between compounds that are etymologically defined as *Taiyu* and those that are not (Mandarin, Hakka), given the fact that, almost by definition, *Taiyu*-speakers are fully bilingual in one of these languages. Whereas the hybridity in orthographic variation displayed by *luo-han* makes it possible to hide certain differences in pronunciation, its oral use in radio and television (as the next step) will make it even more compelling for its language missionaries and activists with access to the national level to codify pronunciation of the standard in the new formal media contexts.

Elaboration of function

The elaboration of function is concerned with implementing and spreading the results of the selection and the codification processes. The issues highlighted in this section regard both the efforts and debates within the camp of writers and novelists creating literary works and those active in reaching a broader public, general and academic. The organisation of language testing, implementing the codified format, and seeing to the production of scientific-academic literature illustrate the elaboration phase in the creation of a linguistic standard.

The primary source materials considered for the building of a literary canon in *Taiyu* are folksongs that are contained in songbooks written in characters. These songs were starting to be compiled during the colonial period; in the 1950s they featured in the local movie industry – known as *Taiyu pian* – and in the 1970s they were included in the *xiangtu wenxue* literary genre. Come the 1980s the *xiangtu wenxue* themes were filmed, thus paving the way for an emerging literature in *Taiyu*. Because writings in *Taiyu* were not recognised as the official script, some of the folksongs took on a representational role and became a significant part of the Taiwanese social movement. Seen from the perspective of traditional Chinese literature, folksongs compensated for the lack of scripts for theatre plays (劇本*juben*) and were seen as a prerequisite for building a literary canon (Liao 2013: 48). But elaboration is not limited to creating literary works only. The standard had to be used as a widely maximum variation in society, and thus steps had to be taken to implement it in as wide a way as possible; and this brings us to education.

The debates over character selection, spelling conventions, and lack of a unified orthography continued to busy the writers' world, and academic conferences came to act as a venue where the practitioners and theorists met. This was possible through the organisation of conferences on Taiwanese literature, initially in Mandarin, but under the impetus of the Taiwan subjectivity discourse, room was created for papers written and presented in Taiwanese. Because conference organisation is supported by academia and funded by the MOE, together with the establishment of graduate institutes and departments of Taiwan(ese) literature, a number of these conferences switched the emphasis from literature theming Taiwan as a geographical entity where the dominant language was Mandarin to that of language and literature conferences in Taiwanese. Taking the lead were the Taiwan programs with a strong linguistic input. It was also shown in the titles of the conference proceedings using POJ and *han-luo* as the obvious markers to reveal that these 'International conferences on Taiwanese literature' were not limited to Mandarin oral and written presentations only. Concurrent is a branching out in conferences that steer away from literature as such, but focus on language and teaching with the support of the Taiwanese Romanisation Association.[9] The politico-ideological distinction made itself felt in either the funding by the co-organiser providing the venue or the names of dignitaries in the opening remarks revealing that it was supported by a mainstream literature group (museum, foundation) or adhered more to the social movement camp with linguistic activist undertones. Of specific interest are the conferences that feature Taiwanese languages and language testing as they provide a platform to zoom into the issues at stake.

As shown in the previous sections, in creating the linguistic standard process, dialectal characters and uncommon standard characters were represented by Romanised forms to make up for the shortage of graphs. In the words of Chen Ming-jen, 'mixing was a convenient way for a transitional stage ultimately leading to full Romanisation of written Taiwanese' (Klöter 2003: 60, communication with Chen). Besides its significance for the codification of form, Chen's words also illustrate concerns raised for the elaboration of function. This becomes clearer when taking a look at the motivations of some of the Taiwanese language makers/practitioners. For instance, Klöter's interview with Huang Yuanxing (黃元興) – one of the *han-luo* practitioners – reveals that Huang called himself a strong proponent of non-institutional support stemming from his conviction that 'both governmental institutions and college-educated philologists [are] too distant from the view, daily lives and authentic language use of ordinary Taiwanese speakers' (Klöter 2003: 47–48). Let us relate Huang's conviction to Haugen's (1972: 109) theorisation that identifies three procedures in the construction of a new standard: First 'the comparative' that equals making a hypothetical mother tongue, second 'the archaizing' which is guided by some mother tongue that existed in older traditional writings, and third 'the statistical' which is a combination of those forms that have the widest usage, in the hope that they will most easily win general acceptance. Huang's convictions place him as being in favour of the 'statistical' approach in selecting a norm, whereby the widest use possible is the language spoken in the private domain. He distances himself from 'the governmental institutions and college-educated philologists' whose proponents favour the 'archaizing approach' in selecting a norm, and are representative of the authenticity debate (purists).

Diversity of this kind of opinion fuelled the debate whereby the notion of authenticity in terms of first or oldest use and true to its character-script etymology became paramount in deciding appropriate character selection. Disagreements over the authenticity of a character came to the fore and featured precisely in academic conferences aimed at setting standards for language testing. In 2001 the MOE had allowed the instruction of *Taiyu* and other local languages (Hakka and indigenous) to be included in the elementary and secondary school curriculum, and for which a language testing exam was created. By 2006, the 'Union for nation-wide Taiyu proficiency qualification' (全民台語能力檢定聯盟, abbreviated to 全民台檢) was established and set up their annual conferences during which its members (mainly academics and POJ sympathisers) debated and discussed a number of language testing models to delineate the *Taiyu* equivalent of the standardised tests for the English language (TOEFL, etc.). Opinions differed on the advantages of adopting a norm-referenced test versus a criterion-referenced test, and the popular model of the Common European Framework of Reference for Languages (CEF): Learning, teaching, assessment adopted by the Council of Europe in 1996. In 2009, the NCKU Center for Taiwanese Languages Testing profiled itself in conducting Taiwanese-language proficiency testing. However, this was more a by-default decision, because the official nationwide Taiwanese test developed by the National Language Committee (NLC) of the MOE was cancelled due to a budget halt by KMT legislators in February 2009 (Chiung and Lim 2010: 11.3–11.4). Under the pressure of grassroots organisations, the MOE promised to subsidise local governments and for testing to be conducted by cities and counties rather than the central government. Related obstacles to these governmental setbacks during the 2008–2016 years of the Ma administration were the criticisms of academics in the field of language testing in educational science departments, but without a linguistic background in Taiwanese and commissioned by the KMT-led government to develop the Chinese-language proficiency testing methods, including those for 'Southern Min' (*Minnanyu*), as 'Taiwanese' (*Taiyu*) was now officially referred to. The repeated demands for the MOE to advance the instruction of *Taiyu* in education and work towards its professionalisation continue to show a history of being thwarted when the KMT is in power and has the majority of legislators.

Academic conferences and teaching manuals fulfil one aspect of the elaboration in society. Of equal importance is the professionalisation of vocabulary acquisition, and by preference its dissemination as widely as possible, not only in written practice but especially at the spoken level. Spoken language is not mastered by everyone in the same way, and therefore revitalisation is not only about instruction to reverse the increasing decline of competent day to day speakers. It also requires acquisition of a specialised jargon and a corpus building of the vocabulary, such as the medical, legal, and other scientific, professionally oriented language clusters that can compete with those in Mandarin. Reality shows that younger personnel in the professional world are not necessarily capable of assisting elderly persons speaking Taiwanese. Itemisation of medical, legal, and other technical vocabulary proves more needful than the collection of folksongs. To follow suit its codification in pedagogical materials is needed to develop a school curriculum. Concurrent forms of normalisation involve using *Taiyu* in the broadcast media and other public domains to press for language legislation. To date, Taiwan-language legislation is still in the making; it is drafted as the National Languages Development Act (*guojia yuyan fazhanfa* 國家語言發展法) and educational institutions are given until August 2022 to opt for any other national language (e.g. Taiwanese, Hakka, indigenous) as the official medium of instruction and/or a mandatory school subject.[10] This kind of language planning policy is clearly derived from dominant language ideology; it does not disturb the diglossic schema and its hierarchy of values, but rather attempts to improve the standing of Taiwanese within the existing framework. Much is about engaging with the dominant Mandarin policy that devalued Taiwanese as 'not a language', and its activism that is now conducted on the national level is all about proving that it 'is' a language and thus an important act of validation in the effort to change language attitudes and through them, language practices.

Finally, the popularisation of digital technology and social media undertaken by dedicated groups of teachers, authors, artists, performers, amateur linguists, filmmakers, and broadcasters facilitate in reaching a broader audience and promote local language learning initiatives.[11] The public auditing the academic conferences consists of, for the most part, sympathisers involved in oppositional politics, grassroots movements, and language activists, including Hakka and indigenous languages social movements. During the Chen administration (2000–2008), this core group politically aligned with the DPP enlarged its network and consolidated its base, but witnessed a setback during the Ma administration (2008–2016) in reaching a larger audience at the pace they were planning for language legislation. Achievements remained on the level of how conferences on Taiwanese languages and teaching offered a platform that generated a greater awareness for the multilingual and multicultural branding of Taiwanese society. The return to power of the DPP with the presidential election victory in 2016, and again in 2020, witnessed an enhanced participation inclusive of Hakka and the indigenous languages and their respective activism. Similar attempts are being undertaken for Hakka and the indigenous languages along the lines of Haugen's standardisation matrix. However, it would be erroneous to conclude that there is a consensus in society and among the parties involved that language legislation will succeed in evoking social change in the form of a language shift from Mandarin to Taiwanese or another local language. Hence, we come to the last section: The role of social acceptance.

Acceptance by the community

The final category in Haugen's matrix on the social level is that of acceptance. The meaning of matrix requires that social acceptance must be in resonance with the other three categories: Selection, codification, and elaboration. As mentioned in the introduction, Haugen's model is based on the transition from dialect to standard. This brings us to the underlying ideology that keeps the social acceptance of *Taiyu* in its linguistic progress towards a standard in an unfortunate grip. However, it need not be, and it is in the discussion of social acceptance that the relation of *Taiyu* to its association with *Taidu* comes to the fore.

The Haugen model showcases the transition from vernacular to standard. In the project of nation-building, this translates as the efforts undertaken by linguists and cultural activists to elevate a vernacular – or dialect – local variant of the languages spoken to the status of a national language. The local variant is locked in a dialectical substandard setting, it is of a lesser value, and this linguistic subordination is also socially felt. Precisely this struggle to counter social subordination is part of Taiwanese identity formation, and illuminates the association with *Taidu*. Perceptions about *Taiyu* in society at large range from descriptions as a dialect, the language spoken at home by the elder generation, qualifying as mother tongue, but at the same time it is also the language of opposition, an electoral language for political participation that has been successful in achieving the transition to democracy, a signifier of cultural identity, and a marker of socio-political identification with Taiwan (see Goudin 2009; Chang and Holt 2014; Dupré 2017). The tension this created is the relation to Mandarin in the struggle from *Taiyu* dialect to *Taiyu* standard, and the complexity of the struggle becomes clearer when taking a closer look at the length to which some of the interpretations of that transition go. Truly so, the ensuing process could not have taken place without the achievements of the democratisation of society, generating profound political change that affected the existing social hierarchy, exemplified with a progressive Taiwanisation and oppositional politics winning the victory. Linguistically speaking, the inclusion of *Taiyu* as part of the National Languages Development Act demonstrates that a high degree of standardisation has been achieved. However, socially speaking, the ideological component inherent in this kind of language activism strives towards turning around the hierarchy and the emerging standard overtakes the existing dominant one. This interpretation to replace Mandarin with

Taiyu is farfetched at this stage, though if that is the intent, *Taiyu* as the emerging standard language first needs to attain the same level of equality as Mandarin. This draws the attention to 'who' understands 'what' by 'equality'?

The previous sections have alluded to the existence of a considerable amount of in-group disagreements, exemplified with the three competing discourses in the orthography debate: Full character writing, POJ, and *han-luo* writing, likewise the co-existence of at least two different scripts for transcription: Church POJ adherers, and the Tâi-lô practitioners. Along the way, another challenge surfaced. Reference is made to the disagreements between what constituted 'mother tongue writing' (*muyu shuxie* 母語書寫) and 'mother tongue literature' (*muyu wenxue* 母語文學) in defining the scope of Taiwanese literature. During the period of 1987–1996, the literary world witnessed the controversy over Taiwanese literature (*taiyu wenxue lunzhan*台語文學論爭) when authors composing literary works in *Taiyu* faced criticism from the established group of writers who had spearheaded the *xiangtu wenxue* – native soil – since the late 1970s and those who had made fame as literary figures merited for their talented writing and international recognition. Also taking part in the controversy were scholars in literature departments who were supportive of creating 'Taiwanese literature' in its Taiwan-centric subjectivity discourse while still having to engage with writers and colleagues in Chinese literature departments. That group was upholding their leading status as representing 'Chinese literature on Taiwan' and its traditional thematic periodisation, which was challenged by the emerging field of Taiwanese literature no longer limited to the genre of native soil (see Wang 2007). The edited volume *Rectifying the Name of Taiwan Literature* (台灣文學正名) (Cai 2006; Liao 2013: 111–123) brings together a number of essays written in the wake of the 2000 power change demonstrating how the camp of *Taiyu* writers became entangled over designating what constitutes 'Taiwanese' literature, and more specifically how to distinguish it from the literature written in Mandarin (Taiwan ROC and China PRC). The controversy between these different literature camps deepened when the *xiangtu* writers called themselves the authors of 'true Taiwan literature' to distinguish themselves from the China literature camp, but not necessarily identifying with the ones composing literary works in *Taiyu* irrespective of its orthographic choice. In May 2011, it came to an open confrontation – with extensive newspaper coverage – between NCKU linguist Chiung Ui-bun and Huang Chun-ming (黃春明), Taiwan's most prolific writer and icon of *xiangtu wenxue*, engaging Chen Fang-ming (陳芳明), distinguished professor of Taiwanese literature at NCCU, in support of Huang's claim that 'Taiwanese literature does not equal literature in *Taiyu*'. The controversy delayed Chiung's academic promotion, to give an idea of the seriousness and sensitivity of the matter in Taiwan politics, and keeping in mind that Chiung had been prolific in voicing his opposing opinion – together with others – when in 2008 the KMT was voted back into power and the MOE adopted the official naming and politically correct term 'Taiwan Minnanyu' (臺灣閩南語) to designate all educational and other official government supported activities involving *Taiyu*.

Of immediate interest is the way that linguists Chiung Ui-bun and Taiwanese poet and academic Li Khin-huann (李勤岸) interpreted the terms Taiwanese language/literature, and what this reveals about ideological standpoints in the process towards standardisation. Li suggested the naming of Sino-Taiwan literature (中華台灣文學) for the Mandarin-written literature, which Chiung split up in *zhonghua minguo wenxue* (中華民國文學, referring to the literature written in Mandarin by ROC nationals) and *zhonghua renmin gongheguo wenxue* (中華人民共和國文學, referring to anyone else writing literature in *putonghua*, or simplified characters), while reserving the term *Taiwan wenxue* (台灣文學) for works written in *Taiyu*, Hakka, or the indigenous Austronesian languages. What this points to is that Chiung's designation of the term *Taiwan wenxue* is inclusive to the other local languages, excluding Mandarin, whereas Li in proposing the term Sino-Taiwan literature, partially reaches out to the groups of concerned literary scholars more interested in promoting a Taiwan Studies that is inclusive of a literature not determined by an écriture in Mandarin, but encompassing all the languages in the Sino-sphere without giving a higher status to one over the other. The work by Shih Shu-mei (2017) and Liao Ping-hui (2016) is recommended reading here on the usage and coinage of the term Sinophone literature. But even if one argues in favour of Sinophone literature encompassing literary works in *Taiyu*, Hakka, Cantonese, and the Austronesian languages as a convenient compromise towards social acceptance, it still touches on two interrelated nerve-racking aspects for those who want to see *Taiyu* equal to (and replacing) Mandarin.

First, 'sino' is inclusive; it denotes an umbrella term that brings into the open the notion of pluri, multi, variation. The acceptance of the term 'Sinophone' depicted with the Chinese character 'hua' (華) instead of *zhongwen* (中文) or guowen/yu (國文/語), opens up to variation, and lifts the language in which the literature is written above its political, read: Nation-state interpretation. Second, replacing *Taiyu* by *Minnanyu* (Southern Min) arranges the language as a variant of the Min language in Chinese dialectology, and calls up the association with 'dialect'. Neither of the two designated terms eliminate the stigmatic perception of the language being 'secondary to' or 'subordinate'. What hits the nerve-racking spot is that the type of language activism operates within the confines of the dominant language ideology that is defined in terms of a language: Dialect relation, and has difficulties moving away from this pattern in adopting a language: Variant approach. Making that shift is easier said than done, because it requires a different approach to what is considered 'inclusive'; seeing the language in its pluri-centricity; that, after all, is what a multicultural and multilingual society stands for. The internal obstacle in making that shift is precisely what encompasses 'pluri' in its relation to the standard. 'How can a standard be pluri-centric?' underlies the bone of contention.

In order to grasp a better understanding, I propose to discuss the language situation in Taiwan in a pluricentric framework as elaborated on in Michael Clyne's edited volume (1992) and following Kloss' (1952, 1967) definition that 'Ausbau languages develop through planned emphasis on differences and divergence from structures and vocabularies of those idioms in their respective environments, with which they are in close genetic relationship' (cited in Tomić 1992: 438).[12] This planned emphasis in '*ausbau-ing*' equally applies to *Taiyu* in its quest for an autonomous language in relation to the other used varieties. The connection with pluricentricity exists in the move away from the relationship 'language versus dialect' to the relationship 'language versus variant' approach.[13] This presupposed pluricentricity assumes the functioning of a unique language (Southern Min as a monocentric language) in more than one distinct nation or statehood centre (Taiwan, China, Malaysia, the Philippines) through more than one distinct norm (*Taiyu, Minnanyu*, Hokkien, Lán-lâng-uē (咱人話)). Such an approach facilitates a framework for research on two genetically closely related idioms designated as dialects of a monocentric language (Tsiang-Tsuan-mix (漳泉濫) in relation to *Taiyu*), as variants of a pluricentric language (Amoy in relation to *Taiyu*) or else as distinct languages (Hakka, Mandarin in relation to *Taiyu*). These designations, in the words of Tomić (1992: 437), 'do not depend on any inherent propensity towards autonomy or heteronomy, but rather follow(s) from the activity of various political agents. When policies change these designations are reexamined and shifted – through systematic emphasis on differences or similarities'.

This is precisely where the problem lies, not only because of the precarious cross-Strait politics, but also the fact that the notion of pluricentricity has not gained much hearing among the *Taiyu* linguists and language planners. The underlying cause is that current language attitudes are still steeped in a history too deeply engrained and interwoven with the official policies and viewpoints on language planning, bringing in ideology that – unnecessarily but understandably – was not open to replacing language versus dialect by language versus variant. Willingness to see the possibility for a language versus variant needs to overcome the difficulty in challenging the deeply rooted mono-cultural/mono-lingual models concurrent with identity that have been imposed onto Taiwanese society since 1945, are historically rooted in Chinese political economy, and equally imposed under Japanese colonial rule that left the population coming out of a social order as the 'second-rate citizen'. It is here that the ideological position of the model of standardisation comes across the strongest in the social acceptance. Pluricentricity works both ways. Considering *Taiyu* as one among many from this pluricentric perspective also draws attention to the prestigious position of Mandarin in society, and anticipates an equal change in its language attitude towards *Taiyu*, more specifically opening up to the idea of others sharing the benefits of its language dominance.

Concluding remarks

The quest for a *Taiyu* linguistic standard is politically inspirited and motivated by a drive for recognition out of contestation with the dominant language ideology and linguistic policy of Mandarin only. Coming out of a 50-year period of being ruled and having undergone the experience of having to accept another language

(Japanese) as the superior one – not to mention the assumed cultural superiority – had created a mindset and the tools of intellectual critique. This generated rhetoric of resistance politically and culturally continued when a repetition of the same scenario occurred in the post-war years, maintaining the status-quo relation between culture and politics, but now the other was Chinese, and of importance here, a continuation of the nation-state model and concurrent to that of the language standardisation at the time. In which aspects does *Taiyu* as a language elucidate the ideology of standardisation with an 'independence' connotation and assume a monocentric position? That is different from inquiring about the political connotation of *Taiyu* (which is not the purpose of this chapter). Let us zoom in on the variant of Taiwanese Romanisation in POJ spelling that shares its orthography with nations that are not politically Chinese, and distinguishes itself as an alphabetic language from the character script as embodiment of Chinese culture. But Taiwanese Romanisation does not go by the name of *Taiwan Minnanyu*. The politically interpreted variant *Minnanyu* functions as a compromise in its co-existence with Mandarin, and constitutes *Taiyu*'s position in the Sinophone-sphere on an equal level with other Sinitic languages sharing the character (graph) orthography. The distinction between *Taiyu* and *Minnanyu* on the national level is one of inclusiveness, characterised by a complacent companionship not to upset the political status quo in the region, hence the addition of 'Taiwan' to *Minnanyu*. However, in its pluricentric function, the term *Minnanyu* allows for the variants spoken elsewhere, i.e. Lán-lâng-uē (咱人話) in the Philippines, *Taiyu* (台語) in Taiwan, Hokkien (福建話) in Malaysia, and embodies a more comprehensive recognition of multilingual policies. To date, written Taiwanese in *han-luo* with Tâi-lô script is only slowly finding its way in the educational mainstream. Much effort and political will is still required to strike a balance in a sociolinguistic environment that problematises the economic and cultural benefits of secondary language learning and acquisition beyond that of English teaching.

Notes

1 I retain the distinction between standardisation and language planning, and view standardisation as one aspect of the process of language planning. This chapter is not concerned with the sociolinguistic discussion of Mandarin to *Taiyu* in terms of linguistic borrowing, nor is there any space to discuss the standardisation of *Taiyu* in relation to that of the other languages such as Hakka and the Austronesian languages.

2 For detailed discussions of Chinese dialectology, see Yan (2006) and Tang (2018).

3 During the Japanese colonial period, a number of Japanese lexical items were borrowed and assimilated into *Taiyu*. For research on this, see Hsieh and Hsu (2006), Chang (1995).

4 With reference to the 'particular social characteristic', mention can be made of the turn-of-the-millennium *taike* (台客) iconisation as the authentic Holo-speakers. The sociolinguistic implications of this phenomenon requires more in-depth study. For a cultural interpretation, see Wang (2006).

5 https://twblg.dict.edu.tw/holodict_new/default.jsp and https://language.moe.gov.tw/result.aspx?classify_sn=23&subclassify_sn=439, visited on 27 March 2020.

6 http://tai.king-an.com.tw/, visited on 27 March 2020.

7 The online dictionary (https://taigi.fhl.net/dic_un/; visited on 17 July 2020) that was firstly named 台華線頂辭典 (original website: http://iug.csie.dahan.edu.tw/TG/sutian/ ; invalid now). Special thanks to Lau Seng-hian Lau (劉承賢) and Tiun Hak-khiam (張學謙).

8 http://ctlt.twl.ncku.edu.tw/jotv.html, visited on 27 March 2020.

9 These conferences are listed on the websites of the Taiwan Languages and Literature Society, for example, see The 7th International Symposium on Taiwanese Languages and Teaching (第七屆台灣語言及其教學國際學術研討會), 2008 www.twlls.org.tw/conference_1_07.php; the 5th Young Scholars Conference on Taiwan Languages (第五屆青年學者台灣語言學術研討會), 2017 www.twlls.org.tw/conference_2_05.php; the Taiwanese Romanisation Association www.tlh.org.tw/; the 1st Conference for Young Scholars on Taiwanese Romanisation (第一屆台灣羅馬字青年學者學術研討會), 2008; and the 7th International Conference on Taiwanese Romanisation (2015 Tē 7 Kài Tâi-oân Lô-má-jī Kok-chè Gián-thó-hōe), 2015 http://ctlt.twl.ncku.edu.tw/conf/2015/, visited on 27 March 2020.

10 https://law.moj.gov.tw/LawClass/LawAll.aspx?pcode=H0170143, visited on 27 March 2020.

11 www.tailingua.com/resources/books/https://en.wikipedia.org/wiki/Taiwanese_Hokkie n, visited on 27 March 2020.

12 Kloss (1952) developed a framework categorising *Ausbau* and *Abstand* language intended to deal with situations in which multiple varieties from a dialect continuum have been standardised, so that they are commonly considered distinct languages even though they may be mutually intelligible. 'Ausbau' in German means 'built-up' and has taken on the sociolinguistic meaning of a 'standard variety with dependent varieties'. 'Abstand' in German means 'distance' and refers to a language that has 'significant linguistic distance from other languages', it need not have 'developed into a standard' or is mutually unintelligible with other languages.

13 Victor Mair refers to topolect in his discussion of Chinese languages (Mair 1991: 7).

References

English references

Chang, Hui-Ching, and Holt, Richard (eds.) (2014) *Language, Politics and Identity in Taiwan: Naming China*. London: Routledge.

Chang, Yü-Hung. (1995) 'The assimilation of Japanese loanwords in Taiwanese Hokkien', in Shuangqing Zhang and Bohui Zhan (eds.) *Chinese Language Studies* 11 (Special issue on the Third International Conference on the Min Dialects). Hong Kong: Chinese Language Research Centre, Institute of Chinese studies, the Chinese University of Hong Kong, pp. 107–122.

Cheng, Robert L. (1994) 'Language unification in Taiwan, present and future', in Murray A. Rubinstein (ed) *The Other Taiwan: 1945 to the Present*. New York: M.E. Sharpe, pp. 357–91.

Clyne, Michael (ed.) (1992) 'Pluricentric languages—Introduction', in *Pluricentric Languages: Differing Norms in Different Nations*. Berlin, New York: Mouton de Gruyter, pp. 1–6.

DeBernardi, Jean (1991) 'Linguistic nationalism: The case of Southern Min', *Sino-Platinic Papers* 25. http://www.sino-platonic.org/complete/spp025_taiwanese.html.

Deumert, Ana, and Vandenbussche, Wim (eds.) (2003) 'Standard languages. Taxonomies and histories', in Ana Deumert and Wim Vandenbussche (eds.) *Germanic Standardizations. Past to Present*. Philadelphia: John Benjamins Publishing, pp. 1–14.

Dupré, Jean-François (2017) *Culture Politics and Linguistic Recognition in Taiwan: Ethnicity, Identity, and the Party System*. London: Routledge.

Goudin, Yoann (2009) *Electoral and Media Fields in Taiwan, Language Use of the Candidates during the 2008 Presidential Campaign*. Saarbrucken, Germany: VDM Verlag Dr. Müller.

Hannesdóttir, Anna Helga (2011) 'From vernacular to national language: Language planning and the discourse of science in eighteenth-century Sweden', in Britt-Louise Gunnarsson (ed.) *Languages of Science in the Eighteenth century*. Berlin, New York: Mouton de Gruyter, pp. 107–122.

Haugen, Einar (1966) 'Dialect, Language, Nation', *American Anthropologist*, 68(4): 922–935.

Haugen, Einar (1972) 'Dialect, Language, Nation' (reprint) in John B. Pride and Janet Holmes (eds) *Sociolinguistics. Selected Readings*. Harmondsworth: Penguin, 97–111.

Heylen, Ann (2012) *Japanese Models, Chinese Culture and the Dilemma of Taiwanese Language Reform*. Wiesbaden: Harrassowitz.

Hsiau, A-chin (1997) 'Language ideology in Taiwan: The KMT's language policy, the Tai-yu language movement, and ethnic politics', *Journal of Multilingual and Multicultural Development*, 18: 302–315.

Hsiau, A-chin (2000) *Contemporary Taiwanese Cultural Nationalism*. London, New York: Routledge.

Hsieh, Shelley Ching-Yu, and Hui Li Hsu (2006) 'Japanese mania and Japanese loanwords in Taiwan Mandarin: Lexical structure and social discourse', *Journal of Chinese Linguistics*, 34(1): 44–79.

Irvine, Judith T.,and Gal, Susan (2000). 'Language ideology and linguistics differentiation', in Paul Kroskrity (ed.) *Regimes of Language*. Santa Fe, New Mexico: School of American Research Press, 35–83.

Jaffe, Alexandra (1999) *Ideologies in Action: Language Politics on Corsica*. Berlin: Mouton, Walter de Gruyter.

Khoo Hui-lu (Hsu Hui-ju) (2019) 'The dynamics of Southern Min in Taiwan. From Southern Min dialects to "Taigi"', in Chris Shei (ed.) *The Routledge Handbook of Chinese Discourse Analysis*. London: Routledge, pp. 596–610.

Kloss, Heinz (1952) *Die Entwicklung Neuer Germanischen Kultursprachen von 1800 bis 1950*. Munich: Pohl.

Kloss, Heinz (1967) '*Abstand* languages and *Ausbau* languages', *Anthropological Linguistics*, 9: 29–41.

Klöter, Henning (2003) 'Writing Taiwanese: The people behind the scripts', in Christina Neder and Ines Susanne Schilling (eds.) *Transformation! Innovation? Perspectives on Taiwan Culture*. Wiesbaden: Harrassowitz Verlag, pp. 45–63.

Klöter, Henning (2005) *Written Taiwanese*. Wiesbaden: Harrassowitz Verlag.

Li, Khinn-Huan (2003) *Lexical Changes and Variation in Taiwanese Literature Text, 1916–1998: A Computer-Assisted Corpus Analysis*. Tainan: Kim-an.

Liao, Ping-hui (2016) 'Modern Taiwan Literature', in Gunter Schubert (ed.) *Routledge Handbook of Contemporary Taiwan*. London: Routledge.

Lien, Chinfa (1995) 'Language adaptation in Taoist liturgical texts', in David Johnson (ed.) *Ritual and Scripture in Chinese Popular Religion: Five Studies*. Berkeley, CA: Institute of East Asian Studies, pp. 219–246.

Lin, Christine Louise (1999) 'The presbyterian church in Taiwan and the advocacy of local autonomy', *Sino-Platonic Papers*, 92.

Mair, Victor H. (1991) 'What is a Chinese 'dialect/topolect'? Reflections on some key Sino-English linguistic terms', *Sino-Platonic Papers*, 29.

Rubinstein, Murray (1991) *The Protestant Community of Modern Taiwan: Mission, Seminary, and Church*. New York: M.E. Sharpe.
——— (2006). 'The presbyterian church in the formation of Taiwan's democratic society, 1945–2004', in Tun-jen Cheng, Deborah A. Brown (eds.) *Religious Organizations and Democratization: Case Studies from Contemporary Asia*. New York: Routledge, pp. 109–135.
Schipper, Kristofer (1985) 'Vernacular and classical ritual in Taoism', *Journal of Asian Studies*, 45(1): 21–57.
Sebba, Mark (2007). 'Ideology and alphabets in the former USSR', *Language Problems & language Planning*, 31(2): 99–125.
Sebba, Mark (2012) 'Orthography as social action: Scripts, spelling, identity and power', in Alexandra Jaffe, Jannis Androutsopoulos, Mark Sebba and Sally Johnson (eds.) *Orthography as Social Action: Scripts, Spelling, Identity and Power*. Berlin: Mouton De Gruyer, pp. 1–19.
Street, Brian (1984) *Literacy in Theory and Practice*. New York: Cambridge University Press.
Street, Brian (2006) 'Autonomous and ideological models of literacy: Approaches from New Literacy Studies', unpublished. https://www.semanticscholar.org/paper/Autonom ous-and-Ideological-Models-of-Literacy-%3A-New-Street/1957884a4cad853a1c6ef f5bf148671e45f6af4f. (Accessed: 15 March 2019.)
Street, Brian V. (1993) 'The new literacy studies, guest editorial', *Journal of Research in Reading*, 16(2): 81–97. https://onlinelibrary.wiley.com/doi/abs/10.1111/j.1467-9817.1 993.tb00039.x. (Accessed: 27 March 2020).
Tang, Chaoju (2018) 'Dialects of Chinese' in Charles Boberg, John Nerbonne and Dominic Watt (eds.) *The Handbook of Dialectology*. Hoboken: Wiley Blackwell, pp. 537–558.
Tomić, Olga Mišeska (1992) 'Macedonian as an Ausbau language', in Michael Clyne, ed. *Pluricentric Languages: Differing Norms in Different Nations*. Berlin, New York: Mouton de Gruyter, pp. 437–454.
Wang, David Der-wei (2007) *Writing Taiwan: A New Literary History*. Duke University Press.
Yan, Margaret Mian (2006) *Introduction to Chinese Dialectology*. Lincom: Europa.

Chinese references

Cai, Jinan ed. 蔡金安主編 (2006)，《台灣文學正名》，台南：開朗雜誌社。
Cheng, Robert L. 鄭良偉 (1993)，《台語電腦文書處理輸入法系統: TW301使用手冊》，台北:前衛出版社。
Chiung, Wi-vun Taiffalo, and Lim, Bi-soat (2010)，〈台語能力測驗研發kap執 - 以2008年教育部委託案kap2009年各縣市委託案為研究對象〉(Development of the Taiwanese Proficiency Test), paper presented at 2010 Tē 3 Kài Tâi-gí Jīn-tsìng Haksut Gián-thó-hōe Lūn-bûn-tsip, National Cheng-kung University, Center for Taiwanese Language Testing, 13 March: 11.1–11.18。
Liao, Ruiming 廖瑞銘 (2013)，《舌尖與筆尖 - 台灣母語文學的發展》，台南:國立台灣文學館。
Lua, Siok-ling 賴淑玲 Iûⁿ, Ún-giân 楊允言 (2010)，〈教育部台灣閩南語推薦用字的比較分析〉(On the recommended Han characters for Taiwan southern min promulgated by Taiwan's ministry of education), *Journal of Taiwanese Vernacular* 《台語研究》，第2卷第1期，頁72-97。
Shih, Shu-mei 史書美 (2017)，《反離散: 華語語系研究論》，台北: 聯經出版公司。

Van der Loon, Piet (1992), *The Classical Theatre and Art Song of South Fukien*. Taipei: SMC Publishing.

Wang, Mei-jen 王美珍 (2006)，〈文化「台」風意味著什麼?「台客文化」的社會 想像與認同形構〉(What does "taike fad" mean culturally: The social imaginary and identity construction of "taike culture"), Master thesis, National Chengchi University, Taipei, Taiwan.

6

DAIGHI TEACHERS' DAIGHI IDENTITY AND THEIR PROMOTION OF STUDENTS' IDENTITY THROUGH LEARNING DAIGHI IN PRIMARY SCHOOL CLASSROOMS

Chia-Ying (Annie) Yang, Yvonne Foley, and Jill Northcott

Introduction

Daighi, a key marker of Taiwanese identity (Zhong 2002; Chen 2008; Her 2009), is going through an intergenerational language shift (Huang 1988; Chan 1994; Hong 2002; Yeh et al. 2004; Census 2010; Chen 2010; Yang 2020). Daighi, meaning 'Taiwanese language', has many alternative appellations. It is variously known as Minnanyu (Yeh et al. 2004; Yang 2008), Tai-yu (Hsiau 1997), Taiwanese (Edwards 1985; Sandel 2003; Liu 2012), Southern Min (Huang 2007; Chen 2010), Taiwanese Min-Nan language (Liu 2012), Taiwanese Holo/Hoklo language, Taiwanese Hokkien, Hokkienese mentioned by Liu (2012) and Edwards (1985), and lastly, Tai-gi (Lim 1996, 1997, 1998; Li 1999; Sandel 2003; Klöter 2009). Daighi is the name used in this study because first, it draws on the phonetic transcription of 'Taiwanese language', which is how the language has been referred to among Taiwanese ever since the Japanese colonial era (Hsiau 2012). Second, this name is pronounced in Daighi rather than in Taiwanese Mandarin (Tai-yu), and spelled in the Daighi tongiong pingim (Taiwanese phonetic transcription system, DT) (see also Yang 2020).

Daighi, it is argued, first became a symbol of Taiwanese identity during Japanese colonisation (1895–1945) (Hsiau 2012), because Japan's colonial language policy 'gave Taiwanese people a common language, and helped to foster a feeling of "Taiwanese identity"' (Scott and Tiun 2007: 55), and since Daighi was the language of the majority, it became the 'Taiwanese language' (Gold 1986; Tsao 1999; Wei 2006; Wu 2009; Hubbs 2013).

Daighi is the mother tongue of the Minnan ethnic group in Taiwan, accounting for 73.3% of the Taiwanese population according to Chen (2010: 82) and Scott and Tiun (2007: 54); and 75% according to Liu (2012: 109) and Chen (2008). However, it is in the process of undergoing an intergenerational language shift. According to the Census (2010), the first language or mother tongue of those under 30 is Taiwanese Mandarin, whereas the mother tongues of those from 30 to 60 are both Taiwanese Mandarin and Daighi, and only those 60 and above are native in Daighi, with a certain percentage (around 37.86% according to Wu 1992: 353–359) bilingual in Japanese.

Perhaps with the increasing awareness of language endangerment or potential death due to this language shift, in 2001, the Taiwanese Ministry of Education (MOE) proposed the Local-Language-in-Education (LLE) Policy, introducing local languages – Daighi, Hakka, and Austronesian languages – into Taiwanese primary school education as optional subjects. On 15 July 2009, a revised LLE Policy was proposed, and implemented on 1 August 2011 as National Curriculum (Ministry of Education, 2009), repositioning local language subjects from optional to compulsory in primary schools. As this LLE Policy (2009) was the implemented policy during the period of my data collection for this study, this policy is the version referred to throughout this chapter. The four aims of the LLE Policy are: (1) To cultivate students' interest in Daighi and their active learning of the language; (2) to help them improve their listening, speaking, spelling, reading, and writing ability, thus enabling them to express their thoughts in their daily lives; (3) to develop their ability to think, communicate, discuss, appreciate, and solve problems in Daighi; (4) to enhance students' ability to learn through Daighi, to broaden their living experiences, and to familiarise them with multiple cultures, in order to meet the needs of modern society (Ministry of Education, 2009). Based on the proposed aims, to develop the Daighi language identity in education, the LLE Policy focuses on the improvement of language proficiency and knowledge of Taiwanese culture.

With the National Curriculum (2009) aims setting out a guideline to focus on language proficiency and culture, this study explores teachers' perceptions of Daighi's association with identity, and how they promote such perceptions in their classroom practices. This chapter first explains theories on identity and teacher agency in the literature review, before examining the use of interviews and classroom observations as data collection tools, and the implementation of a thematic analysis as the main data analysis method. In the findings and discussion section, teachers' perceptions and observed teaching practices are discussed and explained drawing on relevant theories. Lastly, the conclusion section summarises this chapter, and suggests directions for future studies.

Literature review

In the field of language maintenance and shift, education plays a crucial role in '*maintain[ing]* the minority language of the student, *strengthen[ing]* the student's sense of cultural and linguistic identity, and *affirm[ing]* their individual and collective ethnolinguistic rights' (May 2008). Although similar functions are shared, different aspects of language identity are emphasised depending on the specific contexts. This is exemplified drawing on the cases of Welsh, Scottish Gaelic, Luxembourgish, and Catalan.

In the Celtic-language context, 'cultural and linguistic heritage – of family, community, region or nation' (O'Hanlon 2015: 245) are emphasised and Welsh-medium education is a case in point (Williams and Reynolds 2003: 363). Similarly, the findings of Grant's (1983) and Roberts' (1991) studies suggest that in Anglicised urban areas, the rationale behind pursuing Gaelic-medium primary education is the parental desire 'to continue a tradition of Gaelic speaking in the family or a wish to preserve the Gaelic language and culture in Scotland' (O'Hanlon 2015: 245). In the case of Luxembourgish, one of the three official languages (Luxembourgish, French, and German), their Language-in-Education Policy promotes identification with all three languages (Horner and Weber 2008: 87). Horner and Weber (2008: 85) explain that this 'trilingual language-identity' is an ideology based on 'instrumental criteria', and that it is an 'acultural instrument of social integration – as everybody's language – rather than solely a cultural symbol of national identity in an endeavour to justify the ratification of language testing procedures within the framework of citizenship policy' (Horner 2015: 364). Another case in point is Catalan, the preferred language in public domains – administration, media, and public education – as stated in the Statute of 1979 (Casesnoves et al. 2019: 527). According to Casesnoves et al. (2019), the factors favouring the use of Catalan is related to ideology and identity, as the language is critical in the process of Catalonia becoming an independent state. Such identity is addressed as 'ethnic-national identity' by Fainé (2017) (see also Woolard 1989; Berrera 1997; Llobera 2004). Education plays a crucial role in reinforcing the national Catalan identity, through the means of culture promotion and reviving the use of Catalan (Fainé 2017: 47).

Although the link between language and identity is reinforced through education, the conceptualisation and emphasis on identity varies according to the nature of each case. In the case of Daighi, a number of research studies have focused on the Taiwanese population's perception of Daighi and its link to Taiwanese identity (Chen 2008; Her 2009; Liu 2012); language policy and its impact on education (Hsiau 1997; Sandel 2003; Klöter 2004; Scott and Tiun 2007; Wu 2009; Liu 2012; Hubbs 2013); language use in Taiwan (Chen 1998, 2003; Hong 2002; Yeh et al. 2004), and attitudes to Daighi (Van den Berg 1988; Yeh et al. 2004; Yang 2020). However, none of this research has focused on exploring the frontline Daighi teachers' perspective on Daighi and identity, and how this is emphasised in classroom contexts. As Daighi teachers constitute an important agent in Daighi education, this chapter sets out to fill in this gap.

To understand the case of Daighi, this section discusses first, the definition of identity, relevant perspectives on identity theories adopted for this study; and second, why this study employed Biesta et al.'s (2015: 627) 'model for understanding the achievement of agency'.

Identity

Ball and McIvor (2013) explain the strong link between language and identity, as 'language is widely understood by Indigenous Peoples as the vehicle for the

TABLE 6.1 Individual/collective identity types (Block 2007: 43)

Ascription/affiliation	Based on
Ethnic identity	Shared history, descent, belief systems, practices, language and religion, all associated with a cultural group
Racial identity	Biological/genetic make-up, i.e. racial phenotype
National identity	Shared history, descent, belief systems, practices, language and religion associated with a nation-state
Migrant identity	Ways of living in a new country, on a scale ranging from classic immigrant to transmigrant
Gender identity	Nature of conformity to socially constructed notions of femininities and masculinities, as well as orientations to sexuality and sexual activity
Social class identity	Income level, occupation, education, and symbolic behaviour
Language identity	Relationship between one's sense of self and different means of communication, understood in terms of language, a dialect or sociolect, as well as multimodality

intergenerational transmission of knowledge, culture, spirituality and identity' (Ball and McIvor 2013: 20). This study takes a post-structuralist approach to identity, which is defined as 'beyond the search for such "universal and invariant laws of humanity that are operative at all levels of human life" (Ekeh 1982: 128; cited in Ritzer 1992: 498), to more nuanced, multileveled and ultimately, complicated framings of the world around us' (Block 2007: 13). That is, identity is viewed as a complex and multi-layered entity, which can be unpacked through various perspectives. Block (2007: 14) identified seven key perspectives, on identity – 'ethnicity, race, nationality, migration, gender, social class and language' – as shown in Table 6.1.

In the Daighi context, the relevant perspectives drawn on are ethnic identity, national identity, and language identity, and are discussed in more detail below.

Ethnic identity and national identity

Although ethnicity is not explicitly defined in most research (May 2001), and '"ethnic" identity is sometimes used as a synonym of "national" identity...and in some languages, of "racial" identity' (Joseph 2004: 162), Block (2007) distinguishes 'ethnicity' from 'nationality'. The former focuses on culture, whereas the latter focuses on the nation-state. This echoes the definitions proposed by Joseph (2004: 162–163), where '*ethnic* identity is focused more on common descent and on a shared cultural heritage because of common descent, than on political aspirations for autonomy' and '*national* identity, which tend to focus on political borders and autonomy, and are often justified by arrangements centred on shared cultural heritage, but where the ethnic element is inevitably multiple'. Such conceptualisation of national identity is derived from B. Anderson's (1983: 49) widely accepted view of nation – 'imagined political community'. These understandings of ethnic and national identities are adopted to differentiate the mother tongue of the Min 'ethnic' group (Chen 2010; Scott and Tiun 2007; Liu 2012), from a language of Taiwan where multiple ethnic groups co-exist[1] – that is, Daighi.

Language identity

Language identity, or 'ethnolinguistic identity' (Blommaert 2005), is 'a complex notion covering both linguistic and "ethnic" features' (Blommaert 2005: 214). That is, language identity is the link between one's sense of self and a means of communication (Block 2007). Leung et al. (1997: 555) refer to the three types of relationship of such a means of communication as *language expertise, language affiliation,* and *language inheritance* (see also Rampton 1990). In their definition,

> *language expertise* refers to how proficient people are in a language; *language affiliation* refers to the attachment or identification one feels for a language whether or not they nominally belong to the social group customarily associated with it; and *language inheritance* refers to the ways in which individuals can be born into a language tradition that is prominent within the family and community setting whether or not they claim expertise in or affiliation to that language.

These three identity perspectives – ethnic, national, and language identity – are the key perspectives applied in this chapter to unpack identity linked to Daighi.

Teacher agency

As discussed in the Introduction, agency forms the analytic framework this study employs to explore teachers' understanding of Daighi and their own identity, and the importance of teaching this understanding to their students in Daighi classrooms. Instead of adopting the definition of 'agency' as discussed in the literature worldwide – that is, viewing agency as holistic and individualistic social action (Hollis 1994; Fullan 2003; Biesta et al. 2015; Pantic 2015) – this study uses the definition by Biesta and Tedder (2006), which recognises the role of 'socioculture' in agency (Biesta and Tedder 2006) to view agency as mediated action. According to the definition (Biesta et al. 2015: 626), agency is 'not something that people can *have* – as a property, capacity or competence – but is something that people *do*. More specifically, agency denotes a quality of the *engagement* of actors with temporal-relational contexts-for-action, not a quality of the actor themselves'. This statement showcases agency as an act of interaction between the agent and its social context.

Biesta et al.'s (2015) agency model is adopted (see Figure 6.1) to unpack the values identified through interviews. Biesta et al. (2015) explained that this model is guided by two concepts. The first is the 'ecological conception of

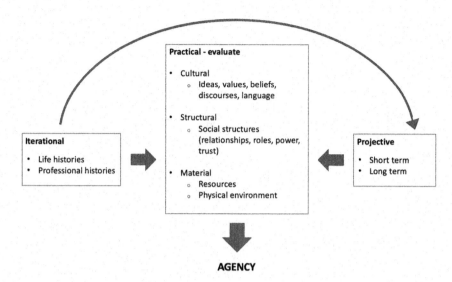

FIGURE 6.1 A model for understanding the achievement of agency (adapted from Biesta et al. 2015).

agency-as-achievement' (Biesta et al. 2015: 627), which views teachers' actions as 'the way in which actors critically shape their responses to problematic situations' (Biesta and Tedder 2006: 11; Biesta et al. 2015). This concept emphasises both teachers as agents whose actions are responsive and shaped by their own beliefs, as well as their understanding of the sociocultural context. The second comprises the ideas in Emirbayer and Mische's (1998) *Chordal Triad of Agency*, which presents agency as 'a configuration of influences from the *past* (iterational), orientations towards the *future* (projective) and engagement with the *present* (practical-evaluative)' (Biesta et al. 2015: 636, original emphasis).

The iterational dimension is defined as '*the selective reactivation by actors of past patterns of thought and action, routinely incorporated in practical activity, thereby giving stability and order to social universes and helping to sustain identities, interactions, and institutions over time*' (Emirbayer and Mische 1998: 971, original emphasis). In other words, the iterational dimension is a reflective process that looks at the impact of past events and professional development on the person's teaching practice. As the focus of this chapter is on the perception of Daighi identity, the discussion of iterational dimension focuses on teachers' life histories, specifically on the transformation from external (*interpsychological*) to internal (*intrapsychological*), as emphasised in the literature (Johnson and Golombek 2016: 4). If put into a second language teacher education context, the focus is on the teachers' internalising of 'the informed habits of mind, productive instructional concepts and practices that support student language learning, and the particular view of L2 teaching', and enactment of these in the L2 classroom (Johnson and Golombek 2016: 7). Unpacking teachers' life histories enables us to understand their motivation in devoting themselves to this profession, and the motivation to engage in professional development support that prepared them to pursue the profession of a Daighi teacher.

Teachers' professional development pursues the short-term and long-term goal of promoting positive attitudes to Daighi. In Emirbayer and Mische's definition (1998: 971), this projective dimension encompasses '*the imaginative generation by actors of possible future trajectories of action, in which received structures of thought and action may be creatively reconfigured in relation to actors' hopes, fears, and desires for the future*' (original emphasis). That is, having the short-term and long-term goal in mind shapes and is shaped by both the professional development plan and the present dimension – the current practice in the classroom.

The practical-evaluative dimension, or the present dimension, is defined as entailing '*the capacity of actors to make practical and normative judgments among alternative possible trajectories of action, in response to the emerging demands, dilemmas, and ambiguities of presently evolving situations*' (Emirbayer and Mische 1998: 971, original emphasis). That is, in a real-time classroom situation, teachers are equipped with knowledge and skills that enable them to make various decisions, which lead to different trajectories. These decisions are analysed according to three aspects – cultural, material, and structural.

> Cultural aspects have to do with ways of speaking and thinking, of values, beliefs and aspirations, and encompass both inner and outer dialogue. This links to life stories in the iterational dimension, and the aspiration of teaching in the projective dimension. Material aspects have to do with the resources that promote or hinder agency and the wider physical environment in and through which agency is achieved. Structural aspects have to do with the social structures and relational resources that contribute to the achievement of agency.
>
> *(Biesta et al. 2015: 30)*

When the cultural aspects lens is applied to analyse my data, teachers' perceptions of their identity and Daighi, and how important it is for their students to share such understanding are illuminated. The structural aspect lens – the relationship between the Daighi teacher and the MOE, schools, and colleagues, and material aspect – the resources and physical environment are also important aspects to explore, as these aspects help the understanding of implicit mediation on teachers' actions (see Yang 2020 for further discussion), but are not discussed in detail due to the specific focus of this chapter.

This chapter draws on three perspectives of identity – ethnic, national, and language – and Biesta et al.'s (2015) teacher agency model to explore teachers' perceptions of Daighi and identity, and Daighi education, as well as the promotion of this ideology through their classroom practices.

Methodology

Twenty Daighi teachers were interviewed and observed: Eleven teachers in Taipei, with six teaching primary 6 and five teaching primary 4, and nine in Changhua, with four teaching primary 6, and five teaching primary 4. This study first drew on the semi-structured active interview[2] as the primary data collection tool. The interviews lasted from 40 minutes to two and a half hours and were followed by two unobtrusive classroom observations,[3] with each class lasting 40 minutes, finishing with a short post-observation interview, which lasted between two minutes and 40 minutes, for further confirmation or clarification purposes.

An inductive approach – the constant comparative method – proposed by Glaser and Strauss (1967) was employed to analyse both interview and classroom observation data. That is, I used sequential comparisons, which involved first developing a list of codes based on one interview, coding the next interview against the list, and adding those emerged codes to the existing list; and second, going through my data again and again to compare statements shared within the same interview, and with other interviews. These codes and extracts were then grouped into categories to develop themes, and related theories and studies were consulted to redefine the analytic framework that best describes this research. This indicates that at this stage, I also engaged with the deductive approach in addition to the inductive approach that I had used when coming up with the codes.

To improve the validity of the findings, peer checking (Dörnyei 2007) was employed at the first cycle coding level. The codes overlapped substantially, which helped assure the validity of this qualitative research. In terms of ethics, the research procedure was approved by the Ethics Committee from the Moray House School of Education and Sport from the University of Edinburgh, UK. Each participant was informed of the focus of this study prior to giving their consent; they were also aware of their rights to withdraw at any stage, and that their identity was anonymised.

Findings and discussions

This section is structured according to relevant aspects of the teacher agency model which provided the theoretical framework for the study (Biesta et al. 2015). The themes identified are categorised according to the characteristics of each dimension identified in the Biesta et al. (2015) model – iterational (past), projective (future), and practical-evaluative (present).

Iterational dimension (past)

As discussed and explained in the literature review, the iterational dimension has to do with the past of the actor, which is critical for stabilising and informing present and future actions (Emirbayer and Mische 1998; Biesta et al. 2015: 626; Johnson and Golombek 2016), and the focused aspect discussed is life histories – personal attachment to Daighi and teachers' identity.

Teachers' strong link to Daighi

The personal attachment to Daighi aspect helps us to understand how teachers perceive their identity in relation to Daighi, which is fundamental to understanding the motivation for their teaching. To many Daighi teachers (19 out of 20 in the study), Daighi is their mother tongue; thus, the sense of identity and responsibility to pass on Daighi emerged as the main reason for the attachment. Take Beth for example:

> It was after I started going to kindergarten, going to school that I started to speak Taiwanese Mandarin. I came to Taipei for a university education, and no one spoke Daighi with me. Whenever I go back home, I especially miss this language. Yes, Daighi to me is the link to my own origin.
>
> *(Beth.TP4.additional discussion.3)*

Beth positioned Daighi as a language that was linked to her family of origin, and this association became more apparent when she left the Daighi-speaking environment to live in Taipei. Richard also stated that Daighi was his mother tongue – his language, and that he had a sense of responsibility and motivation to pass it on to his children and grandchildren. The majority of Daighi teachers perceived themselves as 'inheritors' of Daighi as they were 'born into a language tradition that is prominent within the family and community setting' (Leung et al. 1997: 555), and identify themselves with Daighi and have a sense an attachment to it (see '*language affiliation*', Leung et al. 1997). In terms of '*language expertise*', apart from obtaining the certificate as qualified Daighi teachers, they also needed to complete 36 to 72 hours of professional training prior to commencing their career as Daighi teachers. Additionally, for many of these Daighi teachers, Daighi is also their mother tongue and their main language for communication. Daighi thus meets the types of language identity for these teachers.

Projective dimension (future)

The projective dimension (both short-term and long-term) is informed by actors' expectations of the future, or their vision of the future constructed on the basis of their own beliefs (Embirbayer and Mische 1998; Biesta et al. 2015). The emerged expectations are a projection of the discussion of themes in the iterational dimension. These are: (1) Students acquiring knowledge about Daighi (half of the teachers within the study), being able to speak their ethnic mother tongue (two out of 20 teachers), and linking their identity with Daighi (Richard and Sandra); and (2) to improve students' Daighi skill in listening, speaking, reading, and writing (shared among all Daighi teachers), enabling them to communicate with parents and grandparents in Daighi (six out of 20 teachers), and to use Daighi in their daily lives (seven out of 20 teachers). The teachers' expectations suggest that *language expertise* is one of their clear goals. Additionally, the emphasis on family and linguistic heritage is similar to Celtic-language cases, employed to develop an identity connecting to Daighi ('*language affiliation*'). Recognising students' '*language inheritance*' is another important aspect that teachers work towards, as they aim for their students to use Daighi to speak to their parents and grandparents. The emphasis of identity aspect links to Daighi appeared to be prominent in these expectations and visions, together with teachers' sense of identity and responsibility discussed in the iterational dimension.

Practical-evaluative dimension (present)

The focus of this dimension is on current actions, and cultural aspects are drawn on, which explore ideals, values, beliefs, discourses, and language (Emirbayer and Mische 1998; Biesta et al. 2015). Such aspects are crucial to explore as almost half of the teachers expressed the opinion that teachers' beliefs and aspirations shape their teaching. To teachers, the shared view on the importance of Daighi and its link to identity are categorised into the following three themes: (1) Daighi is 'your' identity; (2) Daighi is a useful communication tool; and (3) Daighi preserves ancestors' wisdom, Taiwanese tradition and culture (see also Yang 2020).

Daighi is 'your' identity

Three aspects are categorised under this rationale: Daighi names, students' ethnic mother tongue, and 'Taiwanese speak Daighi', each of which are explained in the following.

Daighi names

Based on classroom observation notes, three of the Daighi teachers addressed students by pronouncing their names in Daighi, and one teacher addressed students by calling their numbers in Daighi. Ethan, for example, explained that:

> Whenever I start teaching a new class, I always ask the home teacher for the students' name list, and check their pronunciation in Daighi at home before coming to teach them…So, in my class, I asked students to check attendance calling on their peer's Daighi names, as you observed…In a new academic year, I will spend two to three weeks checking attendance myself, teaching them how to pronounce their names in Daighi, and after that, I let them check attendance. After a while, they should not use the name list anymore, but should check attendance by looking at their peers.[4]
>
> *(Ethan.TP6.1)*

To Ethan, it was important that students know how to pronounce their names in Daighi, as students do not have many opportunities to learn this. Like Gloria and Henry who also insisted on addressing students using their Daighi names, no specific reasoning was provided, apart from that they expected their students to know their names in Daighi, and to pronounce them appropriately. Such motivation may link to what Joseph (2004: 1) considers to be one of the two basic aspects to a person's identity: 'their name, which serves first of all to single them out from other people'. Addressing students with Daighi names can also be the first step to develop 'affection connection', or 'identify with and feel attached' to Daighi (see *'language affiliation'* above). Alternatively, these Daighi teachers may be emphasising to students their ethnolinguistic inheritance (see *'language inheritance'* above). On the other hand, three other teachers mentioned calling students by their Daighi names, but they explained that it was challenging for the teachers.

Students' ethnic mother tongue

Daighi is identified by the Daighi teachers as a key to link to grandparents. As discussed in the Introduction, students' grandparents are either bilingual in Daighi and Japanese or monolingual in Daighi, and have little or no Taiwanese Mandarin. This language barrier across generations became a serious issue since a strong family bond is highly valued in Taiwan (Olsen 1974). This was also reflected in the interviews, in which teachers emphasised the function of Daighi as the key to bridging the existing language gap across generations and building a strong bond (see Tosi 1999: 325 on the sense of us-ness). For example, Sandra shared how students using Daighi with their grandparents could strengthen the family bond (Sandra.TP6.4.b.5/6). Beth's view is also a case in point:

> Minnanyu[5] is widely spoken among their grandpa and grandma's generation. So, I hope that they can use Minnanyu to interact with them because Minnanyu is still a much friendlier language [to the grandparents]. It feels that, if you speak Minnanyu and I speak Minnanyu, the feeling of using Minnanyu to communicate to each other gives a sense of zero-distance compared to using the National Language.
>
> *(Beth.TP4.4.b.3)*

Daighi is Beth's mother tongue, and as she shared in an earlier part of the interview, speaking Daighi gives her a sense of being part of the family (see also discussion in iterational dimension above). Beth wanted to share this aspect of Daighi with her students, and hoped that the students would one day come to realise this and value Daighi themselves. This emphasis on family or the community linguistic setting that students are associated with is shared among the Daighi teachers, and they promoted the importance of it in their teaching practices given the critical role family plays in Taiwanese culture. This family heritage focused identity is similar to the Welsh and Scottish Gaelic cases discussed by O'Hanlon (2015), and matches with the *language inheritance* type of language identity discussed in the literature review.

Taiwanese speak Daighi

Another important theme which emerged is the link between Daighi and Taiwanese identity, which is illustrated clearly in Sandra's extract:

> We try our best to enable them [students] to [communicate] <u>through that,</u> through language to find something that <u>they themselves</u> can identify with. <u>For example, we want them to use it a bit more when they go back to visit their grandparents.</u> Then their grandparents find that…you will find this bond of 'usness' with your grandparents, and they also think that you are together with them. This language of our grandparents cannot be thrown away, <u>because you are Taiwanese</u>! Right? And I just encourage them, <u>saying that</u> you were born in Taiwan, no matter whether you are Hakkanese, Minnanren, new immigrants or what, <u>you are all Taiwanese. We Taiwanese have many languages, and Daighi that you are learning now is just one of them, right?</u>
>
> *(Sandra.TP6.4.b.5/6)*

Sandra considered herself responsible for helping students to develop an identity through Daighi. Sandra began with explaining the importance of Daighi and family bond, then extended Daighi's importance to Taiwanese identity. A similar point was also made by Anita and Richard, where they emphasised that students are 21st century Taiwanese citizens, and speaking the Taiwanese language and knowing its culture is essential. Such a perception reflects the strong link between Daighi and Taiwanese identity since the Japanese colonisation era (see discussion in Introduction).

Although not specified, this identity could consist of national identity (Block 2007: 30), where 'individuals are born, raised and educated in a particular locality of a particular nation state', a perception which is similar to the case of Catalan (Casesnoves et al. 2019; Fainé 2017); and language use and identity (Giroux 1992; Wexler 1992; Rampton 1995; Gee 1996; Hall 1996; Schiffrin 1996; Lippi-Green 1997; van Dijk 1997; Miller 2000), whereby speakers 'view their language as a symbol of their social identity' (Kramsch 1998: 3), as a result of developing a language into a part of the students' linguistic repertoire (Norton 1995). On the other hand, it can also be viewed as close to the Luxembourg case, where language-identity is an ideology based on 'instrumental criteria' (Horner and Weber 2008: 85). This theme is closely linked to the next theme that emerged – Daighi is a useful communication tool.

Daighi is a useful communication tool

Another feature brought out by the teachers was that Daighi was a useful communication tool in daily life, even when it came to making a living:

Even if Daighi is not used during your study period of time, once you start working you will definitely use it, because we are all Taiwanese. This matters to your future, either you start your business or take on office job, right? If others use Daighi to talk to you, if you can't understand it, then you are like a duck listening to the sound of lightning [a Daighi idiom to express the situation when someone cannot understand what is being said].

(Sandra.TP6.4.b.5/6)

One of the Daighi values reflected in this observation of Sandra's is that, regardless of the students' ethnicity, Daighi is the second lingua franca in Taiwan next to Taiwanese Mandarin (see Chen 2010: 82; Scott and Tiun 2007: 54; Liu 2012: 109). Therefore, in Sandra's understanding, Daighi was also essential when it comes to making a living. This point was also stressed by Doris, as she explained that she does not expect her students to speak Daighi well, but since Daighi is one of the major languages in Taiwan, it is important that students should at least understand what others are saying (Doris.TP4.5.iii.3).

It is important to note that, linking back to the discussion under 'Taiwanese speak Daighi', these Daighi teachers aimed for their students to learn Daighi not just for their ethnolinguistic background, but because their 'national identity' is Taiwanese, and Daighi is a prominent language.

Daighi preserves ancestors' wisdom, Taiwanese traditions and culture

Similar to Gaelic-medium education, 'maintaining linguistic and cultural heritage – of family, community, region or nation' (O'Hanlon 2015: 245) – is a common theme shared among the Daighi teachers. Ofelia stressed the cultural heritage preservation aspect of Daighi when discussing her teaching practices. She gave an example of how Taiwanese ancestors' accurate observations were reflected in descriptions of the seasons in Daighi, and argued that this feature differed from those of Taiwanese Mandarin:

I want them to think that Daighi is beautiful, Daighi is beautiful; Daighi is knowledgeable. It is a beautiful and knowledgeable language; it is deep, and preserves treasures from our ancestors. They say one sentence, but why do they say it this way? There are reasons behind it. In the past, with one sentence you can describe the whole season; it is completely different from the sayings in our Taiwanese Mandarin. In ancient times there were no technologies like we have today; how did they manage to put it so well and accurately? For each solar term, there exists an idiom…I use these opportunities to tell them that Daighi is not for offensive expressions, absolutely not…Children need to hold this attitude of respect, then they can enjoy learning Daighi. If they think Daighi is something low-class, they won't want to learn it.

(Ofelia.CP6.4.c.6/7)

One of the examples of a solar term idiom in Daighi is '冬至烏，過年酥' (a rainy Winter Solstice Day precedes a sunny Lunar New Year). Sharing knowledge of Daighi's intellectual resources with her students was Ofelia's approach to improve students' motivation to affiliate with Daighi: They might even start to like learning it as they learn to respect it. In a similar vein, Queenie shared that in her class, increasing the awareness of Daighi as a beautiful, elegant language that preserves ancestors' wisdom was the approach to improve students' knowledge of Daighi, and learn the cultural aspect of the language. A Daighi idiom example could be '拍斷的手骨顛倒勇' (a broken bone comes back stronger), meaning failure does not make us weaker; it strengthens us to face the next challenge. Such emphasis by Daighi teachers' on the cultural aspect of identity is consistent with the definition of ethnic identity employed in this chapter, where the emphasis is on 'a form of collective identity based on shared cultural beliefs and practices, such as language, history, descent, and religion' (Puri 2004: 174).

The findings suggest that the majority of the Daighi teachers within this study perceived Daighi as an important link to their own identity (see iterational dimension). Based on this affiliation to Daighi, these teachers also set it as their teaching objective that students should develop an identity with Daighi and improve their proficiency (language expertise) (see projective dimension), either with an emphasis on students' ethnolinguistic background (language inheritance), personal association with Daighi (language affiliation), shared cultural beliefs (ethnic identity), or that they are 21st century Taiwanese (national identity) (see practical-evaluative dimension). In other words, Daighi is perceived as an important aspect of identity for both teachers and students, and this link with identity is emphasised by the Daighi teachers as an important aspect of compulsory Daighi education in primary schools. The teaching practices observed were in line with the implicit identity emphasis of the National Curriculum (2009), focusing on improving Daighi proficiency, knowledge about Daighi and Taiwanese culture, with an additional focus on national identity, language affiliation, and inheritance. Such an emphasis of teachers is also found in other languages – Celtic languages, Luxembourgish, and Catalan – where education acts as a vehicle for reinforcing language identity, culture, and linguistic heritage.

Conclusion

This chapter explored the case of Daighi, where language is viewed as a marker of Taiwanese identity (Zhong 2002; Chen 2008; Her 2009). For historical, sociocultural, and political reasons, Daighi is going through an intergenerational language shift to Taiwanese Mandarin. As a result, the Ministry of Education in Taiwan introduced and implemented the Local-Language-in-Education Policy in 2001, highlighted this ongoing language shift, and aimed to address it by introducing local languages (Daighi, Hakka, and Austronesian languages) into primary school education as optional subjects. The revised LLE Policy in 2009 repositioned local languages as compulsory subjects at primary school level. The National Curriculum 2009 set improving Daighi proficiency and cultural understanding of

Daighi as objectives. Based on this language policy background, this chapter has explored Daighi teachers' perceptions of Daighi and identity, and the importance of identity in Daighi education. The findings suggest that Daighi teachers view Daighi and identity as strongly linked, and they perceive this understanding as an important aspect to be addressed in Daighi education. Their understanding is similar to other cases discussed – Celtic languages, Luxembourgish, and Catalan – and is generally in line with the aims of the National Curriculum (2009).

Future studies

On 9 January 2019, the Ministry of Culture in Taiwan implemented the 'Development of National Languages Act', enacted with the intention to 'recognise the multicultural nature of the nation, and to spur the transmission, revival, and development of national languages'[6] (Taiwan, Ministry of Culture 2019: 1). In the education sector, it is proposed that 'any national language may be used as the language of instruction at schools', and that within three years (in 2022), these languages are included as compulsory subjects at primary, junior high, and high school levels (Taiwan, Ministry of Culture 2019: 3). Further studies are needed to explore the impact of this Language Act, understanding how the emphasis on the multicultural and multilingual nature of Taiwan may have an impact on the National Curriculum, and on learners' development of this multicultural and multilingual identity.

On the other hand, it is also important to explore students' language identity, whether they perceived language as 'only a linguistic system of words and sentences, [or] a social practice in which identities and desires are negotiated in the context of complex and often unequal relationships' (Norton 2016: 476), and how they associate language with their identity. Another aspect to investigate is then how the new multilingual and multicultural language policies influence students' perceptions towards their language identity development.

Notes

1 Although not always clear, according to Huang (1993: 21), the percentages of the four main ethnic groups are 73.3% Minnanren, 13% Mainlanders, 12% Hakkas, and 1.7% Austronesians (see also Hsiau 1997; Scott and Tiun 2007; Liu 2012).
2 Active interview is proposed by Holstein and Gubrium (1995: 4), emphasizing the active engagement of both interviewer and interviewee, on the process of reality constructing and meaning-making.
3 According to Robson (2011: 316), an observational style is 'non-participatory in the interest of being *non-reactive*…[and] is more usually unstructured and informal'. It is, according to Robson (2011: 316), a technique of directly watching and listening to what participants are doing, in order to obtain data concerning 'their views, feelings or attitudes', since these are not obtainable through direct inquiry (see also Yang 2020).
4 The fonts of the extract differ based on the language teachers use. <u>Daighi is with straight underline</u>, Taiwanese Mandarin in normal font, **English in Bold**, *<u>Japanese is in italics and underlined</u>*, and Italian or other languages with dotted underline.

5 Minnanyu is the name used by Beth to refer to Daighi; this is also the name used in National Curriculum to address Daighi.
6 National languages refer to 'all natural languages and sign languages used by the different ethnic groups in Taiwan' (Ministry of Culture 2019: 1).

References

English references

Anderson, B. (1983) Imagined Communities: Reflections on the origin and spread of nationalism, 1st edn, London: verso.

Ball, J. and McIvor, O. (2013) 'Canada's big chill: Indigenous languages in education', in C.B. Kosonen (ed.) *Language Issues in Comparative Education: Inclusive Teaching and Learning in Non-Dominant Languages and Cultures.* Rotterdam/Boston/Taipei: Sense Publishers, pp. 19–38.

Van den Berg, M. (1988) 'Taiwan's sociolinguistic setting ', in R. Cheng and S.-F. Huang (eds.) *The Structure of Taiwanese: A Modern Synthesis.* Taipei: The Crane Publishing Co., Ltd, pp. 241–261.

Berrera, A. (1997) 'Lengua, identidad y nacionalismo en Cataluña durante la tran- sición', *Revista de Antropologia Social,* 6, pp. 105–134.

Biesta, G., Priestley, M. and Robinson, S. (2015) 'The role of beliefs in teacher agency', *Teachers and Teaching,* 21(6), pp. 624–640.

Biesta, G. and Tedder, M. (2006) *How is Agency Possible? Towards an Ecological Understanding of Agency-as-Achievement (Working Paper 5).* Exeter: The Learning Lives Project.

Block, D. (2007) *Second Language Identities.* London: Bloomsbury Academic.

Blommaert, J. (2005) *Discourse.* Cambridge: Cambridge University Press.

Casesnoves, R., Mas, J.À. and Tudela, A. (2019) 'Primary and secondary factors in language maintenance in a medium-sized community language: Catalan in Spain', *International Journal of Bilingualism,* 23(2), pp. 525–552.

Chan, H.-C. (1994) *Language Shift in Taiwan: Social and Political Determinants.* Edited by R. Fasold. Dissertation. ProQuest Dissertations Publishing.

Chen, S.-C. (2003) *The Spread of English in Taiwan: Changing Use and Shifting Attitudes.* Taipei: The Crane Publishing Co., Ltd.

Chen, S.-C. (2010) 'Multilingualism in Taiwan', *International Journal of Sociology of Language,* (205), pp. 79–104.

Chen, Y.-C. (2008) 'The possibility of implementing new policy of language education reconcile and unify different ethnic groups in Taiwan', *Journal of Education Research and Development,* 4, pp. 223–250.

van Dijk, T. (1997) *Discourse as Social Interaction.* London: Sage.

Dörnyei, Z. (2007) *Research Methods in Applied Linguistics: Quantitative, Qualitative and Mixed Methods.* Oxford: Oxford University Press.

Edwards, J. (1985) *Language, Society and Identity.* Oxford: Blackwell in Association with Deutsch.

Ekeh, P. (1982) 'Structuralism: The principle of elementarism, and the theory of civilisation', in I. Rossi (ed.) *Structural Sociology.* New York: Columbia University Press, pp. 122–148.

Emirbayer, M. and Mische, A. (1998) 'What is agency?', *The American Journal of Sociology,* 103, pp. 962–1023.

Fainé, M.C.i. (2017) 'Language, national identity and school: The role of the Catalan-Language Immersion Program in contemporary Catalan nationalism', in K. Kantasalmi and G. Holm (eds.) *The State, Schooling, and Identity: Diversifying Education in Europe*. Palgrave Macmillan.

Fullan, M. (2003) *Change Forces with a Vengeance*. London: RoutledgeFalmer.

Gee, J.P. (1996) *Social Linguistics and Literacies: Ideology in Discourses*. London: The Falmer Press.

Giroux, H. (1992) 'Resisting differences: Cultural studies and the discourse of critical pedagogy', in L. Grossberg, P. Treichler, and C. Nelson (eds.) *Cultural Studies*. New York: Routledge, pp. 199–212.

Glaser, B.G. and Strauss, A.L. (1967) *The Discovery of Grounded Theory: Strategies for Qualitative Research*. London: Weidenfeld and Nicolson.

Gold, T.B. (1986) *State and Society in the Taiwan Miracle*. Armonk, NY: M.E. Sharpe.

Grant, J.H. (1983) *An Investigation into the Feasibility of Establishing Gaelic/English Bilingual Schools on the Mainland of Scotland*. Glasgow, Scotland: The University of Glasgow.

Hall, S. (1996) *Introduction: Who Needs Identity?, Questions of Cultural Identity*. Edited by S. Hall and P. Gay. London: Sage.

Her, O.-S. (2009) 'Language and group identity: On Taiwan mainlanders' mother tongues and Taiwan mandarin', *Language and Linguistics*, 10(2), pp. 375–419.

Hollis, M. (1994) *The Philosophy of Social Science: An Introduction*. Cambridge: Cambridge University Press.

Holstein, J.A. & Gubrium, J.F. (1995) *The Active Interview* (Vol. 37). Thousand Oaks, CA: Sage.

Horner, K. (2015) 'Language regimes and acts of citizenship in multilingual Luxembourg', *Journal of Language and Politics*, 3(14), pp. 359–381.

Horner, K. and Weber, J.J. (2008) 'The language situation in Luxembourg', *Current Issues in Language Planning*, 9(1), pp. 69–128.

Hsiau, A.-C. (1997) 'Language ideology in Taiwan: The KMT's language policy, the Tai-Yu language movement, and ethnic politics', *Journal of Multilingual and Multicultural Development*, 18(4), pp. 302–315.

Hsiau, A.-C. (2012) *Reconstructing Taiwan: The Cultural Politics of Contemporary Nationalism*. Taipei: Linking Publishing.

Huang, C. (2007) 'Language planning for naming and its connotations: A case study in Taiwan', *Current Issues in Language Planning*, 8(3), pp. 305–323.

Huang, S.-F. (1988) 'A sociolinguistic profile of Taipei', in R.-I. Cheng and S.-F. Huang (eds.) *The Structure of Taiwanese: A Modern Synthesis*. Taipei: The Crane Publishing Co., Ltd, pp. 301–335.

Hubbs, E. (2013) 'Taiwan language-in-education policy: Social, cultural, and practical implications', *Arizona Working Papers in SLA & Teaching*, 20, pp. 76–95.

Johnson, K.E. and Golombek, P.R. (2016) *Mindful L2 Teacher Education: A Sociocultural Perspective on Cultivating Teachers' Professional Development*. Edited by K. Johnson and P. Golombek. New York; London: Routledge.

Joseph, J.E. (2004) *Language and Identity: National, Ethnic, Religious*. New York: Palgrave Macmillan.

Klöter, H. (2004) 'Language policy in the KMT and DPP eras', *China Perspectives*, 2004(6), pp. 1–12.

Klöter, H. (2009) 'Re-writing language in Taiwan', in F.-L. Shih, P.F. Tremlett, and S. Thompson (eds.) *Re-Writing Culture in Taiwan*. Abingdon: Routledge, pp. 102–122.

Kramsch, C.J. (1998) *Language and Culture*. Oxford: Oxford University Press.

Leung, C., Harris, R. and Rampton, B. (1997) 'The idealised native speaker, reified ethnicities, and classroom realities', *TESOL Quarterly*, 31(3), p. 543.

Li, H.-C. (1999) *Collection of Essays on Taigi Literature Movement*. Taipei: Chian-ui.

Lim, I.-B. (1996) *Essays on the Taigi Literature Movement*. Taipei: Chian-ui.

Lim, I.-B. (1997) *Essays on Taiwanese Language and Culture*. Taipei: Chian-ui.

Lim, I.-B. (1998) *Language, Culture, and Nation-State*. Taipei: Chian-ui.

Lippi-Green, D. (1997) *English with an Accent: Language, Ideology and Discrimination in the United States*. London: Routledge.

Liu, R.-Y. (2012) 'Language policy and group identification in Taiwan', *Mind, Brain, and Education*, 6(2), pp. 108–116.

Llobera, J.R. (2004) *Foundations of National Identity: From Catalonia to Europe*. New York: Berghahn Books.

May, S. (2001) *Language and Minority Rights: Ethnicity, Nationalism and the Politics of Language*. Harlow, Essex: Longman/Pearson Education.

May, S. (2008) 'Bilingual/immersion education: What the research tells us'. In J. Cummins and N. Hornberger (eds.) *Encyclopedia of Language and Education*. 2nd edn. Berlin: Springer, pp. 19–34.

Miller, J.M. (2000) 'Language use, identity, and social interaction: Migrant students in Australia', *Research on Language and Social Interaction*, 33(1), pp. 69–100.

Norton, B. (1995) 'Social identity, investment and language learning', *TESOL Quarterly*, 29, pp. 9–32.

Norton, B. (2016) 'Identity and language learning: Back to the future', *TESOL Quarterly*, 50(2), pp. 475–479.

O'Hanlon, F. (2015) 'Choice of Scottish Gaelic-medium and Welsh-medium education at the primary and secondary school stages: Parental and pupil perspectives', *International Journal of Bilingual Education and Bilingualism*, 18(2), pp. 242–259.

Olsen, N.J. (1974) 'Family structure and socialization patterns in Taiwan', *American Journal of Sociology*, 79(6), pp. 1395–1417.

Pantic, N. (2015) 'A model for study of teacher agency for social justice', *Teachers and Teaching*, 21(6), pp. 759–778.

Puri, J. (2004) *Encountering Nationalism*. Oxford: Blackwell.

Rampton, B. (1990) 'Displacing the "native speaker": Expertise, affiliation, and inheritance', *ELT Journal*, 44(2), pp. 97–101.

Rampton, B. (1995) *Crossings*. London: Longman.

Ritzer, G. (1992) *Sociological Theory*. 3rd edn. New York: McGraw-Hill.

Roberts, A. (1991) 'Parental attitudes to Gaelic-medium Education in the Western Isles of Scotland', *Journal of Multilingual and Multicultural Development*, 12, pp. 253–269.

Robson, C. (2011) *Real World Research* (3rd ed.). West Sussex: John Wiley & Sons Ltd.

Sandel, T.L. (2003) 'Linguistic capital in Taiwan: The KMT's Mandarin language policy and its perceived impact on language practices of bilingual Mandarin and Tai-gi speakers', *Language in Society*, 32, pp. 523–552.

Schiffrin, D. (1996) 'Narrative as self-portrait: Sociolinguistic constructions of identity', *Language and Society*, 25, pp. 167–203.

Scott, M. and Tiun, H.K. (2007) 'Mandarin-only to mandarin-plus: Taiwan', *Language Policy*, 6, pp. 53–72.

Taiwan, Ministry of Culture (2019) *Development of National Languages Act*, Available at https://law.moj.gov.tw/ENG/LawClass/LawAll.aspx?pcode=H0170143 (Accessed: 25 April 2020).

Tosi, A. (1999) 'The notion of "community" in language maintenance, in L. Verhoeven and G. Extra (eds.) *Bilingualism and Migration*. New York: Mouton de Gruyter, pp. 325–344.

Tsao, F.-F. (1999) 'The language planning situation in Taiwan', *Journal of Multilingual and Multicultural Development*, 20(4–5), pp. 328–375.

Woolard, K. (1989) *Double Talk: Bilingualism and the Politics of Ethnicity in Catalonia*. Standford: Standford University Press.

Wei, J.M. (2006) 'Language choice and ideology in multicultural Taiwan', *Language and Linguistics*, 7(1), pp. 87–107.

Wexler, P. (1992) *Becoming Somebody: Toward A Social Psychology of School*. London: Falmer.

Williams, R.H. and Reynolds, J. (2003) 'Background: The Union of Welsh-medium school parents', in I.W. Williams (ed.) *Our Children's Language: The Welsh-Medium Schools of Wales, 1939–2000*. Talybont (Wales): Y Lolfa, pp. 362–367.

Wu, M.-H. (2009) 'Language planning and policy in Taiwan: Past, present, and future', *Working Papers in Educational Linguistics*, 24(2), pp. 99–118.

Yang, C.-Y. (2020) *Language Maintenance through Primary School Education : The Case of Declaration of Authorship*. Edinburgh, Scotland: The University of Edinburgh.

Yang, Y.-T. (2008) 'The challenges of indigenous language curriculum reform in Taiwan: Multicultural education perspective', *Journal of National University of Tainan*, 20, pp. 25–58.

Yeh, H., Chan, H. and Cheng, Y. (2004) 'Language use in Taiwan: Language proficiency and domain analysis', *Journal of Taiwan Normal University: Humanities & Social Sciences*, 49(1), pp. 75–108.

Zhong, R.-F. (2002) 'The current situation of language policy and actual language use in Taiwan', in *Hakka Public Policy Symposium Proceedings*. Xinzhuang, New Taipei: Executive Yuan Council for Hakka Affairs.

Chinese references

Chen, M.-R. 陳美如 (1998) 臺灣語言教育政策之回顧與展望 *(The Retrospect and Prospect of Language Education Policies in Taiwan)*, Kaohsiung: Fuwen Publishing Co.

Hong, W.-R. 洪惟仁 (2002) '臺灣的語言政策何去何從' (Language policy in Taiwan: where to go?), in *The Proceedings of International Conference on Language Policy: Multiculture and Ethnic Equality*. Taipei: Council for Hakka Affairs, The Executive Yuan, pp. 18/1–19.

Huang, S.-F. 黃宣範 (1993) 語言、社會與族群意識: 臺灣語言社會的研究 (Language, society and ethnicity: Taiwanese sociolinguistic research), Taipei: Crane Publishing Co., Ltd.

Ministry of Education (2009) 國民中小學九年一貫課程綱要語文學習領域(閩南語) (The National Curriculum: Grade 1-9 Curriculum Guidelines – Daighi), available at: https://www.k12ea.gov.tw/files/97_sid17/課程綱要語文學習領域(閩南語)8.26.pdf (Accessed: March 2020).

Taiwan, Legislative Yuan (2010) '99年人口及住宅普查總報告統計結果提要分析' (Census 2010 General Report: Population, Housing, Institutions, Ages, Marital Conditions, Education, Birthplace, and Nationality). Available at: https://www.stat.gov.tw/public/Attachment/21081884771.pdf (Accessed: 25 April 2020).

Wu, W.-S. 吳文星 (1992) 日據時期台灣社會領導階層研究 *(Research on Taiwanese Social Stratification during the Japanese Era)*, Taipei: Cheng Chung Book Company.

7

DISCOURSE AND IDEOLOGY IN THE TAIWANESE ENGLISH-LANGUAGE PRESS DURING KMT PRESIDENT MA YING-JEOU'S EARLY RULE

Lutgard Lams

Introduction

When it concerns a lofty initiative such as the present book's aim of looking into the interplay of language and ideology in a Taiwanese context, various discursive platforms can become the object of exploration. One can focus on official and/or public discourses in written or spoken formats, i.e. text or talk, and approach the semiotics of language use through an analysis of text or imagery or a combination of both in a multimodal approach. Irrespective of the actual units of analysis, what is crucial in a study of the dynamics of ideology and language is an examination of how they operate in discourse, which has been defined as 'a rule-governed system held together by a set of statements that the discursive practice continues to reproduce' (Escobar 1995: 154). The discourses examined in the present study are situated in a Taiwanese context, where points of contention very often revolve around matters of cultural and political identity, besides other issues of sociopolitical and economic reality. These involve political economy, ecology, governance system, people's welfare, and livelihood, all of them typically dividing opinions along left- and right-wing political agendas. In a democratic society, such as contemporary Taiwan (or the Republic of China on Taiwan, as it is named officially), these discourses can be openly debated in political settings, such as the legislature, and in public spaces, including the educational sphere and the media sector.

Taiwan has witnessed three peaceful changes of ruling party after hotly contested election campaigns on the presidential and legislative levels (in 2000, 2008, and 2016). In 2020, the incumbent DPP president, Tsai Ying-wen, was re-elected to a second term in office, gaining a convincing mandate from the electorate on the basis of what must have been deemed effective domestic and foreign policies, and a consistent position on cross-Strait relations. Especially the latter differed substantially from the attitude and actions taken by the former KMT (Kuomintang or Nationalist Party) President Ma Ying-jeou, who initiated a rapprochement with the Chinese political leadership of the People's Republic of China. However, a sizeable proportion of the Taiwanese electorate did not perceive this move sufficiently beneficial to the entire Taiwanese population. The lack of consultation was one of the main reasons for the student revolts or the Sunflower Movement in 2014. Since then, a new political climate of enhanced consultation, transparency, and a stronger focus on local issues has become the 'new normal' on the Taiwanese political scene, and gradually, the former type of Ma Ying-jeou-style governance has been relegated to a memory of the past. Yet, as it is the reflection of yesterday that makes today make sense to mankind, it is useful to recall the spirit or sentiment of the zeitgeist during KMT rule, starting from 2008. The present article thus takes a historical approach to discourses of a not so remote past, a period in which political acts and discourses contributed to present-day positions on a variety of regional and national issues, not in the least cultural and political identities and matters of civic concerns, giving rise to an expansion of social movements and street demonstrations in 2014.

This chapter looks into the prevalence of themes deemed worthy of discussion in the public sphere during the early years of KMT administration (2008–2009) and teases out the dynamics of ideology and language as discernible in a selected corpus of Taiwanese media narratives. It does not examine the changing power structures and the strategies of social groups that led to a political power change in 2016, nor does it present a political analysis of reasons for electoral gains/losses in the particular local election chosen for analysis in this article.[1] The study also does not provide a survey of identity development in the Taiwanese context, which can be easily retrieved through the periodical surveys on identity, conducted by the Election Study Center at National Chengchi University, Taiwan, and more recently, in May 2020, also by the Pew Research Center. Since Taiwan's democratisation, there has been a steady increase in the number of people in Taiwan identifying as Taiwanese. The overall ideological orientation concerning cultural identity (in terms of Sinicisation/localisation) in official speeches of Ma Ying-jeou has been documented in earlier studies (Lams and Liao 2011), but there is a research gap on how this discourse was echoed or contested in the public sphere, in particular in those Taiwanese print media catering to domestic and international audiences alike, i.e. the English-language newspapers. Hence, the study investigates how discourse testifies to what particular thought patterns were underlying the specific media accounts and maps the various issues that captured the attention of the media professionals and other commentators at that point in time. As discourse, within a post-structural epistemological perspective, is viewed as a social practice (Foucault 1972/2010: 50–55, 80; Fairclough 1992), it not only *represents* social ideas, beliefs, values, and norms, but it also *shapes* them and the media are the platforms par excellence for certain discourses to powerfully influence people's thoughts and actions, not in the least at electoral times.

Rather than focusing on the evident discourse moments, such as presidential/legislative campaigns with highly ideological debates, a more low-key event, such as a local election, is selected as the object of analysis. Local elections usually encompass a broader span of issues than the typically ideologically laden topics on the agenda in national elections and yield a more comprehensive picture of what was discussed in the public forum of those days. The 2009 mid-term 'three-in-one elections' (county magistrates and county-level city mayors; county councillors; township mayors) were also viewed as a first indicator of the new administration's early performance ratings.[2]

As for the choice of the traditional newspapers, one needs to return to the historical setting of more than a decade ago, when social media had not yet occupied centre stage in citizens' communicative practices. The specific objects of investigations are narratives from the three English-language newspapers in Taiwan. The prevalent political and societal themes articulated in the English-language press of Taiwan mirror and represent the existing public debates, as mediated in the Chinese-language newspapers. The choice for foreign-language narratives allows investigation of whether and how identity issues are projected to the foreign community. Judging from their mission statements, the papers aim to not only bring the world to Taiwan but especially deliver Taiwanese news to the world. Just like the official PRC media endeavour in soft power propaganda, the Taiwanese news organisations, while operating in a free market climate, function as cultural diplomacy tools. Comments and op-ed pieces are circulated and discussed on online international fora, which in turn may have an impact on academic and political thought and action, abroad as well as on the domestic scene. In the Taiwanese case, the nation-building process is not solely a domestic issue, but the foreign community is a behind-the-scenes major player in this process and is thus a prime target (for Taiwan and China alike) to be discursively influenced.

In addition, and in tandem with their Chinese-language equivalents in Taiwan, these English-language news outlets engage in an ideological struggle concerning identity and nation-building issues for the hearts and minds not only of the foreign community, but also of the domestic audience. The latter comprises a community of English-language learners in Taiwan and those readers who are more interested in these papers for their international outlook, believed to go beyond the local perspectives on Taiwan and China, as narrated in ideologically polarising ways in the partisan Chinese-language press. Within the Taiwanese pluralist media landscape, open to a variety of voices, the vernacular press is notoriously partisan in nature (Lee 1994; Rawnsley 2000; Weston 2013; Sullivan et al. 2019). When it comes to examining the interplay between language and ideology, it is more challenging to find instances of ideological meaning generation, where it is less expected or less conspicuous. Although the main English-language newspapers have also been shown to be divided along partisan lines (Lams 2006, 2008), they may be viewed by some avid readers as less openly antagonistic than their Chinese-language counterparts.

Since Taiwanese citizens constitute a large part of the intended readership, these English-language media outlets also serve as a domestic discourse building tool, especially around electoral times by steering people's choices and addressing the Taiwanese electorate on how to interpret poll outcomes. Obviously, given the limited scope of readership compared to the vernacular newspapers, the potential impact of these English-language media on changing the local political landscape remains minimal. Yet, the present article demonstrates that this locus of the English-language media scene in Taiwan can constitute an interesting testimonial for retrieving what discursive practices were instrumentalised in more or less subtle ideological ways to influence domestic and foreign opinion about the political scene at that particular point in time.

In particular, the analysis investigates the themes discussed in the media accounts and explores whether the formerly hotly debated identity-related issues were still deemed relevant after one year of Ma Ying-jeou rule or whether the public debate already focused more on civic issues. Identity-oriented topics include references to the term 'identity' itself and argumentation about ethnic and cultural divisions within the Taiwanese society, whereas the civic issue orientation covers matters of social, economic, and political concerns as in any modern society at electoral times, in other words, the bread-and-butter issues steering voter behaviour during local elections.

As for method, a content analysis probing into the salience of themes was complemented by a qualitative discourse analysis looking at argumentation lines and ideology underlying the discursive practices. Ideology, from a discourse analytical perspective, is defined as 'any constellation of fundamental or commonsensical, and often normative, beliefs, and ideas related to some aspect(s) of (social) "reality"' (Verschueren 1999: 238). What is naturalised or presented as 'common sense' does not lend itself to easy questioning and is usually carried implicitly. Ideological meaning generation, by and large, revolves around matters of positioning the Self versus the Other, power relations, categorisation and identification processes. In the Taiwanese context, this translates most often in trends of Sinicisation and Taiwanisation or localisation.

Sinicisation and Taiwanisation/localisation processes

Taiwan's democratisation process was consolidated after two rounds of presidential and legislative elections (in 2008 and 2016) led to a peaceful change of ruling hands. These power shifts were based on the rise and fall of political parties and/ or their top representative figures, for 2008 Chen Shui-bian (DPP)/Ma Ying-jeou (KMT) and for 2016 Ma Ying-jeou/Tsai Ying-wen (DPP). Every time, they were closely connected with the emergence and decline of different national identification trends. These issues of national identity have been related to more general processes of (de)localisation in terms of adoption of a more or less Chinese-/ Taiwanese-centric position on the domestic cultural scene as well as in the field of regional/international diplomacy and political economy. The different approach towards cross-Strait relations between the main protagonists in the 2016 and 2020 presidential races bears witness to the sustained importance of this (de) localisation question and related national identification issue. A more outspoken

Taiwan-centric attitude goes hand in hand with the quest for more attention to local Taiwanese matters and greater international visibility for Taiwan in its own right, so as not to be viewed as peripheral to China, and a diversification of economic and cultural exchanges beyond China. A China focus, on the other hand, attaches greater importance to economic integration with China and emphasises the historical and cultural links with greater China.

Ever since the 2014 Sunflower Movement and the more outspoken civil society, demanding governmental transparency and an enhanced consultation process in policy-making, several social groups have become new political forces in Taiwan, some of them foregrounding Taiwanese national identity issues from a Taiwan-centric position, others taking to the streets for civic issues, such as social welfare, housing, unemployment, environment protection, pension reforms, and the like. The inclusion of these civil priorities in the 2016 DPP agenda contributed to its winning ticket, although they had already been articulated during the 2012 electoral campaign, where the presidential candidate, Tsai Ying-wen, had also addressed domestic civic concerns, such as revitalising the economy, social justice, transitional justice, sustainability, regional integration with South-East Asia to avoid over-reliance on China, as well as international cooperation. These civic themes have been the mainstay in President Tsai Ying-wen's inauguration speeches in 2016 and 2020, but they have also consistently been accompanied by repeated localised references to the country of 'Taiwan'. Since Tsai assumed the presidential office, the term 'ROC' has disappeared from the official discursive scene altogether.

Since, just like in any other consolidated democracy, civic issues were already clear on the electoral agenda during the 2012 presidential race in Taiwan, it is worth investigating whether the formerly contentious issues in Taiwanese society, namely inter-ethnic relations and national identification issues, had lost discursive attention in the Ma Ying-jeou era and whether civic issues which often come to the fore in other democracies at electoral times had already taken centre stage prior to 2012.

If the national identification issue should happen to feature on the media agenda, a sub-question then arises concerning the presence/absence of its formerly antithetical character. Identity matters in Taiwanese debates used to give rise to an ethnic-political-cultural inclusion/exclusion formula on three levels.[3] First, the concept of ethnic identity was utilised to distinguish between the various ethnicities on the island, viz. Waishengren (mainlanders), local/native Taiwanese, Hakka, and the original Austronesian population. Second, political partisanship at the period investigated played a divisive role between the pan-blue alliance (including the KMT, New Party, People First Party), and the pan-green alliance (comprising the DPP, Taiwan Solidarity Union). Third, cultural identity set off those people who would emphasise the Chinese cultural inheritance from the Taiwanese who would focus on Taiwan's multicultural characteristics. These polar lines of allegiances, whereby Taiwanisation processes competed with Sinicisation processes and which were mutually exclusive, used to be articulated in Taiwan's polity and society through advocacy by political parties and social groups, state-driven propaganda, concrete policy implementation, and, not least, in the partisan Taiwanese media scene.

Yet, a former study of President Ma's public statements at important occasions from 2008 to 2010 indicates that these polarising positions in the cultural sphere were masked by more ambiguous signifiers, blending Chinese traditional core values with the 'Taiwan spirit' (Lams and Liao 2011). This is how the concept of Taiwanisation was discursively broadened during President Ma's rule. The amalgamation of 'Taiwan spirit' and 'Chinese core cultural values' paved the way for a growing consciousness that political 'Taiwaneseness' and cultural 'Chineseness' were no longer contradictory. It allowed for an inclusive perspective embracing the internal hybridity of cultures and discursively reaching a 'Taiwanised consensus', not least for electoral purposes (Lams and Liao 2011: 92, 94).[4] Although issues of civic concern, such as the fledgling economy, were already on top of the electoral agenda in 2012 and talk about ethnic polarisation made way for an appeal to societal harmony, including harmonious relationships with China, Ma's ensuing proposal of the ECFA (Economic Cooperation Framework Agreement) deal with China as the solution to face the economic challenges of globalisation revealed a China-centric approach. This sparked a societal debate whether globalisation under Ma's policy was equal to further integration with China. The perceived lack of transparency in handling cross-Strait relations and the insufficient consultation with civil society generated ever louder calls for accountable governance and rekindled the debate about cultural and national identity issues (Muyard 2012; Danielsen 2012). Opinion polls conducted since 1992 about political attitudes concerning the unification-independence issue and political party preference testify to the growing popular identification with Taiwan during the Ma era.[5] Since the 2008 KMT return to power, self-identification as Taiwanese soared to 60% in a reaction to the perceived lack of consultation about the enhanced cross-Strait exchanges, which were viewed as putting Taiwan's sovereignty at risk (Tseng and Chen 2016).

If these English-language newspapers should be seen to (unconsciously) subscribe to the blended and less antagonistic notion of 'Taiwanised consensus', could it be that other issues – rather than the divisive identity issue – took centre stage, due to wider societal processes in the second half of the last decade, such as globalisation and regionalisation, on the one hand, and local domestic political and institutional developments on the other hand? Global factors, such as worldwide recession, could have an impact on domestic economic prospects and consequently, electoral voting behaviour. Taiwan did not remain spared from the 2008 global recession. Its unemployment rate saw an increase from 3.81% in April 2008 to 6.13% in August 2009 (Tien and Tung 2011: 82). By the end of 2009, income inequality had become increasingly salient, further aggravated by domestic factors, such as active speculation in the stock market and a swift increase in real estate prices.

Similarly, a stronger media focus on Taiwanese domestic issues, such as party corruption scandals, personality traits of highly positioned political leaders, institutional reform mechanisms, like the new electoral system,[6] could corroborate the thesis, put forward by Fell (2010: 928), that the major changes in election results from late 2005 onwards were due to the KMT's effective ownership of the anti-corruption issues, the new party leadership, as well as institutional factors, such as the blue camp realignment and the electoral reform. According to Fell, the political corruption scandals around the DPP administration starting from mid-2005 played a more significant role in public opinion shifts in the last quarter of 2005 than explanations focusing on cross-Strait relations or national identity (Fell 2010: 939). In this respect, it is worth taking a look at whether domestic partisan political issues in our corpus might overshadow the former focus on the polarising national identity debate along ethnic and cultural lines.

Contextualisation of the narratives: Relevance and poll results of the 2009 mid-term elections

The relevance of choosing the local December 2009 elections for county magistrates, city mayors, county and city councilmen, and township chiefs rather than the following 2010 local elections is twofold. First, these elections are deemed important since city mayors and county magistrates are regarded as 'noble men of the feudal system, who are powerful enough to stage political dissent or collaborate with the incumbent administration' (Kao 2009: 228). Second, the December 2009 elections were the first island-wide recording of public opinion since the KMT resumed office in May 2008. The popularity of President Ma Ying-jeou, who had also taken over the KMT chairmanship in October 2009, had taken a dip in the aftermath of the devastating August 2009 Typhoon Morakot (Rigger 2010). The KMT administration's reaction and rescue measures had been criticised for being slow and inadequate. Hence, the November 2009 elections are to be set against this background of speculation on whether the Ma administration would be given a clean bill of health. The elections were referred to as the 'mid-term' exam of President Ma Ying-jeou (Li 2009, in Fell 2010: 934).

For the 17 positions of county magistrates and city mayors, KMT nominees garnered 12 seats (70.6%), the DPP four seats (23.5%), and an independent runner one seat.[7] While the DPP only captured 23.5% of the seats, the party garnered 45.32% of the overall vote share. This discrepancy between total popular vote and seat distribution is a direct result of the 2005 constitutional reform of the electoral system, shifting from the single vote multiple member district system to the single member district two-vote system. Previously, voters only cast one vote for a candidate in multiple member districts. After the reform, each voter was allowed to bring out two votes, one for a candidate in a single member district and one for their preferred party. In practice, the change meant a move away from proportional representation in the direction of the 'winner takes all' mechanism. The KMT dominated the scene in capturing the majority of the seats, thus sustaining the pattern that had been in place since the 2005 local elections (Fell 2010: 933). Yet, of the total vote share the KMT county magistrates and city mayors only took

2.5% more than the DPP elected officials. KMT expectations had been higher, hoping to reduce swing votes from the KMT to DPP in the wake of President Ma's active support for the KMT candidates (Fell 2010: 934). As Kao argues, President Ma first framed the poll results as not being a 'loss' for the KMT, only a small defeat or not as ideal as expected [不如理想 (bù rú lǐ xiǎng)] (Kao 2009: 229). The unsatisfactory KMT candidate nomination policy and doubts of presidential leadership quality explained the gap between public perception and President Ma's framing of the results (ibid.). Yet, the discrepancy between popular vote percentage and seat allocation, as the result of the 2005 electoral reform, must have equally contributed to the gap in perception as to who turned out to be victorious after all. Since the 'first-past-the-post' electoral system generally favours larger parties, the electoral reform offered the KMT party the leading edge for seat allocation. The KMT's loss of one seat has also been interpreted in terms of the 'rational' choice the Taiwanese citizens made, referring to dissatisfaction with the incumbent administration's perceived lacklustre performance and voters' concern with capital interests and gain (You 2009: 219–20).

Tracing Taiwanisation/Sinicisation processes in the English-language press narratives during the December 2009 'three-in-one' local elections[8]

This part describes the empirical study's methodological approach and presents results of the content analysis examining formal features, such as prominence, origin, and sources of the narratives. This is followed by an outline of the findings about thematic hierarchies. The discourse analysis investigates argumentation lines and other discursive strategies. A discussion about the state of Taiwanisation/ Sinicisation processes in the narratives concludes this section.

Operationalisation: Units of analysis and methodology

The present study zooms in on the prominence and descriptive nature of the identity issue in the media narratives, as well as on other discursive features, such as source selection and argumentation lines. These could reveal the media outlets' oppositional perspectives in view of their historical links to KMT-affiliated actors (for the China Post) and DPP-leaning organisations (for the Taipei Times as a sister newspaper of the pro-DPP Liberty Times). Many articles are authored by Taiwanese journalists as well as foreign experts or pundits on Taiwanese affairs, while some others are taken from CNA, the local press agency, or from the foreign news agencies Reuters, AP, or AFP. Often, articles are translated from the vernacular press as well.

The corpus consists of 221 articles and seven cartoons spanning an eight-day period from 4 to 10 December,[9] and includes all op-ed articles and news narratives about the elections for city mayors, township chiefs, and county commissioners. Research units are the three Taiwanese English-language newspapers (the China

Post (CP), the Taipei Times (TT), and the Taiwan News (TN)). For an in-depth analysis of the news articles only the Taiwan-related accounts were selected, but Taiwan- as well as China-related articles were retained for the op-ed articles because their lower numbers allow a manual analysis. Selection of the period of analysis (2009 local elections) was based on the relevance of electoral periods in a study of salience of cultural and political identity matters in the public Taiwanese sphere. More particulars about the English-language corpus selection are detailed in the introduction.

Structural elements, such as prominence and position of Taiwan- and China-related articles in the newspaper,[10] page layout, genres, and source selection render descriptive quantitative data concerning editorial interest in certain matters and draw the first pencil strokes for the qualitative approach. The discourse analysis was carried out both on a macro- and micro-level. From a macro-perspective, the analytical focus was on an examination of global textual meaning constructs, such as topic selection,[11] argumentation patterns, intertextuality, semiotics of illustrations and headlines. On the micro-level, the analysis of smaller textual units looked at implied meanings, lexical choice-making, or judgemental descriptions of social groups, thus categorising between the Self and the Other. According to social identity theory (Tajfel 1981), groups tend to draw boundaries of exclusion and inclusion. A polarising discursive activity highlights the negative aspects of the Other and the positive attributes of the Self, while marginalising the positive features of the Other and the negative actions or characteristics of the Self. Applied to this case study, any narrative categorisation of groups in terms of a 'Taiwan-centric' or 'China-centric' descriptive attitude can contribute to analytical insights into the state of polarisation when Taiwanisation/Sinicisation processes emerge in the accounts of that period.

The study also investigates whether previous findings about the formal positioning of Taiwan-related articles in the newspapers as well as their ideological alignments (Lams 2006) are sustained, since these ideological aspects are, in the Taiwanese case, closely related to matters of identity. As indicated earlier, three major dimensions used to be the subjects of discussion and division in Taiwan's public sphere: Ethnicity, political partisanship, and culture. Therefore, the discourse analysis kept these dimensions in mind while tracing the survival or disappearance of elements pointing at binary oppositions in these fields.

Formal features: Prominence, origin, and sources of Taiwan-related articles

First, a brief comparative description of formal features, such as the prominence of the Taiwan-related articles (in terms of quantity and position), indicates salience or perceived importance of Taiwanese local matters and serves as a prelude for the discussion on the state of Taiwanisation/Sinicisation in the three dimensions of ethnicity, partisanship, and culture.

TABLE 7.1 Op-ed articles about Taiwanese affairs

	China Post	Taipei Times	Taiwan News
Editorials	4	6	5
Columns	3	14	0
Letters to editor	0	4	0
Cartoons	0	7	0

Prominence: Genre and quantity of Taiwan-related articles

What generally stands out, from a quantitative perspective, is that the Taipei Times (TT) devotes more commentaries to local Taiwanese affairs (see Table 7.1). Fourteen out of fifteen columns in the TT were devoted to Taiwan compared to one opinion article about China. The China Post (CP), on the other hand, only brought five columns in total, in which three dealt with Taiwan and two with China. No comments discussing Taiwan or China affairs made it to the pages of the Taiwan News (TN). As for editorials, i.e. the genre in which the paper is most likely to show an overt ideological position, the TT brought seven editorials, six of which discussed Taiwan affairs and one reported on Chinese media censorship. The CP also published seven editorials, four of which related to Taiwan and one to China. All five editorials in the TN treated Taiwanese current affairs. The TT is the only paper that also prints the genre 'Letters to the Editor', and four of the six letters argued in favour of Taiwan with another letter criticising China. Cartoons only appear in the TT and all seven brought derogatory illustrations about Ma Ying-jeou's administration. As concerns the genre of news articles, the CP featured 164 articles (including 41 briefs), the TT 104 (including five briefs), and the TN 61 (including ten briefs). Clearly, fewer articles are printed in the TN, but format has to be taken into account. At the time of analysis, the daily was printed on a tabloid-size paper, but counted more pages, some of them filled with full-page ads. This is how the total count of TN articles is still smaller than in the other two corpora. The CP prints more articles than the TT, as it also includes more human interest stories and soft news articles. More significant, however, is the discrepancy between both papers in the number of op-ed articles about local affairs, as shown in Table 7.1. The TT features 20 Taiwan-related opinion articles, while the CP devotes only seven editorials/columns to local matters.

Prominence: Position of Taiwan-related articles

Both the TT and the TN position their Taiwan-related articles on the first pages of the newspaper, which points to the prominence they give to local affairs. By contrast, the CP relegates the local accounts to the end of the paper. Ideologically significant domestic news is often printed within the bottom half range of the page. This stands in shrill contrast to similar news stories that are deemed front-page news in the other two papers. An example is the treatment of the apology by Premier Wu Den-yih for calling the pro-independence camp 'idiots'. While this appears in a small article at the bottom of the last page in the CP, it is the top article on the front page of the TT on 10 December, which also devotes a full editorial to this speech act with the headline 'One third of the nation are idiots' (One third 2009e: 8). China-related articles feature on the 'International News' pages of the TT and the TN, whereas the CP positions the China articles either on the Asia-Pacific News page or on the local news pages, if there is a link to Taiwan. The CP also includes a special 'Focus on China' page on Mondays and a weekly column on 'Ancient Chinese Anecdotes' featuring on the local news page. By contrast, the TN remains particularly silent about China. Unlike the CP, the TT and TN treat Chinese stories as international affairs and foreground local Taiwanese news topics. Clearly, this quantitative and semiotic difference in attention to China-/Taiwan-related topics discloses a continuity with findings in previous studies about these newspapers' ideological allegiances to partisan lines (Lams 2006, 2008).

Origin of articles and voices

As concerns authorship, most remarkably, all three comments on the Taiwanese elections printed in the China Post are written by Chinese sources either in China, Singapore, or Hong Kong. Fewer Taiwanese political observers get the floor, when compared with the Taipei Times. Increasingly, articles from the China Daily and other Chinese networks appear in the CP. Unlike the 1990s, in 2009 the CP and the TN appear to rely more heavily on own staff reporters for the news articles, a feature already apparent in the TT since its inception. The TT and TN also print more articles originating from the Taiwanese news agency, CNA, than before. Although the analysis did not include a detailed count of voices that were heard or silenced, privileged or sidelined, on the whole, it can be argued that the CP allocates ample news room to government voices defending policies, whereas opposition voices tend to feature more frequently in the other two papers. Implications for Taiwanisation/Sinicisation processes will be dealt with in the concluding discussion.

Discursive features: Thematic choices, argumentation lines, and other discursive practices

A comparative look at what themes preoccupied the authors of the narratives and editors of the papers provides valuable information on the extent to which domestic, civic issues were part of the 2009 public debate and dimmed the former focus on exclusionary identity sentiments in the ethnic and cultural sense. This content analysis is followed by findings of the in-depth qualitative analysis of argumentation patterns to shed light on the nature of the Taiwanisation/Sinicisation processes and how they operate in the narratives. The discourse analysis also examines other discursive practices, such as descriptive markers with positive/

negative connotations thus categorising the Self and the Other into the positive in-group and the negative out-group, use of deontic modality markers in the op-ed articles with assertive statements, and strong advice as to how political parties should act or rebrand themselves for maximum electoral success, or framing of the poll outcomes to highlight victory or minimise defeat of their favourite party.

Thematic choices

The narratives examined present a wide array of domestic issues, belonging to the hard and soft news genres. Examples of the hard news topics are legislative by-elections, vote-buying problems during elections, the US beef-import referendum, Ma's China policy and economic exchange mechanisms, such as ECFA, and the talks between the two semi-official bodies across the Strait, the Taiwanese SEF (Straits Exchange Foundation), and the Chinese ARATS (Association for Relations Across the Taiwan Strait). What resorts under soft news are accounts on arts, performances, the environment, sports, social affairs, and health care. Issue-oriented topics prevail, although certain topics, such as Ma's China policy with ECFA, and the SEF/ARATS talks, belong to both categories – 'issue' as well as 'identity' – as they also involve matters of national identity. Overall, a growing civic nationalist spirit shines through the corpus. Socio-economic themes are prominent, which is not surprising, given the global 2008 recession. The globalisation/regionalisation factor has become an extra constituent of the discourses. Topics like the ECFA debate and the importance of regional economic integration are widely debated but cannot be disentangled from the underlying national identity question, since it involves two oppositional approaches, namely deeper integration with China under the conditional framework of the 'one China principle', or engaging additional trading partners besides also dealing with China but without the conditional straitjacket imposed by Chinese conditions. It is precisely this point which shows a stark contrast in the KMT/DPP agendas of the 2012, 2016, and 2020 presidential and legislative elections.

Common themes in the three papers emerge from some human interest stories, such as a Taiwan designer winning a foreign prize or medical care complaints, but also the widespread vote-buying practices, which are seen to undermine the democratic aspect of the elections. This criticism of the government is rendered in the TT by the semiotics of a cartoon depicting the government's punishment of the small fish only.

Rather than divisive identity debates along ethnic and cultural lines, clearly domestic partisan issues representative of the blue and green alliance agendas come to the fore. The underlying partisan ideology of the newspapers can be retrieved by a glance at more specific topic selections. The examples, discussed below, are not a loose amalgamation of themes, but they accumulatively invite the reader to detect a partisan pattern. For example, the TT and TN themes like the DPP victory in Yilan, the Kaohsiung Incident, and the opposition to ECFA intertextually reinforce each other in their 'Taiwan-centric' ideological underpinning.

The China Post articles reporting the election results minimise the KMT loss in defence of its China policy including the Economic Cooperation Framework Agreement (ECFA) proposal. By contrast, the other papers highlight the DPP gain and the growing popularity of its chairwoman, Tsai Ying-wen. In the Taiwan News and Taipei Times, articles panning the ECFA proposal abound. The symbolic nature of the Yilan victory in recapturing the formerly lost DPP seat is played out in both dailies. Yilan's unique cultural identity is foregrounded as not a peripheral entity to Taipei but as an independent, small democratic centre with an outward-looking cultural vitality. In the day before the elections, the editorial in the TN describes the Yilan significance as a 'microcosm for Taiwan's political development to its history as the cradle of the DPP's Taiwan-centric Green Administration' and presents its readers with the following dilemma:

> This choice parallels the dilemma facing all of Taiwan's 23 million people of whether to accept a marginal status as a 'spoke' in the continental 'great Chinese economic sphere' as promoted by Ma and his KMT administration or to take a 'different road' by developing into a small but dynamic democratic 'center' oriented toward the Pacific and world community. The choice of Yilan's 180,000 voters may well prove decisive for Taiwan's future choices.
>
> *(Taiwan's choices 2009f: 9)*

Other themes that mark a difference in treatment between the China Post and the other two papers are the 30-year anniversary commemoration of the Kaohsiung Incident and the protests against the listing of Taiwanese institutional bodies under a Chinese name at the Copenhagen climate summit as well as the incorporation of Taiwan into the Chinese pavilion on the Shanghai 2010 Expo website. These are Taiwan-centric prime topics that feature prominently in the TT and the TN and are silenced in the CP. The TN devotes much attention to cultural themes, such as a Taiwanese film director winning a prize in India, thus drawing world's attention to Taiwan's film industry, or the 'Voices of Taiwan', which is a new CD collection compiling works of famous Taiwanese music composers. Whereas the TN hardly prints China-related articles, the China accounts in the TT cast China in a negative light by broaching themes, such as media censorship, human rights abuses, and China's attempts at undermining Taiwan's international space. These topics do not appear in the CP, which no longer demonises the communist Other, but instead presents a mix of neutral, positive, and negative aspects of China. An example is a comment on 10 December speculating on how the sixth-generation leadership in Beijing will be chosen. The TT also reserves space for media ethics and the decline of human rights under the Ma administration with its emphasis on the economy and a perceived lingering of the old KMT authoritarian reflex. A double criticism is levelled against Ma Ying-jeou and China in a TT comment on 6 December (Ma silent 2009c: 8). The Chinese government is said not to hide its intent to 'annex' Taiwan and eliminate the ROC and the Ma government remains silent. A presupposition about Ma's acceptance of 'one China' leads the author to surmise that Ma does not think Chinese sovereignty over Taiwan is harmful to the nation. In an adjacent comment on the same page, arguing in favour of a referendum on ECFA, the question arises whether the 'one China' principle is the premise for government negotiations on ECFA. Clearly both articles are intertextually linked through their concern about Taiwan's sovereignty.

Argumentation patterns and symbolic construction of meaning

As for consistency in chains of reasoning, we mainly focus on the editorials and comments, since these are the genres which allow for most explicit lines of argumentation. Coherence in the logic of commentaries of the Taipei Times is reached by repeatedly establishing causal links between President Ma's proposed deals with China and a perceived threat to Taiwanese sovereignty, national security, and challenges to the domestic labour market. It is argued that national interest should come above profit. Both the TT and TN print disparaging comments about President Ma and the KMT administration and argue in favour of the DPP. Without steering explicitly, the editorial in the TN implicitly assists in the DPP campaign one day before the election by projecting a beautiful future for Yilan if the DPP comes out victorious:

> A DPP victory will also constitute a rejection of subordinate integration with the 'greater Taipei metropolitan area' and an affirmation of the Yilan Road's project of transforming the once marginalized region into 'an unique creative, cultural and beautiful city'.
>
> *(Taiwan's choices 2009f: 8)*

The TN editorial on 8 December moves to a more explicit mode of showing its DPP alignment. The article, headlined 'DPP must accent Taiwan's dignity', argues for a re-establishment of a Taiwan-centric government. After a positive characterisation of the DPP with an enumeration of the DPP Green Administration's values of democracy, Taiwan-centric culture, social equity, community participation, and environmentally sustainable development, advice is given to the party as to how to profile itself in the future. It is suggested that the DPP should maintain unity while also persisting in reform and re-examination. It should 'formulate a feasible and attractive "Taiwan" vision that does not entail subordination to the PRC' (DPP must accent 2009a: 9). Taiwan's dignity is linked up with the perceived DPP victory in the following proposition: 'The reaffirmation of Taiwan's dignity by voters from Yilan to Yunlin after 19 months of erosion may indeed be the greatest legacy of Saturday's polls and the DPP's most potent asset in the future' (DPP must accent 2009a: 9). Similarly, in the editorial on 8 December, the TT offers advice to the DPP that it should not cry victory too early since results are not sufficiently positive to represent a shift in the green camp's fortunes. The DPP should rebrand its wrongly understood 'anti-China' image and should divest itself from the nationalistic and exclusionary image it had during the Chen administration. The DPP chair Tsai Ying-wen is advised to devise a positive brand, namely the DPP being 'for' many things instead of 'anti-China' (Tsai soars 2009h: 8).

In its descriptive strategies, the Taiwan News labels the KMT a 'right-wing Chinese nationalist party' with a near 100% consistency in its editorials. Ma's government is held responsible for deteriorating relations with Japan. A comparison between the different construction by the China Post and the Taiwan News of the reasons for the resignation of the former Japanese Interchange Association Representative, Masaki Saito, to Taipei reveals interesting information concerning historical interpretations. The headlines read 'Ma's vendetta hurts Taiwan-Japan ties / Truth leads to feud' (TN 2009d, 9 December: 6) and 'PM Yukio Hatoyama's Asia fraternity doctrine' (CP 2009, 10 December: 8). The TN's editorial first presents a survey of President Ma's 'clumsy actions, dissatisfying the Japanese government', and then argues that 'Ma's manifestation of a revanchist Chinese nationalism reversed the long-term impression of amity between Taiwan and Japan' (Ma's vendetta 2009d: 6). A tacit boycott was reportedly carried out by the government against the Japanese Representative, who eventually resigned. So-called right-wing KMT legislators had demanded Saito's expulsion for 'insulting'[12] the ROC by calling the island's status unresolved. President Ma is reported to have

> publically and incorrectly claimed that the 1952 'Treaty of Taipei' had transferred sovereignty over Taiwan and the Penghu islands to the 'ROC' as part of his drive to claim that 'Taiwan belongs to the ROC' instead of being a democratic independent state in its own right.
>
> *(Ma's vendetta 2009d: 6)*

In the subsection 'Truth leads to feud', it is then stated that Saito had

> corrected Ma's error since the Treaty of Taipei only reaffirmed the content of the September 1951 San Francisco Treaty in which Tokyo 'abandoned' sovereignty over Taiwan and the Penghu Islands but did not mention to whom, if anyone, sovereignty had been transferred.
>
> *(Ma's vendetta 2009d: 6)*

Clearly, a hotly contested point in history is naturalised as the 'truth' and Ma's position is negatively framed as erroneous. The article ends on the note that, 'if the Ma government truly has the interests of Taiwan at heart, it will cease treating relations with Asia's most important democracy in such a cavalier fashion' and the warning that 'the KMT government's blind insistence on a pro-China tilt in spite of Saturday's ringing electoral defeat gives scant cause for hope' (Ma's vendetta 2009d: 6). The inference implied is that Ma's interest in Taiwan is of a rhetorical nature. When comparing this with the editorial of the China Post discussing Representative Masaki Saito's departure, the opposite interpretation of Taiwan history is advanced, with a China-centric ring along KMT lines. Saito is said to have been 'fired' by the new PM Hatoyama, who was ready to improve relations with China, for a 'diplomatic gaffe' that may make better relations with China difficult. In a paraphrase of Saito's statement, it is mentioned twice that Saito actually argued that Taiwan belonged to the ROC. This runs counter to the interpretation in the Taiwan News's editorial, which ran the day before the one in the China Post. This is how texts dialogically engage in mutual negotiation without explicitly referring to this intertextual function.

In both the Taipei Times and the Taiwan News, the results of the elections are given an ideological interpretation in that the DPP gain of seats is viewed as a 'no-confidence vote of the KMT government craven unilateral tilt towards Chinese Communist party ruled PRC' (Taiwan's people 2009g: 6). In its editorial of 7 December, the China Post, however, presents a different reading of the results (KMT's 'mid-term' defeat 2009: 8). While the DPP gain of seats is minimised, the KMT's image is reinforced by stating that the KMT performed quite well in view of the economic global crisis. If any setback is to be admitted, non-ideological causes are brought forward, such as the KMT's loss of one seat, taken by an independent candidate who was no longer supported by the KMT in its 'clean hands' policy of refusing nomination of candidates with a criminal record. The few news analyses about the elections posted in the CP follow the same non-ideological explanation. In one analysis, Chinese and HK media are said to attribute the KMT's poor result to corruption charges in the election and the government's lacklustre performance, especially with the much-criticised Typhoon Morakot relief efforts. In another comment, the Taiwanese chair of the General Chamber of Commerce states that the results have nothing to do with the KMT administration's overall economic policy and cross-Strait policy, 'with the latter enjoying an approval rating of over 60 per cent' (KMT should improve 2009: 20).

Discussion about the state of Taiwanisation/Sinicisation processes in the narratives

While a limited corpus of the election coverage cannot generate overall conclusions about general positions taken in the newspapers, an ideologically consistent line in the articles under investigation still surfaces from the various investigative angles taken (interest in local Taiwanese themes, voices and origin of articles, argumentation). This offers ample indications about the state of Taiwanisation/ Sinicisation processes during the period of investigation. In the China Post, the previously noted signs of Sinicisation are continued and intensified. By the same token, Taiwanisation in the sense of printing topics that feature high on the green agenda, such as the Kaohsiung Incident commemoration or the quest for more international recognition for Taiwan is absent in the CP accounts. The opposite holds for the two other papers, highlighting those very themes and privileging 'green' sources. In this sense the tension between various ideologies is still alive.

What does this mean for the state of Taiwanisation in the ethnic, (party)-political and cultural domains?

Antagonist patterns in the ethnic realm have become obsolete in the media narratives, at least in the corpus under investigation. Hardly any references are made to ethnicity or ethnic cleavages within Taiwan. The notion of 'New Taiwanese', as it was devised by the KMT President Lee Teng-hui in the midst of the ethnic divisive discourses of the 1990s appears to have been instrumental in forging a strong awareness of being Taiwanese irrespective of ethnic backgrounds. A shift away from the preceding years of the DPP administration, however, is that little mention is made of 'Taiwan identity', safe for some instances in the Taiwan News and Taipei Times. New self-profiling terms have replaced the old references to 'Taiwan subjectivity' or 'Taiwan consciousness', namely 'Taiwan values, Taiwan spirit', thus emphasising some sort of 'authenticity', which merges the ethnic and cultural spheres. This seems to be the new common ground shared across Taiwanese civil society, but more prominently present in the TN and TT than in the CP. Yet, beyond this centrist core, centrifugal aspects of Sinicisation and Taiwanisation are still apparent in the CP and the other two papers respectively. Sinicisation in the CP appears in the sense of highlighting the positive aspects in China/Taiwan cooperation, adopting an inclusive attitude towards mainland Chinese opinions on Taiwanese affairs, and emphasising Chinese culture and ancient Chinese customs. References to 'local, Taiwanese unique culture', i.e. localisation, only appear in the other two papers, but the theme does not occupy a major place.

Other issues pertaining to the political sphere have taken centre stage instead of the 'Taiwan identity' theme. Two binaries permeate many accounts, the party-political 'green' versus 'blue' dichotomy, and the China/Taiwan binary. Antagonism between the blue and green alliances is not surprising given the electoral time period and remains a constant feature in contemporary Taiwan political discourse. The media's participation in negative campaigning and explaining polling results with an underlying ideological preference appear to be part of the electoral reporting game (Lams 2008). Some of the above examples illustrate the strategies of positive Self- and negative Other-presentation: The CP privileges 'blue' sources in favour of the KMT and downplays the party's loss in popularity, whereas the TN demonises the KMT and puts the DPP on a pedestal. The TT also tends to foreground negative aspects of the KMT, while all the same arguing that it was the party's chairman, President Ma, who failed the test of being able to attract more KMT seats, rather than the party itself. This argument finds an echo in the analysis of Michael Y. You, who points out the lost personal charm of Ma Ying-jeou, his poor governing performance, and the deficient KMT candidates' nomination policy as reasons for the KMT defeat (You 2009: 219). The China/Taiwan nexus is the second binary, which also remains prevalent in contemporary Taiwanese debate. The defence of the Taiwanese people's 'will' and Taiwan's 'dignity' function as the common denominator or the core interest everyone seems willing to fight for. It can be viewed as the centripetal force within the Taiwanisation/Sinicisation nexus.

Yet, what is understood by 'dignity' may well be subject to 'one word, various interpretations'. This is the locus where the Taiwanisation/Sinicisation nexus plays out its centrifugal forces. For the China Post, which generally defends the KMT government policy of China rapprochement and gives ample forum to its advocates, a sovereign ROC should cooperate with China and in the face of regional free trade agreements and globalisation should not get marginalised. Besides presenting a different historical version of the political status of Taiwan from the one defended in the TN, the CP also frequently argues in favour of a sustained cooperation with China. Literal quotes from President Ma are taken up with the message that the MOU on cooperation concerning financial supervision between the two sides of the Taiwan Strait was signed under the principles of 'reciprocity and dignity' and there is no question of 'status downgrading or sovereignty being compromised' to affect the interests of Taiwan (Government resolute 2009: 1). Chinese experts are given media room in the China Post to air their views on the likely consequences of the local poll results for cross-Strait relations and Ma's China policy. By contrast, for the other two papers, the TT and the TN, 'dignity' means defending a sovereign nation, to be identified as Taiwan, and not 'to accept marginal status as a "spoke" in the continental "great Chinese economic sphere"' (Taiwan's choices 2009f: 9).

Conclusion

Looking back at discourses of earlier political eras, for example at what themes were deemed important or lost prime attention during electoral periods under the Kuomintang rule of Ma Ying-jeou can facilitate a better understanding of the underlying reasons for the political power change in 2016 and developments in the Taiwanese civil society of the past decade, including the Sunflower Movement and the increased role of social media as a mobiliser of public opinion. Although this paper does not aim to provide an analysis of electoral rationale for the change of ruling party after the 2016 polls, a flashback to the previous political period, clad in a different societal climate, still generates a fresh look on some of the underlying reasons for electoral behaviour. Indeed, discourses during former President Ma's rule can be said to have prepared the discursive soil for the various ideological lines and agendas in the 2012 and 2016 elections.

The present study shows how former ethnic and cultural polarities with their zero-sum positioning games dividing up Taiwanese society are no longer constructed in an antagonistic fashion in the selected English-language media narratives about the 2009 local elections. The dialogue on the variety of policy issues presented in the election accounts indicates that Taiwanese civil society by 2009 had moved on from an antagonistic phase of identity-building to a Taiwanised agora with room for discussion on issue-oriented topics, just like any other mature democratic society. This finding confirms the above-mentioned argument, put forward by Fell (2010), that a civic issue, such as political corruption, may have played a more significant role in public opinion shifts of late 2005 than explanations focusing on purely identity-related matters (Fell 2010: 939).

In addition, by 2009, the 'globalisation/regionalisation factor' had become an important constituent of the discourses, as is evident from prominent socio-economic themes, like the ECFA debate and the importance of regional economic integration. This echoes Tien and Tung's argument that economic issues are politi-cised at times of local elections (Tien and Tung 2011: 83) as well as You's position that voter's choices are made in terms of capital and gain (You 2009: 219).

From the corpus investigated, it appears that a new social arena within Taiwan's public sphere had been opened up where the two major political formations had entered a new phase of the self-identification process to gain popularity. Judging from the themes broached in the media narratives, it can be argued that the pro-cess of 'Taiwanisation' had by 2009 moved into a policy issue-oriented (instead of a purely ideology-oriented) civic nationalism as a new form of 'Taiwanised consensus'.

In parallel with the absence of antagonistic discursive features concerning mat-ters of ethnicity, little mention was made of Taiwanese identity issues. Yet, divi-sive aspects of Sinicisation and Taiwanisation in the cultural realm appeared in the China Post and the other two papers respectively. It shows a marked continuity with previous ideological positioning of these news outlets (Lams 2006, 2008). Whereas positive elements of China/Taiwan cooperation and Chinese cultural elements were highlighted in the CP, which also gave ample room to mainland Chinese expert opinions on Taiwan electoral politics, the other two papers under-lined the local, Taiwanese unique culture. In this sense, a dichotomy was still vis-ible, albeit less antagonistic than before. Few polarising arguments in favour of an outspoken Chinese or Taiwanese cultural identity made it to the editorial pages. The TN, for example, advised the DPP to shed its misunderstood exclusionary image and to brand itself as a party 'for many things' instead of 'anti-China'. Old terms like 'Taiwan subjectivity' and 'Taiwan consciousness' disappeared and made way for a new sense of a common 'Taiwan spirit' and 'Taiwan dignity'.

It appears that, in 2009, this 'Taiwanised consensus' had already consolidated feelings concerning 'Taiwan as homeland with Taiwanese characteristics'. The landslide DPP victory in the 2016 and 2020 presidential and legislative elec-tions featuring a localised agenda bears witness to this trend, although the party's 'Taiwanised' campaign platform alone cannot explain the electoral results. Space for remaining antagonisms was mainly found in the political realm along two bina-ries, namely blue/green party-political alignments and positions concerning cross-Strait relations. Whereas the China Post generally defended the KMT government policy of China rapprochement and argued in favour of cooperation between a sovereign ROC and China, the other papers worried about 'status downgrading or Taiwan's sovereignty being compromised'. Differences between the papers of those days reflect partisan interests and party platforms. The CP supported the KMT focus on Taiwan's national interest in terms of economic benefit, whereas the other papers followed the DPP line insisting on Taiwan's security interest and the likely negative impact of ECFA on local labour. The TN, for example, labelled the KMT a 'right-wing nationalist party', as the KMT gave primacy to improving the economy, maintaining social order, and promoting the rule of law in contrast with the DPP, which privileged social justice with themes such as social equality, human rights, gender, and social minority groups.

Although the analysed smaller text units and linguistic mechanisms, such as lexical choice-making, reveal polarising categorisation processes, derogatory terms about the out-group were no longer as salient as during the former DPP era. Like in any mature democracy, policies and social matters took the central position in the media narratives, at least during the electoral period examined. Common issues in which political parties were aligned were vote-buying problems, the success of Taiwanese artists abroad, a hike in health insurance premiums, environmental protection plans, and rise in low-income households. The debates in which the blue and green camps diverged involved the government-proposed ECFA deal with China and the referendum on US beef imports. These constituted the new discursive terrains, fertilising partisan concerns and realigning the political camps along different lines from the old divisive ethnic or cultural antagonisms. The dialogic nature of the heated media debates on all these issues demonstrates how Taiwanese civil society by 2009 had already turned into a mature open forum based on a perception of 'Taiwanised consensus'. Yet, the articulations in the Taipei Times and Taiwan News of various claims and argumentations against KMT policies can be seen as a clear precursor to the popular unrest during Ma Ying-jeou's second term in office and the DPP landslide victory in 2016.

Notes

1 For literature on the December 2009 local elections, see Braig (2010).
2 This local election was followed by a series of parliamentary by-elections in January and February 2010, and in November 2010 another mayoral election in the five major metropolitan areas. For more information about the 2010 election, see Hung-Mao Tien and Chen-Yuan Tung (2011).
3 Media debates on identity issues in Taiwan, especially from the late 1990s onwards, often exemplified polarized modes of thinking and disregarded the complexity of for-ever shifting identification phenomena.
4 The notion of 'Taiwanized consensus' can be conceived of 'as the crystallization phase in which the political parties might be perceived as having adopted the notion of "Taiwan as homeland with Taiwanese characteristics" as common ground to continue its domestic democratization and self-identification in the international realm' (Lams and Liao 2011: 65).
5 For changes in the Taiwanese/Chinese identity of Taiwanese as tracked in surveys by the Election Study Center, National Chengchi University, Taiwan, see the database at http://esc.nccu.edu.tw/course/news.php?Sn=166, visited on 27 January 2016.
6 The electoral system was constitutionally reformed in 2005, halving the number of legislators from 225 to 113 and changing from a multiple-member-district system to one of mainly single-member districts.
7 Candidates for the city and county councils had to vie for 592 seats, which were won by 289 KMT nominees, 128 DPP candidates, four representatives of smaller parties,

and 170 independent candidates. In 211 townships, the race was fought amongst 470 candidates, resulting in 121 KMT, 34 DPP, and 56 independent town chiefs.

8 The term 'three-in-one' election stems from the three functional levels of election, namely, for county and city magistrates and mayors, township chiefs, and county and city councilmen.

9 As concerns news articles, the China Post (CP) featured 164 articles (including 41 briefs), the Taipei Times (TT) 104 (including five briefs), and the Taiwan News (TN) 61 (including ten briefs). All comments were subdivided in the following generic categories: Editorials (CP: five; TT: seven; TN: five), columns (CP: five; TT: 15; TN: zero), letters to the editor (TT: six), and cartoons (TT: seven).

10 Although the China-related articles were not subjected to in-depth discourse analysis, formal aspects, such as headlines, main topics, and positioning in the newspaper were taken into account.

11 The various topics in the news and op-ed articles were checked for their orientation towards 'electoral issue' or 'identity'. Examples of issue-oriented topics are, just as in other democratic countries, legislative by-elections, scandals (corruption or others), electoral system reform, vote-buying, social affairs (health care, pension reform, housing problems, unemployment, income disparities), environmental issues, and the like. Identity- and ethnicity-oriented topics comprise discussions on national sovereignty, ethnic differences, Chinese cultural heritage and Taiwanese multiculturalism, and partisan electoral platforms concerning national identity. Some topics like cross-Strait relations, ROC China policy, SEF/ARATS talks, and economic exchange mechanisms, such as ECFA, have links to both the 'issue' and 'identity' categories.

12 The inverted commas are used in the original text and create a distancing effect thereby undermining the legislators' argument.

References

Braig, S. (2010) 'Signs of change? An analysis of Taiwan's December 2009 local elections', *Journal of Current Chinese Affairs*, 39 (1): 175–197.

Danielsen, M. (2012) 'On the road to a common Taiwan identity', in Peter C.Y. Chow (ed.) *National Identity and Economic Interest: Taiwan's Competing Options and Their Implications for Regional Stability*. New York: Palgrave McMillan, 135–152.

Escobar, A. (1995) *Encountering Development: The Making and Unmaking of the Third World*, Princeton: Princeton University Press.

Fairclough, N. (1992) *Discourse and Social Change*, Cambridge: Polity Press.

Fell, D. (2010) 'Was 2005 a critical election in Taiwan? Locating the start of a new political era', *Asian Survey*, 50 (5): 927–945.

Foucault, M. (1972/2010) *The Archaeology of Knowledge*. New York, NY: Vintage Books.

Kao, Y.K. (2009) '2009年縣市三合一選舉的後續政治效應 [An Analysis to 2009 three-in-one local elections in Taiwan and its impact afterward]', *Taiwan Democracy Quarterly*, 6 (4): 227–233.

Lams, L. (2006) 'A pragmatic study into ideological investments of the ROC English-language newspapers from a diachronic perspective', *National Chiayi University Inquiry of Applied Linguistics*, 1: 145–172.

Lams, L. (2008) 'Media panic or manic: The 2004 Taiwan parliamentary election in the local English-language press', *The Taiwan International Studies Quarterly* 4 (4): 145–184.

Lams, L. and Liao, L.W. (2011) 'Tracing "Taiwanization" processes in Taiwanese presidential statements in times of cross-strait rapprochement', *The Journal of Current Chinese Affairs*, 40 (1): 63–98.

Lee, C.C. (1994) 'Sparking a fire: The press and the ferment of democratic change in Taiwan', in C.C. Lee (ed.) *China's Media, Media's China*. Boulder, CO: Westview Press, 169–170.

Li, M.H. (2009) 藍: 低於11席就敗選 [Blues: Lower than 11 seats is a defeat], 聯合報 [United Daily News], December 5, 2009, p. A1

Muyard, F. (2012) 'Taiwanese national identity, cross-strait economic interaction, and the integration paradigm', in Peter C.Y. Chow (ed.) *National Identity and Economic Interest: Taiwan's Competing Options and Their Implications for Regional Stability*. New York: Palgrave McMillan, 153–186.

Rawnsley, G. (2000) 'The media and popular protest in pre-democratic Taiwan', *Historical Journal of Film, Radio and Television*, 20 (4): 565–580.

Rigger, S. (2010) 'Ma's puzzling midterm malaise', *Brookings Northeast Asia Commentary*, 37, 12 March; retrieved from www.brookings.edu/opinions/2010/03_taiwan_president _ma_rigger.aspx

Sullivan, J., Feng, C.S., Rawnsley M.Y. and Smyth, J. (2019) 'The media in democratic Taiwan', in J. Sullivan and C.Y. Lee (eds.) *A New Era in Democratic Taiwan*, Oxon: Routledge, 104–121.

Tajfel, H. (1981) *Human Groups and Social Categories Studies in Social Psychology*. Cambridge: Cambridge University Press.

Tien, H.M. and Tung, C.Y. (2011) 'Taiwan in 2010: Mapping for a new political landscape and economic outlook', *Asian Survey* 51 (1): 76–84.

Tseng W.C. and Chen, W.H. (2016) 'Taiwanese' identity hits record level', *Taipei Times*, January 26, 2016, retrieved from http://www.taipeitimes.com/News/front/archives/201 5/01/26/2003610092.

Verschueren, J. (1999) *Understanding Pragmatics*. London: Arnold.

Weston, T. (2013) 'Taiwanese newspapers and politics in China's shadow', in W.H. Yeh (ed.) *Mobile Horizons: Dynamics across the Taiwan Strait*. Berkeley: Institute of East-Asian Studies, 208–234.

You, M.Y. (2009) '2009年台灣三合一選舉的觀察與分析 [Some observations and analyses on the 2009 local governmental election of Taiwan]', *Taiwan Democracy Quarterly*, 6 (4): 217–225.

Cited newspaper articles:

Taiwan News (2009a) 'DPP must accent Taiwan's dignity', Editorial, December 8, 2009, p. 9.

Taipei Times (2009b) 'KMT Caucus apologizes for poll results', December 09, 2009, p. 8.

Taipei Times (2009c) 'Ma silent on crucial issue of sovereignty', Commentary, December 06, 2009, p. 8.

Taiwan News (2009d) 'Ma's vendetta hurts Taiwan-Japan ties/Truth leads to feud', Editorial, December 9, 2009, p. 6.

Taipei Times (2009e) 'One third of the nation are idiots', Editorial, December 10, 2009, p. 8.

Taiwan News (2009f) 'Taiwan's choices and the Yilan Road/Restoring Taiwan's pride', Editorial, December 4, 2009, p. 9.

Taiwan News (2009g) 'Taiwan people's message to Ma, Hu and Obama', Editorial, December 7, 2009, p. 6.

Taipei Times (2009h) 'Tsai soars, but image needs a tweak', Editorial, December 08, 2009, p. 8.

China Post (2009) 'Government resolute on ECFA / Ma stresses talks with Beijing under principles of transparency, equality and sovereignty', December 8, 2009, p. 1.

China Post (2009) 'KMT should improve efficiency: Business sector', December 7, 2009, p. 20.

China Post (2009) 'KMT's 'mid-term' defeat', Editorial, December 7, 2009, p. 8.

China Post (2009) 'PM Yukio Hatoyama's Asia fraternity doctrine', Editorial, December 10, 2009, p. 8.

8

IDENTITY/IDEOLOGY MATTERS IN CROSS-STRAIT TRANSLATION

A case of Mandarin Chinese versions of Peter Hessler's *River Town*[1]

Pin-ling Chang

Introduction

The special status quo across the Taiwan Strait, where Chinese hegemony is increasing its global influence in political, economic, and cultural aspects and claiming Taiwan to be part of its territory, and where the democratising Taiwanese entity enjoys autonomy and resists being seen as a province of China by many other countries in the world and the two unequal powers share the same language and culture (in a broad sense), may be described as one of the most suitable contexts for ideology and identity research in translation studies, as the hegemony-resistance relationship between China and Taiwan may be embodied in cross-Strait translations of the same source texts that involve the political and social realities of either side. This chapter begins with a brief sketch of Taiwan's national identity development against Chinese interference and a review of ideology and identity research in translation studies. Then, after a brief introduction to the Mandarin Chinese versions and studies of US writer Peter Hessler's China-themed book *River Town: Two Years on the Yangtze* (2001), this chapter examines the Taiwan version of *River Town* at the lexico-grammatical level by employing the discourse-historical approach (DHA) to critical discourse analysis (CDA), with 'China (including its government and people)', 'the Chinese government's political control and indoctrination', and the 'Taiwan independence issue' selected as special topics for analysis to see whether the Taiwanese translator showed resistance to Chinese hegemony in her translation. The analysis results indicate that the Taiwanese translator has shown a tendency to present China as the Other and also discursively constructed her Taiwanese national identity in her translation, and that the interpretation of the 'China' in Hessler's eyes in the Taiwan version mirrors the hegemony-resistance relationship between China and Taiwan.

Taiwan's national identity development against Chinese interference

While China claims Taiwan to be part of its territory, Taiwan, as an independent political entity that is not widely recognised as a country on the international stage, may be best described by the term invented by Jonathan Manthorpe (2005) – a forbidden nation. Taiwan's current diplomatic predicaments might begin with the Kuomintang (KMT)-led Republic of China (ROC) government's retreat to Taiwan in the wake of its defeat by the Communist Party of China (CPC) in the Chinese Civil War around the mid-1940s. Since its arrival in Taiwan, the KMT had adopted Sinicisation policies, such as making Mandarin Chinese the national language, promoting Chinese cultural tradition (Confucianism in particular), and emphasising the historical relations between Taiwan and mainland China (Hsiau 2010). Under the KMT authoritarian rule, the people of Taiwan were taught or forced to develop Chinese national identity, which, to most of the native inhabitants of Taiwan, was being built amid their resentment against the KMT's Chinese nationalist hegemony and the privilege enjoyed by those who fled from China and settled in Taiwan, their desire for human rights and freedom, their estrangement from the mainland governed by the other China (the People's Republic of China, PRC), and their disillusion with the KMT's empty boast about re-seizing the mainland from the PRC and making the ROC the only one legitimate China (Makeham and Hsiau 2005). Then, in the early 1970s after the replacement of the ROC at the United Nations with the PRC, the appeal for indigenising Taiwanese culture and politics began to sprout, and the democratisation of Taiwan as well as the development of Taiwanese nationalism has been boosted since the 1980s, which may be seen as a sharp contrast to communist China's increasingly authoritarian control over its people and a direct contradiction of China's false claim about its sovereignty over Taiwan. Despite Taiwan's diplomatic predicaments amid the increasing global acknowledgement of China's One China principle, there has been a generally steady rise in recent decades in the percentage of the people in Taiwan who see themselves as Taiwanese (see Figure 8.1). In particular, whenever the people of Taiwan strongly feel the threat from China against the democracy and independence of Taiwan, there tends to be a surge of Taiwanese nationalist sentiment, which may be well supported by the fact that one of the peaks of Taiwanese national identity in Figure 8.1 appeared in 2014, when Taiwan's Sunflower Student Movement occurred as a show of Taiwan's resistance to Chinese hegemony (Chang 2020). As one's identity may be observed from his/her language use, this chapter aims to find linguistic evidence for Taiwanese nationalism by examining how China is interpreted and represented in cross-Strait Mandarin translations, which may not only help present the abstract but increasingly strong sense of Taiwanese identity in concrete form but also demonstrate how a Taiwanese translator may show his/her resistance to Chinese hegemony.

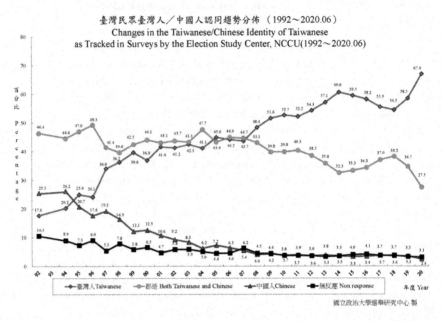

臺灣民眾臺灣人／中國人認同趨勢分佈 （1992～2020.06）
Changes in the Taiwanese/Chinese Identity of Taiwanese
as Tracked in Surveys by the Election Study Center, NCCU(1992～2020.06)

FIGURE 8.1 The changes in the Taiwanese/Chinese identity of the people of Taiwan between 1992 and 2020. Courtesy of the Election Study Center National Chengchi University (2020).

The link between ideology/identity and translation

In recent decades, the link between ideology/identity and translation on the micro-level has become one of the main research foci in translation studies. Every decision or choice the translator makes in the process of translating may be under the influence of his/her surrounding 'socio-political milieu' (Alvarez and Carmen-África Vidal 1996: 5) and of the translational presuppositions that the translator 'will build [...] according to the book to be translated and the audience envisaged' (Schiavi 1996: 15). The impact of the translator's national or cultural identity on his/her translation has also been extensively explored. The selection of source texts and the manipulation of target texts have proved to be a means of building or reshaping national identity in many countries (e.g. Venuti 2005). The translator's conscious or subconscious intervention leads to the fact that translated texts are hardly free from adulteration, hence Bassnett's suggestion for reassessing the role of the translator (1996: 22). Different approaches, such as critical discourse analysis (CDA) and textual analysis, have been employed in translation studies to explore the relationship between translation and ideology (Fawcett and Munday 2009), and the translator's ideological presence in his/her rendition has been found to be achieved through lexico-grammatical choices and various strategies, such as omissions, rewriting, and summarising (Munday 2008: 15).

For example, Munday analyses translations of political speeches, interviews, and writings concerning some revolutionary political figures in Latin America through a textual approach combined with the linguistic toolkit developed under critical linguistics (CL) and CDA and finds 'negative ideologically driven evaluation' to be clearly visible in the 'descriptions, epithet and naming strategies' used in target texts (2007: 214). Also, as opposed to an active structure where 'the agent responsible for performing the action' is specified, the passive voice may be used to create a sense of objectivity or to distance oneself from the text (Baker 2018: 114–115), which means the translator may highlight or obscure the agent or actor in target texts through the use of the active or passive voice. Ideology is also being explored in interpreting studies (Beaton-Thome 2015). In Chang's simultaneous interpreting experiments that investigate the signs of hegemony and resistance embodied in the Chinese-English simultaneous renditions of trainee interpreters from China and from Taiwan against the backdrop of the fact that China and Taiwan have long been in a hegemony-resistance relationship over the One China principle, the results show that the majority of the participating Taiwanese trainee interpreters linguistically resist the One China principle, demonstrate Taiwanese national identity, and construct the image of China as the Other in their renditions through the discursive strategies specified in the discourse-historical approach to CDA (Chang 2012: 192–220). Specifically, through referential and perspectiva-tion strategies, China may be referred to as 'this country', 'China', or 'their moth-erland' when the word 'motherland' is used by a Chinese political leader in the original to describe the relationship between China and Taiwan; the Taiwanese trainee interpreters also discursively construct Taiwan as a country or nation in the cross-Strait political speeches (Chang 2012: 215–216).[2] Compared with inter-preting studies, the link between ideology/identity and translation has been more extensively investigated (e.g. Tymoczko and Gentzler 2002; Muñoz-Calvo and Buesa-Gómez 2010), yet evidence from comparison of multiple target texts pro-duced for the same source text has been very limited in the field of translation studies due to copyright restrictions (Munday 2008: 20), let alone evidence from the cases where the translators of the multiple target texts possess different or antagonistic ideologies/identities against one another, thus making the investiga-tion of the cross-Strait Mandarin Chinese translations of the same source text very likely to be significant in the field of translation studies.

Translations and studies of Peter Hessler's *River Town* in the cross-Strait context

US journalist and writer Peter Hessler is one of the few award-winning US authors in recent decades to have written heavily about China and to have also been highly acclaimed in China. He was dispatched by the US Peace Corps in 1996 to Fuling, a remote hillside town by the Yangtze in the centre of Sichuan Province, Southwest China, and taught English at a teachers college there. During his two-year voluntary service, he was keenly aware of what was happening inside and outside the college, getting to know local people by learning and practising Mandarin with them, and pondering over the political and social problems of China, all of which later became the content of his first China-themed book, *River Town: Two Years on the Yangtze* (2001), which won the Kiriyama Prize and was shortlisted for the Thomas Cook Travel Book Award. While the book quenched the West's thirst for knowing more about China, its Mandarin Chinese translation intended for the Chinese market (also referred to as the China version in this study) was translated by Hessler's former colleague at Fuling, Xueshun Li, and has also gained in popularity among Chinese people who wish to know how China is understood by the West. In Taiwan, the Mandarin Chinese translation of *River Town* was produced by Taiwanese translator Meichen Wu (also referred to as the Taiwan version in this study). Through a rough examination of both Mandarin Chinese versions, it is easy to find many words, phrases, and passages that are politically sensitive under the CPC's authoritarian rule omitted or modified in the China version, while the Taiwan version is in general faithful to the original.

The popularity of *River Town* in China has also aroused interest from Chinese researchers in different fields. Some look at how the image of China was constructed by the Other through analysis of the narrative discourse in *River Town* (e.g. Yin 2019). However, given that their research data was from the China version instead of the English original of *River Town*, it begs the question as to whether the construction of the image of China found in such studies was more or less a reflection of the translator's ideology. Some other researchers in the field of translation studies compare the China version and the Taiwan version of *River Town* (e.g. Gao and Zhao 2019; Wang 2019). Wang (2019) discovers some differences between both versions in linguistic style and in translation of mostly culture-specific terms, such as ideology-free (proper) nouns used by Chinese locals, and he attributes those translation differences to the fact that the two translators have different 'cultural' identities (2019: 50). Likewise, while Gao and Zhao conclude that the Taiwanese translator's failure to restore the Chinese dialectal uses in her translation of *River Town*, such as *Chaoshou* that refers to dumpling soup in the Chinese province of Sichuan (where the river town in question is located), may be partly because her political ideology prompted her to 'prevent Taiwanese readers from having intimate contact with the culture of the motherland' (2019: 130), the dialectal translation examples provided in the study may not properly explain their own link with the Taiwanese translator's political ideology. As a whole, some of the differences between the cross-Strait Mandarin translations of *River Town* have been noted (only) in China but not approached from the perspective of national identity issues, which understandably may be attributed to the practice of the One China principle in China. In light of the special status quo across the Taiwan Strait, where the citizens of democratic Taiwan and of communist China share the same language and culture in a broad sense but have different or opposing political ideologies and national identities in term of whether

Taiwan is part of China, the cross-Strait translations of Hessler's *River Town* are in fact a very adequate case for research into the link between one's ideology or identity and his/her translation. Therefore, this chapter will examine the Taiwan version of *River Town*, with a few translations from the China version serving as a contrastive reference in the discussion of special translation examples (see the following section of the DHA analysis and results of the Taiwan version of Hessler's *River Town*). Meanwhile, some clarifications and explanations from the editors of the China and Taiwan versions of *River Town* and from the Chinese translator have been obtained, which confirmed that both of the Mandarin Chinese versions were subject to very little intervention from the editors (Fuca 2017a; 2017b).[3] Accordingly, the special translation examples found in this study may be attributed to the choice of the translators themselves, thus allowing the confirmation of the link between one's ideology/identity and his/her translation.

Discourse-historical approach (DHA) to critical discourse analysis employed in ideology and identity studies

Critical discourse analysis (CDA), which emerged in the early 1990s and branches out into several approaches, is increasingly employed in studies of the relationships among translation, ideology, identity, and power (Kim 2020). For CDA practitioners, discourse, namely language use in writing and speech, is a form of social practice, and by examining lexico-grammatical choices, genres, or types of discourses within specific contexts, CDA can demystify ideologies embedded in discourse, uncover inequalities and power struggles, and further address social problems (Fairclough and Wodak 1997). In particular, CDA 'intervenes on the side of dominated and oppressed groups and against dominating groups' and 'openly declares the emancipatory interests that motivate it' (Fairclough and Wodak 1997: 259). Of all the CDA approaches that differ in research focus, social domains, and theoretical legacy (Fairclough and Wodak 1997), the discourse-historical approach (DHA), developed mainly by Ruth Wodak, has been made the main methodological focus of the present study. Wodak (1986) developed the DHA from her study of anti-Semitic discourse during the Waldheim Affair in Austria by uncovering the anti-Semitic ideologies embodied in texts and discourses about Kurt Waldheim, who was accused of his participation or complicity in Nazi crimes against Jews during World War II when he ran for the 1986 Austrian presidential election. Different from the other CDA approaches, the DHA aims to 'transcend the pure linguistic dimension' and 'include, more or less systematically, the historical, political, sociological and/or psychological dimension in the analysis and interpretation of a specific discursive occasion' (Reisigl and Wodak 2001: 35). In another DHA-employed study (Wodak et al. 2009) that investigates how Austrian national identity is being constructed through discursive strategies and shifts of Austrian national identity amid EU integration, some linguistic strategies and devices are found to be used for discursively constructing national identities, such as using the deictic 'we' and its other dialectal forms to signify inclusiveness as opposed to 'they' used to refer to 'others' or linking 'they' groups with derogatory and negative attributions (ibid.: 141–142). The application of the DHA is three-dimensional, including: (1) Initial identification of specific discursive topics or contents, (2) investigation of discursive strategies, and (3) examination of linguistic means and the linguistic realisations within contexts (Reisigl and Wodak 2001: 44), and the discursive strategies may include referential/nomination strategies, predication strategies, perspectivation/framing/discourse representation strategies, intensifying/mitigation strategies, and argumentation strategies (Reisigl and Wodak 2001: 44–84). For instance, social actors may be constructed and represented by use of referential or nomination strategies. Predication strategies may involve linguistic devices which explicitly or implicitly express 'evaluative attributions of negative and positive traits' (ibid.: 45), while through strategies of perspectivation, framing, or discourse representation, speakers demonstrate linguistically their stance and their involvement in discourse. Intensifying and mitigation are two opposite strategies, and both may influence the original illocutionary force of utterances. Argumentation strategies, of which topoi (plausible argumentation schemes) and fallacies are two main features, help justify positive and negative attributions of specific persons or groups (ibid.: 45). As the DHA is effective in uncovering discursive strategies used on issues about racism, ethnicism, and nationalism (Reisigl and Wodak 2001: 44), it has been used to explore the discursive (re)construction of one's identity and (re)presentation of the Other in both translation and interpreting studies (e.g. Chang 2012). Therefore, it should be appropriate to employ the DHA in the present study to investigate whether and how a Taiwanese translator, amid the hegemony-resistance relationship between China and Taiwan, may show resistance to Chinese hegemony and demonstrate his/her national identity in his/her renditions.

DHA analysis and results of the Taiwan version of Hessler's *River Town*

In his book *River Town*, Hessler provided in the first person many descriptions of the people and events he encountered in China and his reflections on how the Chinese government's authoritarian rule affected its people. The book was generally written in a reporting style, and many criticisms or not-so-positive comments were conveyed in the passive voice or in an implicit or euphemistic way. In this study, the Taiwan version of *River Town* is the main target of the DHA analysis, and the specific topics for analysis include 'China (its government and people)', 'the Chinese government's political control and indoctrination', and the 'Taiwan independence issue' in order to investigate whether the hegemony-resistance relationship between China and Taiwan may be linguistically embodied in the Taiwan version. According to the results of the DHA analysis at the lexico-grammatical level, it is found that although the Taiwan version of *River Town* is generally very faithful to its original, the Taiwanese translator is found to have discursively showed resistance to Chinese hegemony, demonstrated her Taiwanese national

TABLE 8.1 The discursive strategies and linguistic means used by the Taiwanese translator in her translation of *River Town* and selected examples of realisations

Discursive strategies	*Linguistic means*	*Selected examples of realisations*
Referential strategies	Using active structure to foreground the social actor that is responsible for the action	ST: … because they were constantly being indoctrinated <u>by the Communist Party.</u> (Hessler 2001: 23) TT: … 因為<u>共產黨</u>不斷向他們灌輸思想。(Hessler 2012a: 67) BT: … because <u>the Communist Party</u> was constantly indoctrinating them.
	Specifying the social actor that is responsible for the action through addition	ST: <u>These things</u> were no longer said, …(Hessler 2001: 9) TT: 現在，<u>中國政府</u>不再這麼說了 … (Hessler 2012a: 50-1) BT: Now, <u>the Chinese government</u> no long said [these things].
	Replacing objects/ places with the social actor that is responsible for the action	ST: …, along with <u>the legal changes that allowed</u> the new free-market economics. (Hessler 2001: 114) TT: …, 伴隨而來的還有<u>法令的改變——政府容許</u>自由市場經濟了。(Hessler 2012a: 168) BT: … along with <u>the legal changes—the government allowed</u> free-market economics.
	Converting phrases to clauses to make the social actor inferable	ST: … the displaced peasants (Hessler 2001: 105) TT: … 農民被迫離開家園 (Hessler 2012a: 158) BT: … peasants were forced to leave homes
	Using the terms 'China' or 'Chinese people' instead of pronouns to specify the social actor	ST: … to some degree one would expect China's historical disasters to provide lessons that prevented <u>their</u> blind repetition] (Hessler 2001: 110) TT: … 在某種程度上，你會期待中國的歷史災難可以提供一些教訓，使<u>中國人</u>不再盲目地重蹈覆轍。(Hessler 2012a: 163) BT: … to some degree, you would expect China's historical disasters to provide some lessons that prevented <u>Chinese people</u> from blindly repeating mistakes.
	Using full or more complete names to specify the social actor	ST: … suddenly <u>the Party</u> interfered. (Hessler 2001: 44) TT: 而突然之間，<u>共產黨</u>出面干涉了。(Hessler 2012a: 90) BT: suddenly, <u>the Communist Party</u> showed up and interfered.
	Using deixis to highlight the social actor	ST: But there was always a great deal that surrounded us: the campus and its rules, <u>the</u> country and its politics (Hessler 2001: 44) TT: 但是，我們一直被許多事物包圍著：校園和它的規則、<u>這個</u>國家和它的政治。(Hessler 2012a: 90) BT: But we had been surrounded by many things: the campus and its rules, <u>this</u> country and its politics.
Predication strategies	Using less positive or more negative attributes when the original can be interpreted in more than one way	ST: I ran alone, and in a <u>crowded</u> country that sort of solitude was worth something. (Hessler 2001: 72) TT: 我自己一個人跑，在一個<u>人滿為患</u>的國家，這種孤獨是珍貴的。(Hessler 2012a: 121) BT: I ran alone, and in an <u>overpopulated</u> country such solitude was precious.
	Using allusions to highlight China's authoritarian rule	ST: In their stories, Robin Hood stole from the rich and gave to the peasants, and almost invariably he ended up in prison. Sometimes he was executed. …But almost always Robin Hood was caught; there were no illusions about the idealized green world of Sherwood Forest. There are few trees in China and <u>the police always get their man</u>. (Hessler 2001: 37) TT: 在他們的故事裡，羅賓漢偷取富人的財物，送給農民，而最後，他幾乎都得坐牢。有時候，他被處死。…但是，羅賓漢幾乎總是遭到逮捕。學生們對修伍德森林 (Sherwood Forest)理想化的綠色世界沒有幻想。中國的樹很少，而<u>警察總是抓到他們想抓的人</u>。(Hessler 2012a: 81)

(Continued)

TABLE 8.1 (Continued) The discursive strategies and linguistic means used by the Taiwanese translator in her translation of River Town and selected examples of realisations

Discursive strategies	Linguistic means	Selected examples of realisations
		BT: In their stories, Robin Hood stole from the rich and gave to the peasants, and finally, he almost always went to prison. Sometimes, he was executed....But Robin Hood was almost always arrested. The students had no illusions about the idealized green world of Sherwood Forest. There are few trees in China and <u>the police always get the man they want to catch</u>.
	Changing the original word order or sentence structure to highlight negative implications	ST: <u>Their faith wasn't so much specifically in Party theory as in the notion</u> that people like them could—and should—contribute to society, despite its flaws. (Hessler 2001: 345) TT: <u>他們所相信的不是黨的理論，而是一個觀念</u>；儘管社會有缺點，像他們這樣的人仍然、而且應該對社會有所貢獻。 (Hessler 2012a: 427) BT: <u>Their faith wasn't in Party theory but in the notion</u>: people like them still, and should contribute to society despite its flaws.
	Using straightforward predicative nouns/adjectives or changing the perspective to replace euphemistic terms in the original	ST: And often in Fuling they shouted other <u>less innocent terms</u>—yangguizi, or "foreign devil"; da bizi, "big nose"... (Hessler 2001: 65) TT: 在涪陵，人們常以其他<u>比較帶有惡意的</u>名稱呼叫我，例如「洋鬼子」或「大鼻子」。 (Hessler 2012a: 114) BT: In Fuling, people often shouted at me with other <u>more spiteful terms</u>, such as "foreign devil" or "big nose".
Perspectivation strategies	Using pronouns to show detachment	ST: ... the Chinese looked at <u>the</u> people and saw how they had been shaped by the land. (Hessler 2001: 6) TT: ... 中國人望著<u>他們的</u>人民，看到了土地如何塑造他們。 (Hessler 2012a: 47) BT: ... the Chinese looked at <u>their</u> people and saw how the land had shaped them.
	Replacing first-person pronouns with the country name to show detachment	ST: I didn't agree that <u>our countries'</u> political differences were so neatly (and morally) explained by these contrasting attitudes toward the individual and the group. (Hessler 2001: 111) TT: 我不認為這種對於個人和群體的相反態度，為<u>中國和美國</u>的政治差別提供了適當的(以及道德上的)解釋， (Hessler 2012a: 164) BT: I didn't think that these contrasting attitudes toward the individual and the group provided adequate (and ethical) explanation for political differences between <u>China and America</u>.
	Adding local deixis to show detachment	ST: I disliked Mao intensely. This was not unusual for a waiguoren; there weren't many reasons to like him when you came from <u>outside</u>. (Hessler 2001: 134) TT: 我非常不喜歡毛澤東。對於一個外國人而言，這並非不尋常。如果你來自<u>中國以外的地方</u>，你沒有許多理由喜歡他。 (Hessler 2012a: 189) BT: I disliked Mao intensely. For a foreigner, this was not unusual. If you came from <u>a place outside China</u>, you didn't have many reasons to like him.
	Using plural first-person pronouns to show involvement	ST: <u>China</u> was Communist but it wasn't. Nothing was quite what it seemed, (Hessler 2001: 9) TT: <u>我們認為中國</u>是一個共產主義國家，但其實它並不是。沒有一件事如表面所呈現的， (Hessler 2012a: 50) BT: <u>We thought China was</u> a Communist country but in fact it wasn't. Nothing was quite what it seemed;
	Using repetitions of words/phrases to show involvement	ST: There was the same sense of future glory in China, but the past was far more <u>brutal</u> than anything that had ever happened in America, which complicated things. (Hessler 2001: 23) TT: 在中國，人們也同樣感覺到未來的榮耀，但是，他們的過去遠比美國歷史上的任何事件<u>粗暴而殘酷</u>，於是，事情就變得複雜了。 (Hessler 2012a: 67) BT: In China, people had the same sense of future glory, but their past was far more <u>violent and brutal</u> than anything that had ever happened in America, so things became complicated.

(Continued)

TABLE 8.1 (Continued) The discursive strategies and linguistic means used by the Taiwanese translator in her translation of River Town and selected examples of realisations

Discursive strategies	Linguistic means	Selected examples of realisations
	Using second-person pronouns to engage the reader	ST: <u>The tension in the big cities was palpable;</u> conversations with Uighurs didn't last very long before they started complaining. (Hessler 2001: 212) TT: <u>你可以清楚感知大城市的緊張氣氛</u>。和維吾爾人交談沒多久，他們就開始抱怨。(Hessler 2012a: 276) BT: <u>You could clearly perceive the tense atmosphere in the big cities.</u> Conversations with Uighurs didn't last very long before they started complaining.
Intensifying strategies	Using intensity markers such as emphasising particles	ST: These incidents were mildly disturbing, but mostly they were <u>pathetic</u>. What was the point of censoring an article about the Mississippi River? (Hessler 2001: 174) TT: 這些事件只讓我受到一點困擾。我主要是覺得這種作法<u>非常可悲</u>。為什麼他們要刪改一篇關於密西西比河的故事？(Hessler 2012a: 232) BT: These incidents only mildly disturbed me. I mostly thought this practice was <u>very pathetic</u>. Why did they delete and modify a story about the Mississippi River?
	Adding intensifying verbs/modal verbs	ST: It seemed incredible that in a modernizing country of China's size many people <u>turned to</u> rumor as the most reliable source for information about current events. (Hessler 2001: 144) TT: 這似乎令人難以置信：在一個像中國這麼大、且正在進行現代化的國家，許多人<u>竟然必須</u>把傳聞當成時事資訊最可靠的來源。(Hessler 2012a: 201) BT: It seemed incredible: in a modernizing country of China's size, many people <u>should have to</u> take rumour as the most reliable source for information about current events.
	Using intensifying verbs/verb phrases	ST: The debates continued until finally in 1987 the government tired of this version of democracy and <u>silenced it</u>. (Hessler 2001: 105) TT: 辯論持續著，最後，在一九八七年，政府終於厭倦了這種民主政治的翻版，<u>要大家閉嘴</u>。(Hessler 2012a: 158) BT: The debates continued; finally, in 1987, the government tired of this version of democracy and <u>made everyone shut up</u>.
	Adding evaluative adjective/ noun phrases to unpack the meaning of the original euphemistic or implicit words/ phrases	ST: I thought about Anne's father, the math professor who had spent eight years of the Cultural Revolution <u>working</u> in a Sichuan coal mine, ... (Hessler 2001: 132) TT: 我想到安的父親，在文化大革命期間，這位數學教授在四川的煤礦坑做了八年的<u>苦工</u>。(Hessler 2012a: 187) BT: I thought about Anne's father; during the Cultural Revolution, this math professor did eight years of <u>hard labour</u> in a Sichuan coal mine.
	Specifying vague expressions according to the context	ST: He was completely uneducated but he had interesting ideas; sometimes <u>he talked about the need for more democracy and other political parties,</u> and these were views I never heard on campus. Once I mentioned Hong Kong, but he simply looked bored—<u>it meant nothing to him</u>. (Hessler 2001: 172) TT: 他沒有受過教育，但是，他有一些有趣的想法。有時<u>他會說，中國需要更多的民主和其他政黨</u>，這是我在校園裡不曾聽過的想法。有一次我提到香港，但他只覺得很無趣。<u>對他而言，香港回歸中國沒有任何意義</u>。(Hessler 2012a: 230) BT: He was uneducated but he had some interesting ideas. Sometimes <u>he said that China needed more democracy and other political parties.</u> This was a view I never heard on campus. Once I mentioned Hong Kong, but he simply looked bored—<u>to him, Hong Kong's return to China didn't have any meanings</u>.
Mitigation strategies	Using indirect speech or adding direct object to make China or Chinese people the performer of the action	ST: "Now we have so much freedom," she said, in a sort of fierce whisper. "We are so free. We have so much freedom now." I stood there awkwardly, nodding as if I understood. <u>I couldn't imagine thinking</u> that life in the college was any sort of true freedom, although I knew that I would feel differently if I had spent the Cultural Revolution in China. (Hessler 2001: 137)

(Continued)

TABLE 8.1 (Continued) The discursive strategies and linguistic means used by the Taiwanese translator in her translation of River Town and selected examples of realisations

Discursive strategies	Linguistic means	Selected examples of realisations
		TT: 「現在我們有許多自由，」她以用力但壓低的聲音說：「我們很自由，現在我們有許多自由。」我不知所措地站在那裡，不時點頭，彷彿我了解。<u>我無法想像有人認為這座學校的生活有任何自由可言</u>，雖然我知道，如果我經歷中國的文化大革命，我會有不同的看法。(Hessler 2012a: 193)
		BT: "Now we have so much freedom," she said in a fierce whisper. "We are so free. We have so much freedom now." I stood there awkwardly, nodding from time to time as if I understood. <u>I couldn't imagine someone thinking</u> that life in the college was any sort of freedom, although I knew that I would feel differently if I had experienced the Cultural Revolution in China.
Omitting positive adjectives used in the original		ST: Education Is the Foundation upon Which <u>a Powerful Nation</u> Is Built (Hessler 2001: 78)
		TT: 教育是<u>立國</u>的基礎 (Hessler 2012a: 128)
		BT: Education is the foundation upon which <u>a nation</u> is built.
Swapping the subject with the object in comparative structure to downplay the praise of the Han Chinese languages		ST: In Xinjiang I found myself gravitating to Chinese restaurants and shops, and especially I liked talking with the Sichuanese, who had migrated to Xinjiang in large numbers. After a summer on the road <u>it was good to hear their slurred tones again—much more soothing than the Turkic trills of the Uighur tongue.</u> (Hessler 2001: 215)
		TT: 在新疆，我發現自己喜歡去中國館子和商店，我尤其喜歡和那些大批大批移居到新疆的四川人交談。旅行了一個夏天後，再度聽到他們那種含糊的腔調讓我覺得很舒服。<u>和四川話相比，維吾爾話那種土耳其語的顫音就沒有這麼撫慰人心了</u>。(Hessler 2012a: 278)
		BT: In Xinjiang I found myself gravitating to Chinese restaurants and shops, and especially I liked talking with the Sichuanese, who had migrated to Xinjiang in large numbers. After traveling for a summer, it made me comfortable to hear their slurred tones again. <u>Compared with Sichuanese, the Turkic trills of the Uighur tongue was less soothing</u> ;
Using determiners to downplay the praise of China		ST: This agreement rewarded <u>Chinese contributions</u> to the Allied victory by granting former German concessions like Qingdao to the Japanese... (Hessler 2001: 372)
		TT: 中國在第一次世界大戰中，對協約國的勝利<u>做出了一些貢獻</u>，但是，這個條約卻將先前德國的租界地(例如青島)送給日本人，作為對中國的回報。(Hessler 2012a: 456)
		BT: China in the First World War <u>made some contributions</u> to the Allied victory, but this agreement repaid China by granting former German concessions (like Qingdao) to the Japanese.

identity, and constructed the image of China as the Other in her translation through referential, predication, perspectivation, intensifying, and mitigation discursive strategies, with referential strategies most widely used, mitigation strategies least widely used, and more than one discursive strategy often used simultaneously. Table 8.1 gives an overview of the discursive strategies, linguistic means, and selected examples of realisations found in the DHA analysis of the Taiwan version, which will be followed by the discussion of two other special translation examples regarding the Taiwan independence issue and the One China principle, with their China version counterparts provided for comparison. The determination and categorisation of discursive strategies and linguistic means found in this study mainly follow the explanations and instructions provided by Reisigl and Wodak (2001: 44–84). In presenting the selected translation examples, the focal points are underlined, and three codes are used for easy reference: ST – English source text; TT – Mandarin Chinese target text; BT – the researcher's back translation of the TT.

The translation examples regarding the Taiwan independence issue/One China principle

As *River Town* is a memoir of Hessler's life in China, Taiwan was only briefly mentioned on a few occasions. However, the differences between the Taiwanese translator and her Chinese counterpart in dealing with the texts involving the Taiwan independence issue or the One China principle are remarkable and thus discussed in the following.

Example 1:

ST: 'Most Americans think <u>Taiwan is like a separate country</u>', I said. 'It has its own government and economy. But Americans know <u>the history and culture are the same as the mainland's</u>. So maybe they think <u>it should return to China</u>, but only when <u>the people in Taiwan</u> are ready. Most Americans think this problem is much more complicated than Hong Kong'. (Hessler 2001: 310)

TT-Taiwan version:

「大多數美國人認為<u>台灣是另一個國家，</u>」我說：「台灣有自己的政府和經濟制度，但是美國人知道，<u>台灣和中國的歷史和文化是一樣的</u>。所以他們認為，也許<u>台灣應該回歸中國</u>，但是，唯有當<u>台灣人</u>準備好了才能這麼做。大多數美國人認為，這個問題遠比香港複雜。」　(BT: 'Most Americans think <u>Taiwan is a separate country</u>', I said. 'Taiwan has its own government and economic system, but Americans know <u>Taiwan and China have the same history and culture</u>. So they think maybe <u>Taiwan should return to China</u>, but only when <u>the people in Taiwan</u> are ready. Most Americans think this problem is much more complicated than Hong Kong'.) (Hessler 2012a: 388)

TT-China version:

"大多数美国人觉得，<u>台湾看上去像是另外一个国家，</u>"我回答道，"它有自己的政府和经济体制。但美国人也知道，<u>它跟大陆具有相同的历史和文化</u>。所以，他们也许觉得<u>它应该回归大陆</u>，但只有在<u>老百姓愿意</u>的情况下才行。大多数美国人认为，这个问题比香港问题要复杂得多。"　(BT: 'Most Americans think <u>Taiwan looks like a separate country</u>', I replied. 'It has its own government and economic system. But Americans also know <u>it and the mainland have the same history and culture</u>. So they maybe think <u>it should return to the mainland</u>, but only when <u>the ordinary people</u> are willing to do so. Most Americans think this problem is much more complicated than the problem of Hong Kong'.) (Hessler 2012b: 336)

In the second underlined part of the source text in Example 1, Hessler referred to China as the 'mainland'. The Chinese translator was seemingly faithful to the original by retaining 'the mainland' in his rendition, yet he was in fact following one of China's translation norms regarding the One China principle that the two sides of the Taiwan Strait should be referred to as 'Taiwan and the mainland' instead of

'Taiwan and China' (He and Li 2011: 8–9), which makes Taiwan 'an island' subject to the Chinese 'mainland'. My assumption is then supported by his following rendition of 'China' in the original into 'the mainland' in the third underlined part. The Chinese translator even went so far as to replace 'the people of Taiwan' in the original with 'the ordinary people' in his translation, thus conforming to the claim of the Chinese government – 'Taiwan's future must be decided by all Chinese people rather than by only Taiwan residents' (Cheng and Chang 2014). In contrast, the Taiwanese translator omitted the preposition 'like' in the first underlined source sentence and made Taiwan a country in her rendition through the intensifying strategy. Also, although Hessler used 'the mainland' to refer to China in the second underlined part of the source text when discussing the cross-Strait situation, the Taiwanese translator chose to use the term 'Taiwan and China' instead, which not only still conveys the meaning of the original but also through the referential strategy gives a sense that Taiwan and China are on an equal footing.

Example 2:

ST: It was impossible to grasp all of the varied forces that had affected Mr. Xu's life and would continue to affect him in the future – the war, <u>the Taiwan split</u>, the Cultural Revolution; the dammed river and the new city; his pretty daughter in Xiamen with her cell phone and driving lessons. (Hessler 2001: 316)

TT-Taiwan version:
　　我無法完全了解所有過去影響他的生命、而且未來還會繼續影響他的生命的那些力量：戰爭、台灣和中國的分裂、文化大革命、築起水壩的河流、新的城市，以及他那住在廈門、有手機且上過駕駛課的漂亮女兒。(BT: I could not understand completely all those forces that had affected his life in the past and would continue to affect his life in the future – the war, <u>the split between Taiwan and China</u>, the Cultural Revolution, the dammed river, the new city, and his pretty daughter, who lived in Xiamen, had a cell phone and had attended driving lessons.) (Hessler 2012a: 395)

TT-China version:
　　我根本无法掌握曾经影响，并将继续影响徐先生生活道路的各种力量——比如战争、台湾和大陆的分隔、改革开放、大江截流、新城崛起、漂亮的女儿远在厦门用上了手机、学会了驾驶。(BT: I could not grasp at all a variety of forces that had affected and would continue to affect Mr. Xu's life path – such as the war, <u>the split between Taiwan and the mainland</u>, the reform and opening-up, the large river being dammed, the new city emerging, and [his] pretty daughter far away in Xiamen using a cell phone and learning how to drive.) (Hessler 2012b: 342)

In Example 2, Hessler used the term 'the Taiwan split', which, within the context, indicates the separation between Taiwan and China. The Chinese translator was again adhering to the One China principle by referring to the two sides of the Taiwan Strait as 'Taiwan and the mainland' just as found in Example 1. In contrast, while the Taiwanese translator also chose to make the meaning of 'the Taiwan split' more explicit, she used the term 'Taiwan and China' in her translation, thus conveying the original meaning without any indication that Taiwan should be subject to the rule of China and also demonstrating her Taiwanese national identity through the referential strategy. Clearly, as shown in Examples 1 and 2, the ways in which both translators dealt with the Taiwan independence issue or the One China principle in their translations mirror the hegemony-resistance relationship between China and Taiwan.

Conclusion

The DHA analysis at the lexico-grammatical level of the Taiwan version of Hessler's *River Town* in this study focuses on the topics of 'China (including its government and people)', 'the Chinese government's political control and indoctrination', and the 'Taiwan independence issue', and the results show that the Taiwanese translator has discursively shown resistance to Chinese hegemony, demonstrated her Taiwanese national identity, and constructed the image of China as the Other in her translation by selecting translation or discursive strategies to expose the negative sides of 'China' in Hessler's descriptions. Specifically, she used several referential strategies, such as foregrounding the social actor (China in a broad sense in this study) through the active structure, specifying the social actor through addition, replacing things/places with the social actor as the performer of the actions, and converting phrases into clauses, all of which highlighted the CPC's authoritarian rule of its people or made inferable within contexts those who should be responsible for the actions. Also, through the predication strategies, including using less positive or more negative attributes, predicative nouns, adjectives, and non-literary allusions or changing the original word order/sentence structure, the Taiwanese translator showed the negative sides of China in a more explicit way, thus presenting the image of China as the Other. While employing the perspectivation strategies such as using third-person pronouns, local deixis, or replacement of first-person pronouns with the country name to show her detachment from China, the Taiwanese translator also showed her involvement and engaged the reader in her reconstruction of the negative image of China by resorting to plural first-person pronouns, second-person pronouns, and repetitions of words/phrases. In terms of using the intensifying strategies, her linguistic means of specifying expressions that had been vague in the original effectively uncovered the traces of Chinese people's resentment against their CPC government. When dealing with cases where the author gave positive or neutral comments on China, the Taiwanese translator downplayed the praise through the mitigation strategies such as omitting positive adjectives, using determiners or indirect speech, or swapping the subject with the object in comparative structure. As found through the DHA analysis, the Taiwanese translator tended to make explicit the negative connotations about China in the original and distance herself from China, thus presenting China as the Other in her translation. She is also found to have demonstrated her Taiwanese national identity by presenting

Taiwan as a country on an equal footing with China. All the above evidence shows that despite the fact that translators may be subject to the constraints of the source text, they may still have their identities and ideologies embodied in their translations to some extent, consciously or subconsciously, and that the Taiwan version of *River Town* has more or less represented the hegemony-resistance relationship between China and Taiwan. While it is arguable that one translated work may not proportionately reflect the development of mainstream ideology and identity in its target culture, it has also been increasingly recognised that the translator tends to deal with translation on the basis of his/her cognition and knowledge and caters to the envisaged audience (e.g. Schiavi 1996: 15; Munday 2008: 11; Tan 2018). Accordingly, the findings of the DHA analysis of the Taiwan version of Hessler's China-themed book *River Town* in this chapter may be well said to have echoed the upward trend in the development of Taiwanese national identity as shown in Figure 8.1, presented the abstract sense of Taiwanese national identity in concrete form, and even reflected the entangled but antagonistic relations between Taiwan and China.

Notes

1 This research is funded by Taiwan's Ministry of Science and Technology under grant no. MOST 104-2410-H-033-028 – and MOST 107-2914-I-033-018A1.
2 It is also found in Chang's study that Chinese trainee interpreters may refuse to recognise Taiwan as a country in rendering a Taiwanese political leader's speech, and that they follow the One China principle by discursively constructing both China and Taiwan as 'mainland and Taiwan' or 'the two sides of China' (Chang 2012: 213–215).
3 Special thanks must be given to Dr Yanke Fuca, chief editor of Gasu Publishing Company 八旗文化 which introduced Hessler's books to Taiwan, for relaying the interview questions to Chinese translator Xueshun Li and Chinese editor Jiren Zhang.

References

English references

Alvarez, R. and Carmen-África Vidal, M. (1996) 'Translating: A political act', in R. Alvarez and M. Carmen-África Vidal (eds.) *Translation, Power, Subversion*. Clevedon: Multilingual Matters, pp. 1–9.

Baker, M. (2018) *In Other Words: A Coursebook on Translation*. 3rd edn. London: Routledge.

Bassnett, S. (1996) 'The meek or the mighty: Reappraising the role of the translator', in R. Alvarez and M. Carmen-África Vidal (eds.) *Translation, Power, Subversion*. Clevedon: Multilingual Matters, pp. 10–24.

Beaton-Thome, M. (2015) 'Ideology', in F. Pöchhacker (ed.) *Routledge Encyclopedia of Interpreting Studies*. London: Routledge, pp. 187–188.

Chang, P. (2012) *Hegemony and Resistance as Shown in Critical Discourse Analysis of Trainee Interpreters from the P.R.C. and Taiwan in Mandarin-English Simultaneous Interpreting*. Unpublished PhD thesis. Newcastle University.

Chang, P. (2020) 'Civil resistance through online activist translation in Taiwan's Sunflower Student Movement', in R.R. Gould and K. Tahmasebian (eds.) *The Routledge Handbook of Translation and Activism*. London: Routledge, pp. 499–514.

Cheng, C. and Chang, M. (2014) 'Taiwan's future a matter for all Chinese to decide: Beijing', *Central News Agency*, 11 June. Available at: https://focustaiwan.tw/cross-strait/201406110007 (Accessed: 13 August 2020).

Fairclough, N. and Wodak, R. (1997) Critical discourse analysis. In T. A. van Dijk (ed.) *Discourse as Social Interaction* (*Discourse Studies: A Multidisciplinary Introduction*, Vol. 2). London: Sage, pp. 258–284.

Fawcett, P. and Munday, J. (2009) 'Ideology', in M. Baker and G. Saldanha (eds.) *Routledge Encyclopedia of Translation Studies*. 2nd edn. London: Routledge, pp. 137–141.

Hessler, P. (2001) *River Town: Two Years on the Yangtze*. New York: HarperCollins.

Hsiau, A. (2010) 'A 'generation in-itself': The authoritarian rule, exilic mentality, and the postwar generation of intellectuals in 1960s Taiwan', *The Sixties: A Journal of History, Politics and Culture* 3(1): 1–31.

Kim, K.H. (2020) 'Critical discourse analysis', in M. Baker and G. Saldanha (eds.) *Routledge Encyclopedia of Translation Studies*. 3rd edn. London: Routledge, pp. 119–124.

Makeham, J. and Hsiau, A. (eds.) (2005) *Cultural, Ethnic, and Political Nationalism in Contemporary Taiwan: Bentuhua*, New York: Palgrave Macmillan.

Manthorpe, J. (2005) *Forbidden Nation: A History of Taiwan*. New York: Palgrave Macmillan.

Munday, J. (2007) 'Translation and ideology: A textual approach', *The Translator* 13(2): 195–217.

Munday, J. (2008) *Style and Ideology in Translation: Latin American Writing in English*. London: Routledge.

Muñoz-Calvo, M. and Buesa-Gómez C. (eds) (2010) *Translation and Cultural Identity: Selected Essays on Translation and Cross-Cultural Communication*. Newcastle upon Tyne: Cambridge Scholars.

Reisigl, M. and Wodak, R. (2001) *Discourse and Discrimination: Rhetorics of Racism and Antisemitism*. London: Routledge.

Schiavi, G. (1996) 'There is always a teller in a tale', *Target*, 8(1): 1–21.

Tymoczko, M. and Gentzler, E. (eds.) (2002) *Translation and Power*. Amherst: University of Massachusetts Press.

Venuti, L. (2005) 'Local contingencies: Translation and national identities', in S. Bermann and M. Wood (eds.) *Nation, Language, and the Ethics of Translation*. Princeton: Princeton University Press, pp. 177–202.

Wodak, R. (1986) *Language Behavior in Therapy Groups*. Los Angeles: University of California Press.

Wodak, R., Cillia, R. d., Reisigl, M. and Liebhart, K. (2009) *The Discursive Construction of National Identity*. 2nd edn. Edinburgh: Edinburgh University Press.

Chinese references

Election Study Center National Chengchi University政治大學選舉研究中心 (2020) 臺灣民眾臺灣人/中國人認同趨勢分佈 (1992年06月-2012年06月) (Changes in the Taiwanese/Chinese identity of Taiwanese as tracked in surveys by the Election Study Center, NCCU (1992-2020.06)). Available at: https://esc.nccu.edu.tw/course/news.php?Sn=166 (Accessed: 20 July 2020).

Fuca, Yanke 富察延賀 (2017a) Facebook messenger conversation with Dr Yanke Fuca, 17 August.

Fuca, Yanke 富察延賀 (2017b) Facebook messenger conversation with Dr Yanke Fuca, 21 August.

Gao, Xiaoxian 高晓仙 and Zhao, Guoyue 赵国月 (2019) '乡土语言'的异语写作与文化回译 (The non-native language writing of folk languages and its cultural back-translation), 外国语文(双月刊) (*Foreign Language and Literature* (bimonthly)). 35(6): 125–31.

He, Qun 何群 and Li, Chunyi 李春怡 (2011) 外交口译 (Diplomatic Interpreting), Beijing: 外语教学与研究出版社 (Foreign Language Teaching and Research Press).

Hessler, P. (2012a [2006]) 消失中的江城 (River Town: Two Years on the Yangtze, Translated by Wu, Meichen 吴美真), New Taipei City: Gasu Publishing Company.

Hessler, P. (2012b) 江城 (River Town: Two Years on the Yangtze, Translated by Li, Xueshun 李雪顺), Shanghai: Shanghai Translation Publishing House.

Tan, Zaixi 谭载喜 (2018) '文学翻译中的民族形象重构:'中国叙事'与'文化回译'' (Literary translation as a means for reconstructing national image: the narratives of China and the back-translation of its culture), 中国翻译 (Chinese Translators Journal) 2018: 17–25, 127.

Wang, Lipeng 王力鹏 (2019) '彼得·海斯勒《江城》无本回译浅析' (Analysis of textless back translation of Peter Hessler's *River Town*), 广西教育学院学报 (*Journal of Guangxi College of Education*), 2019(1): 46–51.

Yin, Ping 尹萍 (2019) '彼得·海斯勒'中国三部曲'的中国形象建构' (A study on the narrative discourse of the construction of Peter Hessler's China image), 齐齐哈尔大学学报 (哲学社会科学版) (*Journal of Qiqihar University (Philosophy & Social Science Edition)*), 2019(1): 104–6.

9

THREE FACES OF AN ASIAN HERO: COMMEMORATING KOXINGA IN CONTEMPORARY CHINA, TAIWAN, AND JAPAN

Edward Vickers

Introduction: Who was Koxinga?

I first encountered Koxinga during my earliest visit to Taiwan, in 1993. Passing through Tainan, I stumbled across the city's 'Cultural Artifacts Exhibition Hall' (台南市民族文物館). The foreign visitor unable, as I then was, to read Chinese, could divine from paintings and minimal English text the message that Koxinga was a Chinese warrior famous for expelling Dutch colonialists and 'recovering' Taiwan for China. Only years later did I learn that this Chinese hero had a Japanese mother; later still, that she hailed from my current home island, Kyushu.

That transformation of my own crude understanding of Koxinga corresponds to changing Taiwanese interpretations of his legacy since the 1990s. This phenomenon is of significance for comprehending both the evolving discourse of Taiwanese distinctiveness, and cross-Strait divergence in visions of the island's past and future. Like an earlier work on the same theme, the current chapter is thus 'a study of how the perception and manipulation of historical symbols change in response to new historical circumstances' (Croizier 1977: Preface). Writing in the era of Maoism in China and martial law on Taiwan, the American historian Ralph Croizier noted that 'Koxinga remains a hero to all modern Chinese' (1977: 86). In the more than four decades since, 'historical circumstances' have immeasurably altered, with implications for official and popular discourse on 'Chineseness', 'Taiwaneseness', and Koxinga's significance thereto. The time has thus come to reassess the symbolism of Koxinga's heroism, and its manipulation by rival political actors in a post-Cold War East Asia riven by resurgent nationalism.

Who, then, was Koxinga? Born in 1624 in Hirado, in present-day Nagasaki Prefecture, Zheng Sen (to use his infant name) was the son of Tagawa Matsu, a local woman, and Zheng Zhilong, known to Portuguese and Dutch contemporaries as Nicholas Iquan, an up-and-coming trader, buccaneer, and baptised Catholic from Fujian Province. As China's Ming Dynasty weakened, the authorities sought to co-opt Zheng senior, who thus transitioned from outlawed adventurer to legitimate businessman and imperial official. At the age of about seven, the young Koxinga was brought to Fujian by his father, who, aspiring to cement clan respectability through entry into the scholar-bureaucrat elite, arranged for the boy to be schooled for the civil service examinations. The youthful hero proved an apt scholar, becoming a first-degree holder (*xiucai*) at the age of 15.

However, the collapse of the Ming Dynasty in the 1640s precluded a scholarly route to wealth and glory. The Zhengs, father and son, initially threw in their lot with the old dynasty, pledging fealty to the Ming pretender, the Tang Wang (or Lung Wu Emperor). The latter reciprocated by bestowing on Zheng junior the imperial surname (Zhu / 朱), and the name '*Chenggong*' (成功: 'success'). The corresponding title, 'Lord of the Imperial Surname' (國姓爺 / *Guoxingye*), gives rise to the name by which he is traditionally known in Europe: Koxinga (used throughout this paper, except in quotations). As Ming resistance crumbled, Zheng Zhilong defected to the Manchu Qing, prompting a split with his son. Koxinga's Japanese mother, only recently arrived in China, was killed around this time when Qing troops captured the family base of Xiamen in Fujian.

Exploiting the Zhengs' maritime power, Koxinga was able to mount a remarkably sustained rearguard action against Qing forces. In 1659, he launched an attack on Nanjing that nearly succeeded in capturing the southern capital, but poor strategy and hubris instead led to a crushing defeat. Now confined to his island base at Xiamen, Koxinga struggled to retain and supply his remaining followers. His response was to invade Taiwan and expel the Dutch, longstanding trading partners and rivals. After months of stubborn resistance by the greatly outnumbered Dutch garrison, his forces triumphed in early 1662. The Dutch withdrew, and Koxinga set about transforming the island into an agricultural colony for his troops, beginning the process of establishing a regular administration from his new 'Eastern Capital' at Tainan.

It is possible that this success prompted thoughts of further conquest, since Koxinga wrote to the Spanish governor in Manila threatening to invade. But before he could make good on such threats, a mysterious illness struck him down in June 1662, at the age of just 39. An adulterous affair by his son, Zheng Jing, reportedly hastened his death by driving him wild with rage. That same son succeeded him, decamping to Taiwan in 1663 after losing Xiamen to the Qing. Zheng Jing continued to harry the Manchus along the Fujian coast, reestablishing a base there during the revolt of the 'three feudatories'. However, with Qing authority firmly reestablished across South China by the late 1670s, Zheng forces were once again confined to Taiwan. Having pacified the mainland, the Qing decided to snuff out this last redoubt of Ming loyalism. The task was entrusted to Shi Lang, a former Zheng henchman, who led a naval expedition that in 1683 finally defeated Zheng forces and secured the surrender of Koxinga's grandson, Zheng Keshuang.

The many faces of heroism

In his 1977 study, Croizier noted that these 'bare bones' of Koxinga's life have formed the basis for various colourful narratives of heroism over the succeeding centuries. First came his postmortem metamorphosis 'from symbol of anti-Manchu resistance to [Qing]-sponsored exemplar of Confucian loyalty' (5). In the popular and official imagination, Koxinga's unfilial refusal to follow his father in defecting to the new regime was trumped by his loyal devotion to the fallen dynasty and the ruler to whom he had pledged fealty. By 1787, this sworn enemy of the Manchus had been inscribed in the imperially certified Confucian pantheon of 'loyal and pure' (忠潔) officials (35). Meanwhile, on Taiwan, he was celebrated as a folk hero who had opened up the island to mass settlement by Han Chinese. 'In Chinese folklore it is a short step from culture hero to deity' (41), and Koxinga swiftly accomplished that transition. In 1930, a Japanese survey found him venerated as chief deity in 57 temples across the island; he was a secondary deity in many more (42).

Like the Qing before them, Japanese colonial administrators were keen to co-opt the Koxinga legend for their own purposes. Shortly after seizing Taiwan in 1895, they remodelled Tainan's Koxinga Temple, constructed in 1875 by the Qing Governor, as a Shinto shrine. Downplaying his Ming loyalism and, more generally, his Chinese identity, they instead stressed his local significance. As Croizier puts it, 'he was not just half-Japanese: he was all Taiwanese' (60). Gradually, at the hands of colonial propagandists, Koxinga was more completely 'Nipponised', with his traditional virtues of loyalty, determination, and courage credited to the influence of his Japanese mother.

If in Japanese-occupied Taiwan Koxinga remained a 'paragon of an essentially prenationalistic political loyalty and culture' (61), in China he became a proto-typical Chinese nationalist. The Qing sponsored his Tainan temple in an effort to buttress dynastic loyalty in the face of foreign encroachment. However, he soon became a potent symbol for anti-Manchu champions of 'China for the Chinese'. This nationalist reinvention was influenced by intellectual currents in Japan, where Chinese students, imbibing pseudo-Darwinian notions of racial struggle, hailed him both for opposing the foreign Manchus, and for demonstrating the capacity of the 'yellow race' to defeat the 'white race' (55). Following the fall of the Qing in 1911, rhetoric of unity amongst the 'five races' of the new Chinese Republic overtook earlier anti-Manchuism, and celebration of Koxinga was for some time more subdued (except in his native Fujian). The Japanese invasion in the 1930s spurred a renewed enthusiasm for this exemplar of anti-colonial resistance – somewhat ironically, given his Japanese antecedents, which were invariably ignored or downplayed (57).

The Kuomintang-Communist Civil War, and consequent division of China, inaugurated a fresh contest over Koxinga's legacy. In Taiwan, the old temple, latterly a Shinto shrine, was once again repurposed to celebrate this Chinese 'national hero' (see below). The KMT accounts emphasised his manifold contributions to

Taiwan's development, but always 'in the larger context of national [i.e. Chinese] recovery' (69). Koxinga thus served as an avatar for the KMT itself: Desiring to trumpet its achievements on Taiwan, but insisting on the island's status as a mere 'base for recovery' of the mainland.

While on Taiwan the KMT's association of Koxinga with anti-imperialism was relatively muted, for their Communist (CCP) rivals this was crucial. The 1962 tercentenary of Taiwan's 'recovery' coincided with a spike in KMT-CCP tension, and both sides marked the anniversary with considerable fanfare (73). Equating US support for the KMT with Dutch colonialism, the CCP invoked Koxinga as an inspiration for Taiwan's 'liberation'. A decade later, rapprochement with the Americans prompted a toning down of this anti-imperialism. Nonetheless, unlike other 'national heroes' from the old ruling classes, Koxinga was never denounced during the Cultural Revolution. His image, Croizier wrote, remained 'intact waiting in reserve for the time when historical heroes might once again be involved in the name of national defence and also for any change in the Taiwan situation which might again make armed liberation a high priority item' (74).

Revisiting Koxinga's legacy today

The 'Taiwan situation' has indeed undergone dramatic change over the succeeding decades. In 1982, the 'one country, two systems' model for Taiwan's 'peaceful reunification' was written into the PRC Constitution. Despite emphatic rejection of that prescription by the KMT, the more emollient policies of a post-Mao regime focused on economic growth, along with Taiwan's growing international isolation, paved the way for a limited rapprochement in the late 1980s and early 1990s. Schooled as they were in Marxist historical materialism, China's rulers believed that mutually beneficial economic ties would swing popular sentiment their way in restive peripheral regions from Tibet to Taiwan. The '1992 Consensus', negotiated by informal representatives of the ROC and PRC, sealed a *modus vivendi* based on common acknowledgement of 'One China' and enhanced commercial and cultural ties, further expanded from 2008 under the KMT President Ma Yingjeow (Vickers 2010, 2017). More recently, however, Beijing's increasingly brutal crackdowns on assorted critics have intensified Taiwanese unease, contributing to the 2016 and 2020 electoral victories of the independence-leaning Democratic Progressive Party (DPP). In May 2020, the word 'peaceful' was pointedly omitted from the reference to Taiwan's 'reunification' in the Chinese premier's annual work report to the National People's Congress (Straits Times 2020). Whether 'armed liberation' is back on Beijing's agenda, and what that might imply for Koxinga's role in Communist propaganda, remain open questions.

The fate of Koxinga's reputation through earlier cross-Strait vicissitudes nonetheless offers a fascinating window into the evolving political and cultural importance of heroic figures from the Chinese past. As we shall see, Koxinga in fact emerged early from Cultural Revolution cold storage. The new emphasis on 'peaceful reunification' that accompanied Beijing's awkward embrace of capitalism lent fresh importance to his symbolic embodiment of cross-Strait unity. From the 1980s, official definitions of heroism underwent a significant shift, as old 'class enemies' were rehabilitated and figures from 'minority nationalities' were accorded greater prominence, reflecting efforts to heal the divisions of the Mao era (Yan and Vickers 2019). But as Croizier observed, Koxinga had never been denounced during the Mao era; his heroic status unimpugned, he was available for rapid deployment on the propaganda front line.

In Taiwan, the situation was somewhat more complicated, reflecting the island's remarkable transition from one-party state to pluralistic democracy, and the debate over national identity thereby unleashed. Croizier had speculated that 'Taiwan independence' might emerge as a 'third claimant' to Koxinga's legacy, even though much pro-independence literature seemed 'ambivalent about him' (1977: 75). That ambivalence was hardly surprising, given the efforts of the Chiang regime to associate itself with the Zheng Dynasty; a 1970 survey found that a sample of mostly 'native Taiwanese' (i.e. not 'mainlander') secondary students overwhelmingly associated Koxinga with the virtues of 'loyalty' and '[Chinese] patriotism'. Croizier quotes a pro-independence informant telling him that 'Koxinga as a person is not important', but that 'the 20,000 people who came with him are important: they are the most ancient ancestors of most of the present Taiwanese' (75). As noted above, the orthodox Chinese nationalist interpretation of Koxinga's legacy still prevailed in Tainan as late as 1993.

By then, however, Taiwan's political tides were turning rapidly, especially in the hero's old southern stamping grounds. In 1993, the KMT lost Tainan County to the pro-independence DPP, with the Tainan City mayoralty following in 1997. County and City (merged in 2010) have been held by the DPP ever since. Meanwhile, following the arrival of full democracy in the 1990s, the ROC presidency has twice changed hands, the DPP taking power for the first time under Chen Shui-bian in 2000. There had already been a significant shift in identity discourse under the KMT's Taiwan-born President Lee Teng-hui. It was under Lee that the school curriculum, from 1997, first featured substantial coverage of Taiwan's own history, narrated from a Taiwanese perspective (Corcuff 2005). During the 1990s, museums also began to devote greater attention to exhibiting and exploring various aspects of the Taiwanese past (Vickers 2009), a trend that received further impetus under the post-2000 DPP administration.

Meanwhile, beyond 'Greater China', diplomatic and commercial shifts, growing tourism, and a burgeoning transnational heritage 'industry', have shaped interest in this harbinger of early modern 'globalisation'. In Japan's Nagasaki Prefecture, as we shall see, local actors in Koxinga's birthplace of Hirado have sought to tap growing interest in Taiwan and the PRC while also slotting the hero into a distinctive local narrative. Hirado has thus been one more venue for contesting interpretations of Koxinga's legacy.

Western interest in or awareness of Koxinga remains generally slight, although 2011 witnessed the publication of a major scholarly reevaluation of his military record (Andrade 2011). Andrade relates the conflict with the Dutch to a debate between advocates of a 'Eurocentric' interpretation of modern history, emphasizing Western scientific, technological, and commercial superiority, and 'revisionists' who 'see the rise of the west as part of a...deep [Eurasian] history of shared innovations in which Asian societies were prime movers' (8). This debate over the historical East-West balance of power and knowledge reflects contemporary interest in China's 'rise', and that of Asia more broadly. Andrade offers a nuanced critique of the 'revisionist' position, arguing that, while older claims for comprehensive Western superiority in technology and arms were overblown, the fact that Koxinga's forces were nearly defeated by the vastly outnumbered Dutch testifies to significant European advantages by the early 17th century.

Rather than engaging directly in such debates, this chapter analyses how Koxinga's historical significance has been interpreted for public consumption across East Asia over recent decades. It relates to a larger project on the role of history in negotiating identities around China's periphery, encompassing Hong Kong, Tibet, Mongolia, and Xinjiang, as well as Taiwan. That project examines shifting identity discourse in museums, memorials, and public culture, while also making some reference to school curricula and history textbooks. A key theme involves tensions between attempts to articulate a vision of China as 'multicultural' – encompassing both Han and non-Han ethnic groups – and increasing official and popular interest on the Chinese mainland in celebrating 'China's superior traditional culture', essentially identified with the Han alone. As we shall see, this tension between multiculturalism and Han chauvinism has special relevance for interpreting Koxinga's legacy, though in ways that reflect the distinctiveness of the Taiwanese 'case'.

It was originally my intention, before writing this essay, to visit sites related to Koxinga in mainland China as well as Taiwan and Japan. However, the Covid-19 crisis scuttled a planned trip to Fujian in early 2020, compelling me to rely primarily on second-hand sources for the discussion of mainland China. While much information is available online, or in exhibition catalogues and essays relating to symposia held in Taiwan, this cannot fully substitute for first-hand observation of the commemorative sites themselves. But the sources are nonetheless sufficient to support some tentative conclusions, so, rather than abandon the enterprise entirely, I offer this analysis as a record of a work in progress.

Contesting Koxinga's legacy in Hirado, Japan

Since the collapse of its colonial empire in 1945, Japan has been relegated very much to the margins of the Koxinga cult. Nonetheless, the status of Hirado (平戸) as the hero's birthplace has made it an important arena for Chinese and Taiwanese commemorative efforts. And this, in turn, has helped sustain significant local interest in using the Koxinga legend to promote Hirado's history and culture, and its attractions as a tourist destination.

Koxinga's career as a Japanese folk hero long predates his deployment as a colonial propaganda tool. His fame in Edo-era Japan was assured by his starring role in a 1715 work by the famous Japanese playwright, Chikamatsu Monzaemon (近松門左衛門), Battles of Koxinga (國姓爺合戰). Here he exemplifies the supreme samurai virtue of loyalty, while engaging in astounding martial feats such as subduing a tiger with his bare hands. In this telling, his Chinese paternity is an exotic detail in the story of an archetypal Japanese warrior-hero (Croizier 1977: 32). Meanwhile, he was also honoured locally in Hirado, with a stele erected in 1852 on the seafront near his reputed birthplace on Kawachi (川内) beach by the local daimyo (lord) of the Matsuura (松浦) lineage.

Koxinga's reputation made him useful to colonial propagandists during the early 20th century, but in the more inward-looking Japan of the post-war era, his star waned. A Koxinga Festival (鄭成功祭) has been held annually on his birthday, 14 July, featuring a traditional dance, the 'Hirado Jangara' (平戸のジャンガラ). But Japanese interest in him has been limited essentially to Hirado, and even there has been spurred largely by external actors.

The website of the Koxinga Memorial in Kawachi records that, in 1962, the ancestral temple of the Zheng Clan in Tainan, Taiwan, donated some 'sand' (砂) to Hirado City, and that 'some time later' a temple was constructed on Maruyama in Kawachi.[1] Interestingly, this Japanese website makes no mention of the significance of the year 1962: The 300th anniversary of Koxinga's expulsion of the Dutch from Taiwan. Moreover, the gap between that symbolic donation of Taiwanese earth and establishment of the Koxinga Temple seems to have been substantial. From at least 1982 onwards, the Zheng Clan Association in Tainan (台南市鄭氏宗親会) sent representatives to participate in the annual Koxinga Festival.[2] In 1994, on the hero's 370th birthday, the association donated a statue to Kawachi's new Koxinga Temple.[3] This shows Koxinga dressed in the robes of a Ming Dynasty official – a distinctively Chinese image contrasting to his traditional portrayal in Japanese folk culture. From the following year (1995), Tainan City sent an official delegation to participate in the annual festival of Koxinga's birth on 14 July.

1995 was also the year when Nan An City (南安市) in Fujian's Quanzhou (泉州) municipality, the ancestral home of the Zheng Clan, formally established a 'twinning' relationship with Hirado, becoming a 'friendship city' (友好都市). Like Tainan, Nan An usually sends delegations to attend the Koxinga Festival. Determined not to be outdone in statue diplomacy by the Taiwanese, in 2014 Nan An donated a monumental concrete statue of Koxinga. This was erected next to the 1852 stele, in what was now designated the 'Koxinga Park' (鄭成功公園) on the Kawachi seafront. This statue, paired with one in Nan An itself, features an inscription hailing the 'hero of Asia'. Meanwhile, in 2008 a smaller statue of the infant Koxinga with his mother was erected through local subscription, to a design created by one of his descendants (Figure 9.1). This was placed next to the shrine where the ceremonies honouring Koxinga are performed every year during the festival marking his birthday.

FIGURE 9.1 Statue of Koxinga and his mother at his shrine in Hirado.

Adjacent to that statue and shrine, in 2013, a new Koxinga memorial was constructed: 'a reproduction of the family home of the East Asian hero', constructed in part with Taiwanese support.[4] From that year, the Taipei Representative Office in Fukuoka began sending a representative to participate in the annual Koxinga Festival. 2013 also witnessed formalisation of ties between Hirado and Tainan, with an 'agreement for the promotion of citizen exchanges' (「台南市民與平戶市民交流促進協議」), according Tainan the status of an 'exchange city' (交流都市). Reflecting Chinese sensitivities, this stopped short of granting Tainan the formal 'sister city' status enjoyed by Nan An. Nonetheless, Nan An was meanwhile intensifying its own efforts to make its mark on Hirado, donating the statue for erection on the seafront the following year.

Scions of the Zheng lineage, as well as officials from Taiwan and Fujian, have thus vied to associate themselves with commemorative efforts in Hirado. But it is hard to tell what impact this has had on local consciousness. The Koxinga Festival is a significant date on the local calendar, bringing opportunities to promote Hirado as a destination for tourism from Taiwan and China; the lobby of a large hotel on the Kawachi seafront features yet another statue of the boy hero and his mother. However, in the context of the broader heritage landscape in Hirado, let alone Japan, Koxinga's profile remains relatively low.

It is noticeable, for example, that Japanese contributions to international exhibitions on Koxinga held in Tainan in 2007 and 2011 (see below) are relatively lukewarm regarding his heroic status. Hirado's Matsuura Museum, housed in the ancestral home of the Matsuura lineage, provided artefacts for these exhibitions. In an introductory essay for the 2007 exhibition catalogue, the museum's head of 'exhibitions and outreach' wrote on 'trading conditions between Hirado and Western Europe', while a colleague contributed a separate paper on 'Hirado as a port'. Rather than focusing on the exploits of the Zheng clan, these essays discuss how Hirado prospered from around 1550, when the Ming embargo on China's external trade made the port an attractive base for Portuguese merchants, until 1641, when the Bakufu decided to confine the Dutch to the island of Dejima in the port of Nagasaki (Okayama 2007: 34–37).

Indeed, in Hirado and Nagasaki today, commemorating early contacts with Europe seemingly takes priority over honouring an 'Asian' hero. For the contemporary Japanese public, European exoticism appears a stronger draw than Asian heroism. Since 1992, a vast theme park, Huis Ten Bosch, featuring an imaginary Dutch townscape, has been one of Kyushu's main tourist attractions. In the early 2000s, the famous Dutch trading post of Dejima in Nagasaki city was reconstructed as a tourist attraction. In Hirado, too, a Dutch warehouse originally erected in 1639 and demolished shortly thereafter at the orders of the Tokugawa Shogunate has been reconstructed at great expense. Opened in 2011, this houses a somewhat scant exhibition on early modern Japan's links to the West. And in 2018, a number of sites in Hirado and elsewhere in Nagasaki associated with the 'hidden Christian' communities of the 17th–19th centuries were granted 'World Heritage' status by UNESCO. In short, in his Japanese birthplace today, the nemesis of the Dutch on Taiwan finds his reputation comprehensively overshadowed by his defeated European enemies.

Koxinga as an icon of One China patriotism in the post-Mao People's Republic of China

In 1982, while Koxinga's Taiwanese descendants marked the 320th anniversary of his victory over the Dutch by attending Hirado's annual festival, a much larger commemorative event took place on the Chinese mainland. That July, a sizeable international conference was convened in Koxinga's old base of Xiamen. In attendance were 121 individuals, including scholars from America, Japan, and Hong Kong, with the Japanese delegation including two scholars from Nagasaki University. A report by one of these, Ichikawa Shinichi, testifies to the flourishing state of Sino-Japanese ties in these years, noting that Japanese participation was facilitated by the Nagasaki authorities, the local television station, and the China-Japan Friendship Association (Ichikawa 1982). By contrast, cross-Strait relations at this point remained largely frozen. Scholars from Taiwan were invited, but the Taipei authorities forbade them to attend. The Kuomintang leadership, still smarting from the ROC's loss of international status following the United States's 1979 switch of recognition to Beijing, were in no mood to connive at Communist appropriation of Koxinga's legacy.

The sensitivity of the timing was exacerbated, for the ROC authorities on Taiwan, by the fact that 1982 also witnessed the enshrining in the PRC Constitution of the 'one country, two systems' formula for reunification. Seen in that context, the Xiamen conference appears as a classic United Front exercise in enlisting sympathetic forces in tacit support of the Party's agenda. Koxinga's reputation had survived the Cultural Revolution relatively unscathed due both to his totemic status as an anti-imperialist champion, and his role in 'recovering' Taiwan for China. Anti-foreign rhetoric, prominent in commemoration of the 1962 tercentenary, appears to have been somewhat subdued in 1982. Ichikawa, referencing a similar conference held in 1962, notes that the 1982 event represented a 'step forward' in terms of scholarship. Chinese participants displayed more interest in the economic and commercial activities of the Zheng clan, and in Koxinga's resistance to the Qing, rather than simply in his recovery of Taiwan from 'colonialists' (Ichikawa 1982: 63). However, one of Ichikawa's Japanese colleagues criticised the Chinese for their 'lack of interest in foreign documents' and neglect of Koxinga's religious significance (63). Nationalist boilerplate predominated among the Chinese presentations, many rehearsing details of the Tainan battles, long a staple of Communist accounts (Croizier 1977: 72). Scholars from Xiamen University spoke on Koxinga's 'great contribution to the recovery of Taiwan' and 'support from Taiwan's Mountain Tribes' for his campaign (Ichikawa 1982: 62), exhibiting a characteristic Communist penchant for underlining the 'unity of all China's fraternal nationalities in the face of foreign imperialism' (Croizier 1977: 72).

Where national unification was concerned, Beijing's sights were by 1982 trained most immediately not on Taiwan, but on Hong Kong, where 'one country, two systems' was due to be piloted. As Croizier noted, interest in Koxinga within Hong Kong was minimal by the 1970s (77). However, there was a small Hong Kong presence at the 1982 Xiamen conference, which included the businessman Yu Xinhe (余新河).[5] As China's economy opened up in the early 1980s, overseas Chinese and entrepreneurs from Hong Kong and Taiwan travelled there both to explore business opportunities and to reconnect with native regions. In many cases, investment and sentiment went together; a lavish donation to an officially prized local scheme could help oil the wheels of commerce. While it is unclear what role, if any, such considerations played here, Yu and another Hong Kong businessman, Lu Zhenwan (吕振万), both born in the Zheng hometown of Quanzhou, funded a major extension of the Koxinga Memorial there, which incorporated the old Zheng clan ancestral temple. Work on renovating and extending it began in October 1982 and was completed in 1987.

The Quanzhou Memorial had originally been established in 1962 (the tercentenary of the defeat of the Dutch) as a satellite of the Koxinga Memorial on Gulanyu Island in Xiamen. In addition to various commemorative artefacts, the Xiamen memorial featured paintings of grateful Taiwan residents welcoming the hero, and of his forces battering a Dutch fortress. A 1985 guidebook also includes images of the Koxinga Shrine in Tainan, with the text commenting that 'although Taiwan has not yet been reunited with the motherland, Chinese people on both sides of the Taiwan Strait are all descendants of the Yan and Huang Emperors and, sharing the same national sentiment, honour and reverence Koxinga' (Zhang 1985: 40). Stressing that the establishment of the Xiamen memorial in 1962 took place in the context of commemorative events on both sides of the Taiwan Strait, the text also references the 1982 conference. The guide concludes with a rousing paean to Koxinga's patriotic example, which inspires all 'sons and daughters of China' to 'struggle for the revival of China and the unification of the motherland' (42).

The tropes of Koxinga commemoration on the mainland appear remarkably consistent from the 1960s to 1990s, notwithstanding considerable social, political, and ideological shifts. In 1994, Fujian's scholar-bureaucrats marked the 370th anniversary of Koxinga's birth with the publication of a collection of essays (Fujian History Journal 1994). In his introductory paper, the head of the local 'Chronicle Association' (福建省地方志学会), Chen Shu-tian, noted that Koxinga lived at a time of 'acute and complex internal and external social contradictions' and 'momentous change', emphasising that the opportunity for heroism was shaped by impersonal historical forces acting through 'the people':

> Externally, Western colonialists ceaselessly invaded the eastern seaboard of our country; internally, the Ming monarchical government was beset by corruption, prompting the peasant rebellion led by Li Zicheng and Zhang Xianzhong, the entry of the Qing army within the passes, and an anti-Qing struggle by soldiers and common people. The people's struggle against... monarchical rule and western colonial invasion thrust Koxinga onto the political stage, and gave him a crucial role to play. He energetically threw himself into the struggle, leading the soldiers and people of the southwest in resistance to the Qing, and gathering a large army to venture eastwards across the ocean, expel the Dutch colonialists, and recover Taiwan. He thus made an imperishable historic contribution to his nation..., and set a glorious example to the peoples of the East and of the whole world of struggle against Western colonialists.
>
> *(Chen 1994: 1)*

The Hong Kong-based benefactor of Quanzhou's Koxinga Memorial, Yu Xinhe, contributed a lengthy essay to the same collection on 'Koxinga as an International Hero' (Yu 1994). Writing as head of the 'Hong Kong and Provincial Koxinga Commemoration Association', Yu stresses Koxinga's role in defeating Dutch 'colonialists', and hails his international fame. However, this commemorative effort had no obvious cross-Strait dimension; while several Zheng clan members contributed, they do not appear to have been Taiwan residents.[6] Reflecting strict political messaging in the post-Tiananmen years, the 1994 special issue prioritises Marxist-patriotic orthodoxy over United Front outreach.

While the achievement of the '1992 consensus' may have reassured some PRC officials of the stability of the Taiwan-mainland status quo, the rise of Taiwanese 'nativism' during the 1990s, culminating in the victory of the DPP in the presidential election, radically challenged any lingering hopes of smooth progress towards reunification. By the early 2000s, the media in mainland China were fulminating against the DPP administration's policies on culture and heritage, which they dubbed a 'cultural independence ploy' (「文化台独」小动作) (see Vickers 2009). At the same time, it was evident that efforts by Beijing during the 1990s to intimidate the Taiwanese electorate into backing pro-unification candidates had backfired. In the early 2000s, the Chinese Communist Party (CCP) changed tack, and began assiduously to court its old foe, the KMT, appealing to a shared commitment to Chinese nationalism. It was against this backdrop that the cultural authorities stepped up efforts to project a vision of cross-Strait unity grounded less in martial heroics, and more in appeals to shared culture and ancestry.

Embodying this cultural unification counter-ploy was a large new museum opened in Quanzhou in 2006: The China Museum of Fujian-Taiwan Kinship (中国闽台缘博物馆). Here Koxinga retains a prominent role, but not a show-stealing one. A large relief sculpture depicts him in heroic posture, astride a horse; there are images of his defeat of the Dutch, though his Ming loyalism and anti-Manchu resistance are not highlighted (his significance here has everything to do with Taiwan-mainland unity). In depicting Taiwan as Chinese 'from time immemorial', the exhibition highlights its illegitimate sundering from the 'motherland' by Dutch and Japanese 'imperialists'. KMT officials represent China in a diorama depicting the Japanese surrender on Taiwan in 1945. Reflecting widespread official and popular fixation in the early 2000s on the anti-Japan war (a theme central to efforts at CCP-KMT rapprochement; Coble 2007), the exhibition text claims:

> the Taiwan people and the people of China's mainland fought bloody battles hand in hand, shoulder to shoulder and won the great victory in the resistance against Japan. And Taiwan at last returned into the embrace of her motherland. In the struggle for the independence and emancipation of [the] Chinese nation, the people on both sides of the Straits shed their bloods and lay down their lives (*sic*), and fought jointly against the Japanese aggressors, forming an important part of [the] anti-fascism struggle in the world.[7]

The emphasis on resistance to Japanese aggression perhaps dictated a somewhat subdued role for a half-Japanese hero, but this museum was designed primarily to celebrate a shared cultural inheritance (including shared anti-Japanese patriotism) rather than military conflict and heroism. The message of ethnocultural unity is unsubtly proclaimed in the entrance lobby with a vast mural depicting the roots of a tree.[8] Although Communist orthodoxy earlier suppressed the religious aspects of the Koxinga 'cult', here shared religious beliefs are given prominent billing, with the goddess Mazu, widely worshipped in both Fujian and Taiwan, honoured with a monumental sculpture. Reconstructed Taiwanese temples and streetscapes allow mainland visitors to marvel at the preservation of a Chinese cultural 'essence' on Taiwan. Meanwhile, the Chinese name of the museum itself, featuring the term 'yuan' (缘), invokes the concept of a common fate or destiny, underlining the moral that shared culture and ancestry determine unity in a shared future.

Koxinga saw service in the mainland's cultural charm offensive during the early 2000s, as Koxinga-related sites in Fujian and Tainan joined forces for joint celebrations (see following section). And when the KMT candidate, Ma Ying-jeow, won the ROC presidency in 2008, both cultural exchange and cross-Strait tourism received a massive boost. Direct flights between Taiwan and the mainland opened up, tourism boomed, and cultural institutions such as the National Palace Museums in Beijing and Taipei engaged in unprecedented forms of collaboration (Vickers 2011). Seeking to build on their gradual rapprochement with the KMT, the CCP leadership looked both to culture and commerce as means of binding Taiwan more closely to the mainland through mutually beneficial exchanges.

These efforts unravelled rapidly from 2013–2014 onwards, as Taiwanese anxiety over Chinese encroachment fuelled the 'Sunflower Movement', scuppering a much-heralded trade agreement, and paving the way for the DPP's 2016 return to power. Prior to that election, Beijing's efforts to shore up the KMT culminated in November 2015 in an unprecedented meeting between Xi Jinping and Ma Ying-jeow, in their capacity as party leaders. However, following the KMT's electoral defeat, attempts by Beijing to punish the DPP's separatist impertinence, along with intensified repression on the mainland and in Hong Kong, further alienated Taiwanese public opinion. As in the handling of its external relations more broadly, with respect to Taiwan, China increasingly abandoned charm for intimidation.

But the early phase of Xi Jinping's leadership witnessed a continuation of the emollient strategy inherited from his predecessors. The auguries initially seemed promising, since the year of Xi's accession, 2012, also saw the KMT's Ma Ying-jeow re-elected as ROC President. 2012 also marked the 350th anniversary of Koxinga's 'recovery' of Taiwan. Amongst the commemorative events were an exhibition and conference in Beijing itself, hosted by the 'Taiwan Native Place Association' (北京台灣會館), a pseudo-civil society body representing the capital's Taiwanese residents (BTNPA 2012). This exemplified both the continuing enthusiasm of mainland officialdom for rhetoric of shared ancestry, culture, and anti-imperial nationalism, and a widening gulf in sentiment with mainstream discourse on Taiwan.

Koxinga Across the Strait: Exhibition to celebrate the 350th Anniversary of Koxinga's recovery of Taiwan was given a punning title in Chinese (成功在兩岸), translatable as 'Success across the Strait'.[9] On display were images from the plethora of sites worldwide which related to the cult of Koxinga as patriotic hero or folk deity, with the former role very much to the fore. The exhibition opened with encomia from past and present luminaries, including Zhang Xueliang (anti-Japanese warlord) and Guo Muoro (leading Communist historian and ideologue). Included in this line-up was Zheng Yanfen, a Koxinga descendant and Guangdong Province native who, after fleeing to Taiwan after the Civil War, in 1974 founded the Global Zheng Clan Association (世界郑氏宗亲总会). Based in Taipei, it has branches worldwide and has organised international gatherings of Zheng descendants, including a large event in Henan in 1992. Zheng Yanfen is quoted praising his ancestor's 'spirit of migration, revolutionary spirit and patriotic spirit'.

Prefatory remarks by mainland-based figures unanimously echoed these sentiments. The head of Beijing's Taiwan Association (北京市台联会长) declared that 'the spirit of Zheng Chenggong' inspires all 'descendants of the Yan and Yellow Emperors (炎黄子孫)' to 'work together to revitalise the Chinese nation, and once more summon up the heroism of the past (再敲雄風)!' Appealing to 'kinship' in terms of 'common roots and origins' (同根同源), he wrote of 'Chinese culture (中华文化) as an unstoppable life source (割不断的源泉) flowing in the bloodstream of people on both sides of the Strait' (BTNPA 2012: 8). Zheng Jian, a Taiwan-born, Beijing-resident scion of the Zheng clan, emphasised Chinese patriotism, cross-Strait unity, and the need for constant vigilance against the Western and Japanese conspiracy to 'contain' China (10).

These themes were elaborated by Ji Xin, Chairman of the 'Alliance for the Reunification of China' (中国统一联盟), a Taiwan-based association founded in 1988. Ji derived four morals from Koxinga's heroic example (9): The bond of shared culture and racial 'origins' (同根铜钟) between Taiwan and mainland; the hero's 'spirit' of defending China's 'territorial integrity'; the importance of 'correcting' the mistaken ideas about identity harboured by some on Taiwan; and the need further to intensify cross-Strait exchanges. He particularly emphasised the link between reunification, resisting 'the encircling anti-Chinese power of the West (西方反华势力), and bringing about the Great Revival of the Chinese Nation (中华民族才能伟大复兴)'. These remarks precisely echo the key tropes of CCP propaganda as of 2012, not least in evoking memories of Chinese victimhood to reinforce the importance of national strength and 'revival'. Taiwanese separatism is also dismissed as a marginal affair, or (in so far as it is acknowledged) as the product of imperialist 'brainwashing', while there is an assumption that greater cross-Strait exchange will naturally yield peaceful progression towards unity.

However, Zheng Yanfen's successor as head of the Global Zheng Clan Association, Zheng Yangyi, struck a different tone in his preface. Having described the various modes of Koxinga veneration, he concluded by wishing 'success' to the commemorative conference, 'health' to all participants, good fortune, 'peaceful cross-Strait development', and 'the creation of a better future for all our descendants' (11). The orchestrated effusions of Ji Xin and his 'patriotic alliance' no doubt flattered mainland officials, but by 2012 such sentiments were marginal within Taiwan. The measured apoliticism of Zheng Yangyi was far more in tune with mainstream opinion there. But in early 21st-century Taiwan, too, Koxinga has been deployed for overtly political purposes, albeit often in ways diametrically opposed to those seen across the Strait.

Koxinga's legacy in contemporary Taiwan – cross-Strait ambassador or totem of Taiwanese multiculturalism?

In his assessment of attitudes towards Koxinga's legacy, Croizier painted a mixed picture of the situation on 1970s Taiwan. While KMT propaganda appeared successfully to have entrenched the hero's reputation for filial loyalty and emphatically *Chinese* patriotism, precisely such associations helped account for ambivalence amongst independence-leaning Taiwanese (1977: 74–78). As noted above, as of the early 1990s, the public face of Koxinga in Taiwan was still very much that of the Chinese patriot. However, given his diverse repertoire of roles in Taiwan – from Confucian exemplar, folk deity and symbol of Japanese-Taiwanese unity to Chinese national hero – there was, Croizier remarked, 'always the possibility that under different political circumstances Koxinga might well emerge as symbol of yet another cause' (78). And, up to a point, such has indeed proven the case.

The association of Koxinga with a new vision of a 'diverse', 'multicultural' Taiwan distinct from China can be traced back at least to the 'nativisation' (*bentuhua*) movement of the 1990s. As democracy took hold, the DPP's challenge to 'mainlander' dominance of the island's politics saw the party sweep to local power across southern Taiwan from the mid-1990s. Meanwhile, under President Lee Teng-hui, elements within the governing KMT also saw the electoral logic of signalling greater recognition of Taiwan's distinctiveness.

In 1997, pressure for such recognition yielded a significant innovation in the school curriculum, with the introduction of a course, *Knowing Taiwan* (認識台湾), that for the first time mandated substantial instruction in local history for secondary students. The preface to the *Knowing Taiwan: History* text (other volumes dealt with 'Society' and 'Geography') emphasised 'cultural pluralism' as a 'special characteristic' of Taiwanese history. It also portrayed the 17th century as Taiwan's formative phase, when Han people 'plagued by difficulties and dangers' sought to 'escape troubles on the mainland by coming to Taiwan' (NICT 2001: 4; quoted in Vickers 2007). The text portrayed these Han as working together with the island's aboriginal people 'to shape a new territory', and identified 'the heroic spirit of defying danger' and 'overcoming difficulties' as 'unique characteristics of Taiwan's people'.

Especially after the DPP's Chen Shui-bian assumed the ROC presidency in 2000, Koxinga became associated with this narrative of a multicultural Taiwan emerging out of the struggles of the 17th century. Rather than demonising his 'imperialist' opponents, this new approach sought to weave a Dutch thread into the tapestry of Taiwanese multiculturalism. In 2003, Tu Cheng-sheng, the DPP-appointed Director of the National Palace Museum (and formerly editor of the *Renshi Taiwan: Society* volume), organised a special exhibition: *Ilha Formosa – the Emergence of Taiwan on the World Scene in the 17th Century*. This credited the Dutch with making Taiwan 'part of the system of international commerce', while the Cheng (Zheng) regime founded by Koxinga 'developed the island into an independent [maritime] kingdom' (NPM 2003: 2). The exhibition gave star billing to the Europeans and Taiwan's aborigines, with a supporting role for Koxinga as the Netherlanders' nemesis. Stressing the transformative impact of the European arrival in East Asia (Ts'ao 2003: 16), a contributor to the exhibition catalogue noted that Taiwan was 'isolated from Han people' before the mid-Ming (14).

Far from hailing Koxinga's heroic anti-imperialism, the exhibition's account of the siege of Fort Zeelandia adopted a neutral tone, emphasising the closely fought nature of the battle (Lin 2003). In the English exhibition guide, Tu describes both Koxinga and his Dutch counterpart, Coyett, leaving 'the field' as 'honored heroes' (58). But doubt is also cast on Koxinga's heroic status, Tu noting that while 'in both China and Taiwan, Koxinga is portrayed as a national hero in traditional Sino-centric historical literature', Dutch accounts 'tend to highlight the violence and cruelty' of his army, 'showing the troops maltreating soldiers and women alike and killing four missionaries' (59). Tu also stresses the pragmatic rather than patriotic rationale for Koxinga's move to Taiwan (Tu 2003: 53). And in so far as occupation by the Zheng clan provoked eventual conquest by the Qing, he presents it as contributing to Taiwan's fate as a 'marginalized frontier' of the Qing empire (61), when the island was 'little more than an outpost' (62). For Tu and other more outspoken advocates of Taiwanese independence, the expulsion of the Dutch, in paving the way for Taiwan's incorporation into the Chinese Empire, was if anything to be regretted.

Koxinga and his clan received more extensive and somewhat more positive treatment in a ten-volume comic-book history of Taiwan published around this time. This was edited by Wu Mi-cha, doyen of the island's independence-leaning historians, but endorsed both by the KMT's Ma Ying-jeow and by ROC President Chen Shui-bian (Wu 2005).[10] Nonetheless, this nuanced portrayal, occupying one entire volume of the series, stopped well short of uncritical hagiography. Koxinga's story is woven into a larger narrative shaped by a teleology of Taiwanese nation-building, even if the terminology of nationhood is avoided. Koxinga here is part Confucian loyalist and revered founder of Hoklo Taiwan (the 'prince who opened up the mountains'), but also an irascible father and flawed leader whose chief interests lay in China. His ultimate legacy is represented as including Taiwan's incorporation into the Chinese empire, with decidedly mixed consequences for the island's inhabitants, especially the indigenous tribes. His importance for Taiwan is thus indisputable, but he is not a distinctively Taiwanese hero.

The commemorative landscape in Tainan

If the embrace of Koxinga by Taiwanese nationalists has been somewhat guarded, he remains a local hero in southern and central Taiwan. Successive regimes have thus invoked Koxinga to shore up their legitimacy in this region in particular. This is reflected in the vicissitudes of Tainan's 'Temple of the Lord who Opened up the Mountains' (開山王廟), established by the Zheng clan in 1662. In 1875, the Qing authorities constructed a shrine on this site 'in the architectural style of Fuzhou', honouring Koxinga's loyalty to the Ming (hence its full title: 明延平郡王祠). The Japanese restructured the edifice as a Shinto Shrine, the only one anywhere in their empire dedicated to a Chinese god. To mark the 1961 tercentenary of his victory over the Dutch, the KMT regime established a 'Commission for the Restoration of Historical Monuments of the National Hero, Koxinga' which, having gathered

FIGURE 9.2   Tainan's Koxinga Temple (延平郡王祠), with ceremonial gate erected by the post-war KMT regime (replacing a torī gate erected by the Japanese colonial regime).

donations from people 'from all walks of life', restored the temple's Qing-era name but demolished locally distinctive architectural elements, remodelling it in 'the style of northern palaces' (Figure 9.2).[11] Further signalling the Koxinga cult's subordination to secular Chinese nationalism, in 1965 Chiang Kai-shek ordered the statue of the hero-deity moved outside the temple to give it the public prominence appropriate to a 'national hero'. In 2008, Tainan's DPP mayor, Hsiau Tien-Tsai, ordered the statue replaced on the temple altar so as to 'recover the original worshipping conditions'.[12] But meanwhile, a new equestrian statue of Koxinga, donated by the 'people' of Quanzhou, in Fujian Province, was erected nearby (Figure 9.3). A DPP-backed reemphasis on Koxinga as deified folk ancestor was thus accompanied by a mainland-sponsored bid to ensure continued prominence for the Chinese national hero.

Alongside this temple stands a thoroughly secular museum. This traces its origins to a 'Taiwan Records Bureau' (台湾資料館) established under the Japanese in 1932 in the Tainan suburb of Anping. In 1945, this was moved to the old Dutch fort of 'Provintia', and renamed the Tainan Municipal History Museum (台南市歷史館), before in 1964 moving to its current premises in a modernist building next to the temple, when it was once more retitled the Tainan Municipal Cultural Artifacts Exhibition Hall (台南市民族文物館) – its moniker when I first visited in 1993. In 2003, following a restoration, the institution rebranded itself the 'Koxinga Museum' (鄭成功文物館).

FIGURE 9.3 Equestrian statue donated by the city of Quanzhou near the Koxinga Temple in Tainan.

That rebranding took place in the context of a municipal drive to promote Tainan for tourism, and to build commercial links with the Chinese mainland at a time of economic difficulty. In 2002, the city inaugurated a new 'Koxinga Cultural Festival', which from 2004 featured considerable mainland/international involvement, especially from Fujian and Kyushu (TCCAB 2011: 4–5). In 2004, a symposium was convened in Quanzhou, and in 2005 a delegation from Tainan toured Koxinga-related sites in Fujian.[13] There was also a trip to Hirado, Kyushu, to visit the Matsuura Museum. These visits were related to preparations for a 2007 *Exhibition of Koxinga* at Tainan's Koxinga Museum, jointly organised by the municipal Cultural Affairs Bureau, the Matsuura Museum, and the Xiamen Koxinga Memorial Museum (Tainan City Government / NMH 2007). Further joint exhibitions occurred in 2009 and 2010, followed in 2011 by a *Sail with Koxinga* exhibition to mark the 350th anniversary of the hero's landing in Taiwan (TCCAB 2011). A centrepiece of this was a reconstructed 17th-century war junk, docked at Anping and opened to the public (178–180).

Tainan's commemorative landscape during the early 2000s featured diverse and sometimes conflicting messages. Lingering tropes of Chinese nationalism contended with expressions of the new Taiwanese nativism, while political and business elites sought both to sweeten local voters and consumers, and to attract tourism and investment from mainland China. A plaque at the Confucius Temple in 2005 credited Koxinga's successor, Zheng Jing, with building the temple and 'sowing the first seeds of Confucian culture in Taiwan's fertile soil'.

FIGURE 9.4   Entrance to the Zheng clan ancestral shrine in Tainan, flanked by statues of the boy Takamatsu with his Japanese mother (left) and of the adult Koxinga as Chinese national hero (right).

'For over three hundred years', it declared, 'the essence of Chinese culture (中華文化) passed down [within] these sacred halls'. Nearby, the Zheng clan ancestral shrine (鄭成功祖廟) has maintained eclectic ties to China, Japan, and Koxinga descendants worldwide: From 2000 a statue of the boy hero and his Japanese mother (donated by a descendant) has stood by the entrance, joined in 2017 by a bronze statue of the adult warrior donated by the Taiwanese *huiguan* in Beijing (Figure 9.4). But overall, since the 1990s, it is the multicultural aspects of Koxinga's story, rather than the conventional Chinese nationalist account, that have come to the fore.

The trope of multiculturalism was especially prominent in the Koxinga Museum following its rebranding in the early 2000s.[14] Against the backdrop of a large photograph of Koxinga's birthplace on the beach in Hirado, an introductory text hailed the ocean 'as a conduit for the distribution of goods in the 17th century', celebrating Koxinga as 'the most influential maritime figure of his time'. His commercial as well as military prowess were credited with opening up the 'new paradise' (新天地) of Taiwan. Although his achievements in China and Ming loyalism were acknowledged, the multicultural theme was stressed in a section on 'Koxinga's legacies: A Taiwan cultural perspective' (臺灣本土性). Elaborating his 'Cultural Characteristics' (文化特質), the exhibition noted that 'from the official point of view' (Qing, Republican, and Communist), he was celebrated as a 'brave national hero', before explaining other facets of his cultural significance:

As ancestor to many Taiwanese; as folk deity (神明); and as a legendary figure (傳奇人物) credited with fabulous deeds. A further section on 'Koxinga's Legacies: An International Perspective' (鄭成功的影響：國際性) stressed his pluralism in the following terms:

> Having been born in Japan to a mother named Tagawa, and spent the first seven years of his life there, [Koxinga] had a profound attachment to Japan. He returned to China (返回中國) at the age of seven, and until he was 38, the Minnan region of mainland China remained his main stronghold. [Koxinga] thus also had an intimate relationship with China (與中國有密切的關係). Moreover, in the process of recovering Taiwan (光復台灣), he battled and defeated the Dutch, making the name 'Koxinga' famous amongst the Dutch and other Europeans.

The references here to his 'return' to China and 'recovery' of Taiwan reflect the lingering influence of nationalist tropes, but the general thrust echoes the portrayal in the National Palace Museum's *Formosa* exhibition of 2003: Diffidence towards the figure of the Chinese 'national hero', and keenness to highlight the plurality of influences on Koxinga himself, and on 17th-century Taiwan.[15]

Different schools of thought contended more openly in the international, collaborative exhibition hosted by the Koxinga Museum in 2007. Tainan's DPP Mayor, Hsu Tain-Tsair, hailed Koxinga as a 'historical hero' (歷史英雄) and 'local deity', noting that he 'constitutes a link between Japan, China, the Netherlands and Taiwan'. Promoting the Koxinga Festival, 'one of our city's most important annual celebrations', he represents it as a commemoration of Koxinga's 'achievements in the opening up of Taiwan and his impact on the history and culture of Tainan City', but makes no reference to his importance to China (Tainan City Government / NMH 2007: 3). For his part, the Director of Hirado's Matsuura Museum used his preface to the exhibition catalogue less to celebrate Koxinga the personality than Hirado the cosmopolitan entrepôt, while hailing Koxinga and his mother as establishing a 'bridge' between Japan and Taiwan (4). Such cosmopolitan allusions were studiously avoided by the Director of Xiamen's Koxinga Memorial, who deployed stock CCP rhetoric celebrating Taiwan's liberation from 'Western colonial hegemony' and exhorting all 'descendents of the Yan and Yellow Emperors' to strive for the 'revitalisataion of the Chinese nation' (5). However, reflecting the relative openness of scholarly debate on the Chinese mainland in the early 2000s (itself a factor in facilitating exchanges with Taiwan), the Xiamen Memorial's Deputy Director, Chen Yang (Chen 2007), contributed a scholarly assessment of new insights into Koxinga's character, and the circumstances of his death, based on analysis of the diary of Philip Meij (a Dutch East India Company trader involved in the siege of Fort Zeelandia). Chen went so far as openly to acknowledge differences in the interpretation by Taiwanese and mainland scholars of Koxinga's status as a hero – differences evidenced in an essay from the Secretary of Taiwan's National Museum of History (Su 2007: 25).

The narrative of Tainan's Koxinga Museum itself bears witness to an increasingly detached vision of the great man's status. In 2019, the Museum's exhibition described him as a 'household name' (家喻戶曉) in Taiwanese history. 'He played an extremely important role in the history of Tainan City', notes the text, averring that 'very few historical figures have had such an intimate relationship with Taiwanese people'. For a long-revered national hero and deified founder of Hoklo Taiwan, this counts as damning with faint praise.

To some extent, Koxinga has fallen victim to broader shifts in public history in democratic Taiwan. Heroes are no longer as fashionable as they once were; the story of Taiwan is, above all, the story of its people. This shift is evident in the National Museum of Taiwan History (NMTH), newly opened near Tainan in 2011. The permanent exhibition of the NMTH, entitled *Our Land, Our People*, deliberately eschews a 'great man' narrative (NMTH 2012). The Zhengs are described here as trading partners, then rivals, of the Dutch, on whose legacy they built in 'developing' the Tainan region (51). The historian Wu Mi-cha, editor of the comic-book history of Taiwan mentioned above, played a key role in devising the NMTH exhibition (Vickers 2013). The Zheng period is portrayed here as the moment when Han Chinese first came to dominate Taiwan, but this is no longer represented (as under the KMT) as the beginning of Taiwan's history-proper, nor as an occasion for unmitigated celebration (certainly not for the island's indigenous people). The exhibition text notes the Qing Government's hesitation, following its defeat of the Ming-Zheng regime, over whether to retain Taiwan. The decision to bring the island into the Qing Empire signalled 'the ending of one era and the beginning of another' (55): A new chapter in Taiwan's story, but not a notably glorious one.[16]

Conclusion

At the time of writing, our hero looks set to experience a further demotion within the local heritage landscape: In 2020, the Koxinga Museum reverted to its former title of *Tainan City History Museum*. It may be wrong to read too much into this. Koxinga keeps his festival, his iconic status meanwhile reflected in robust sales of tourist knick-knacks and comestibles emblazoned with his image. But it is ever harder today to pin down the basis for his popularity in Taiwan. An immensely colourful relic of a swashbuckling past, for some he has also come to symbolise a pluralistic 'Asian' Taiwan with ties to a wider world. By Hoklo Taiwanese he is still revered as a pioneer, and even worshipped as an ancestral deity. However, his reputation as Confucian paragon is no longer sacred, and his status as Chinese national hero either irrelevant or a source of unease, as is his implication in Han colonisation and the decimation of the island's indigenous people. In democratic Taiwan, Koxinga remains an important symbol, but a contested one, whose complex record and political associations defy easy deployment for propagandistic purposes.

In invoking his multicultural heritage, Taiwanese can count on the somewhat passive collaboration of their erstwhile colonial overlords, the Japanese. However, in today's Japan, commemoration of Koxinga is a purely local affair largely confined to Hirado or Nagasaki Prefecture. There, authorities keen to foster profitable ties with communities on both sides of the Taiwan Strait have leveraged Taiwanese and Fujianese interest, while themselves cleaving to a strictly apolitical vision of their local son. In Hirado as in contemporary Taiwan, though in a far lower key, Koxinga is a symbol of a nostalgically remembered cosmopolitan past. He is a supporting act in a drama celebrating, above all, the European role in Hirado's glory days as an international entrepôt.

In China, meanwhile, Koxinga emphatically retains his status in the pantheon of 'national heroes', if not quite in the front rank (except in his native Fujian). His multicultural antecedents concealed, and the complexity of his relationship with European 'colonialists' ignored, he is celebrated above all for his role in ending illegitimate Western occupation of an island portrayed as immemorially Chinese. But that role was, of course, a violent one, and in so far as the CCP has sought to stress its peaceable intentions towards Taiwan, it has somewhat veered away from the Mao-era fascination with Koxinga's martial exploits. In the early 2000s, a charm offensive characterised by emphasis on ties of blood and culture across the Taiwan Strait saw him celebrated less as a vengeful champion of anti-imperialism, and more as a cultural and ancestral symbol of 'Chinese' unity.

However, the themes of anti-imperialism and militant patriotism, linked to defiance of Western attempts (abetted by Japan) to scupper reunification and thwart China's 'peaceful rise', have never been absent from the CCP narrative. Now that 'one country, two systems' has been dramatically abandoned in Hong Kong, and 'peaceful' rhetoric concerning Taiwan's recovery supplanted by an increasingly blatant threat of force, conditions are perhaps ripe for Koxinga to take a more prominent role in the propaganda struggle. He is potentially a powerful icon for those on the mainland who insist that only action, not talk, will bring Taiwan back into the national fold.

Kinship and culture, meanwhile, have remained key themes of the Koxinga story as told in China. The Xi Jinping regime combines triumphalism over China's geopolitical resurgence with an unapologetically chauvinist vision of 'Chineseness' far closer to that espoused by the KMT under Chiang Kai-shek than the CCP under Mao Zedong. For all its violence and oppression, often justified in terms of 'class struggle', the CCP has long promoted an ostensibly multicultural vision of a China characterised by mutual respect between the Han and 'brother nationalities' (Yan and Vickers 2019). Today, the party has all but abandoned that vision in favour of a celebration of 'China's superior traditional culture' (中国的优秀传统文化)[17] associated with majority Han culture. While brutally suppressing 'minority' culture in Xinjiang, it invokes shared ancestry and tradition in denying the legitimacy of Hongkongers' claims to distinctiveness.

The CCP's early embrace of a multicultural vision along with class-based ambivalence towards figures from the old Han scholar-elite was always trumped in Koxinga's case by anti-imperialist nationalism and the teleology of unification. This was especially so at times, like the early 1960s, when the regime felt threatened by domestic turmoil and external enemies. Today, as economic uncertainty and global crises threaten stability and its performance legitimacy, the party makes increasingly uncompromising demands for deference and obedience both at home and abroad, sidelining even a notional commitment to ethno-cultural inclusivity and 'class struggle'. As China seeks to reassert its dominance within East Asia's moral-political order, Koxinga may assume another role, as exemplary exponent of a muscular Confucianism that batters both recalcitrant foreigners and domestic dissidents into submission.

For the foreseeable future, therefore, it seems likely that the symbolism surrounding Koxinga, rather than bridging the Taiwan-mainland divide, will reflect and reinforce a widening divergence in public sentiment across the Strait. While Beijing harnesses him to a teleology of reunification informed by cultural and biological determinism, mainstream Taiwanese opinion will respond either by further marginalising him, or by enhancing the emphasis on his Japanese antecedents, cosmopolitan ties, and local exploits. In effect, Koxinga's continued relevance in contemporary Taiwan depends largely on the de-Sinification of his memory.

Notes

1 Website of the Koxinga Memorial (鄭成功記念館) at Kawachi, Hirado, https://www.hirado-net.com/teiseikou/about.php, visited on 16 June 2020.
2 Report in Japanese on the 人民中国 website, 21 August 2013, http://www.peoplechina.com.cn/xinwen/txt/2013-08/22/content_562375.htm, visited on 16 June 2020.
3 This and other details regarding Taiwanese cultural diplomacy in Hirado were obtained through personal communication with an official at the Taipei Representative Office (branch) in Fukuoka.
4 This is the description in the pamphlet distributed at the Memorial.
5 I include the Chinese name of Yu and of Lu Zhenwan, below, because I have been unable to find much information about these individuals – others might like to follow this trail.
6 The affiliations of the contributors are not given. The only definitely 'foreign' contribution was by a Dutch scholar, Paulus (包乐史), who contributed a paper on 'the rise of Zheng Zhilong'.
7 It is not clear when, or whether, the exhibition at the Fujian-Taiwan Kinship Museum has undergone renovation or revision. But here the text precisely echoes the exhibition at the Museum of China's War of Resistance against Japanese Aggression in Lugouqiao, near Beijing. As part of a renovation coinciding with the 70th anniversary of the end of World War II in 2015, that exhibition was extended to include a whole new annex narrating Taiwanese resistance to Japanese colonialism. Koxinga and the Zheng clan feature as prologue, praised for ending an earlier colonial incursion and 'recovering' the island for China.
8 The same visual metaphor of tree roots featured in the entrance artwork for a special exhibition in 2019 (the 70th anniversary of the CCP's Civil War victory of the KMT) celebrating the contributions of 'overseas Chinese' to 'New China'.
9 The Chinese name by which Koxinga is most commonly known, 鄭成功, contains the personal name 成功, meaning 'success' or 'achievement', conferred on him by the Lung Wu Emperor, the Ming pretender, during the early days of anti-Manchu resistance.
10 It is also apparently aimed at foreign readers, since the entire text is translated – remarkably well – into idiomatic English. But the bilingual text may also be a selling point for Taiwanese parents.

11 This account is based on the text of the exhibition at the Koxinga Museum in 2009, photographed by the author.
12 This account is provided on a plaque outside the temple, viewed by the author in 2009.
13 This was just one year before the opening in Quanzhou of the 'Museum of Taiwan-Fujian Kinship'.
14 This embrace of cultural diversity was also manifested in the exhibition's trilingual presentation: In Chinese, English, and Japanese. I visited the Koxinga Museum twice during these years, in 2005 and 2009; the exhibition text (especially the English version) was substantially revised between 2005 and 2009.
15 Meanwhile, by 2009, a new National Museum of Taiwan Literature, housed in a lovingly restored Japanese colonial structure nearby by the Koxinga Museum in Tainan, was promoting a vision of Taiwan's literary heritage rooted in multicultural imagery ('Symphonies of Languages, Blossoms of Multiethnic Literatures': 多音交響，族群共榮), including fulsome acknowledgement of Japanese influence.
16 As I discuss elsewhere (Vickers 2013), this exhibition credits the Japanese with the most 'transformative' impact on Taiwan's development.
17 This concept is strongly linked to Xi's rhetoric of the 'Chinese dream'.

References

English references

Andrade, Tonio (2011). *Lost Colony: The Untold Story of China's First Great Victory over the West*. Princeton NJ: Princeton University Press.

Coble, Parks (2007). 'China's "new remembering" of the anti-Japanese war of resistance, 1937–1945', *China Quarterly*, 190: 394–410.

Corcuff, Stephane (2005). 'History textbooks, identity politics and ethnic introspection in Taiwan', in Vickers and Jones (eds.), *History Education and National Identity in East Asia*. London and New York: Routledge, 171–202.

Croizier, Ralph C. (1977). *Koxinga and Chinese Nationalism: History, Myth and the Hero*. Cambridge, MA: Harvard University Press.

NMTH (National Museum of Taiwan History) (2012). *Our Land, Our People: The Story of Taiwan*. Tainan: NMTH.

Straits Times (2020). NPC 2020: China drops word 'peaceful' in latest push for Taiwan 'reunification', Straits Times, Singapore, May 22, www.straitstimes.com (accessed October 28, 2020).

Tu, Cheng-sheng (杜正勝) (2003). *Ilha Formosa: The Emergence of Taiwan on the World Scene in the 17th Century*. Taipei: NPM.

Vickers, Edward (2007). 'Frontiers of memory: Conflict, imperialism and official histories in the formation of post-cold war Taiwan identity', in Jager and Mitter (eds.), *Ruptured Histories*. Cambridge, MA: Harvard University Press, 209–232.

Vickers, Edward (2009). 'Rewriting Museums in Taiwan', in Shih, Thompson and Tremlett (eds.), *Rewriting Museums in Taiwan*. London and New York: Routledge, 69–101.

Vickers, Edward (2010). 'History, identity and the politics of Taiwan's museums: Reflections on the DPP-KMT transition', in *China Perspectives*, 2010(3): 92–106.

Vickers, Edward (2013). 'Transcending victimhood: Japan in the public historical museums of Taiwan and the People's Republic of China', in *China Perspectives*, 2013(4): 17–28.

Vickers, Edward (2017). 'Altered states of consciousness: identity politics and prospects for Taiwan-Hong Kong-mainland reconciliation', in Frieberg and Chung (eds), *Reconciling with the Past*. London and New York: Routledge, 122–137.

Yan, Fei and Vickers, Edward (2019). 'Portraying "minorities" in Chinese history textbooks of the 1990s and 2000s: The advance and retreat of ethnocultural inclusivity', *Asia Pacific Journal of Education*, 39(2): 190–208.

Chinese/Japanese references

BTNPA (Beijing Taiwanese Native Place Association) (北京台灣會館) (2012). *Chenggong Across the Straits: Exhibition to Celebrate the 350th Anniversary of [Koxinga] Zheng Chenggong's recovery of Taiwan* (成功在兩岸：鄭成功收復台灣350周年紀念展). Beijing: BTNPA. (In Chinese).

Chen, Shu-tian (陈树田) (1994). '纪念民族英雄郑成功诞辰三百七十周年' ('Commemorating the 370th anniversary of the National Hero, Koxinga') in 郑成功诞辰370周年：纪念特刊；福建史志增刊 (Fujian History Journal: Special issue commemorating the 370th anniversary of the birth of Koxinga). July 1994, (pp. 1–3). (In Chinese).

Chen, Yang (2007). 'Analysing Zhu Chenggong' (思考朱成功), in Tainan City Government / NMH (eds.) (2007). *Exhibition of Koxinga*, 10–24. (In Chinese).

Fujian History Journal (1994). 郑成功诞辰370周年：纪念特刊；福建史志增刊 (Fujian History Journal: Special issue commemorating the 370th anniversary of the birth of Koxinga). July 1994. Published by the 福建省地方志学会/福建省编纂委员会 (Fujian Local Chronicle Association / Compilation Committee). (In Chinese).

Ichikawa, Shinichi (市川信愛) (1982). 僑郷・閩南（びんなん）探訪記 —福建省鄭成功研究学術討論会（1982年7月）に出席して— ('Overseas Settlement and the Fujianese: Report on participation in an academic symposium on Koxinga-related research held in Fujian Province (July 1982)'), in 東南アジア研究年報 (*Annual Report of Research on East Asia*) [published by Nagasaki University], Issue 23, pp. 55–86 (in Japanese).

Lin, Wei-sheng (林偉盛) (2003). 對峙：熱蘭遮圍城兩百七十五日 ('Confrontation and Opposition: The Siege of Fort Zeelandia'), in NPM (ed.), *Ilha Formosa*, 75–104.

NICT (National Institute for Compilation and Translation / 國立編譯館) (2001). 認識台灣：歷史 (*Knowing Taiwan: History*). Taipei: NICT. (In Chinese) (first edition published 1997).

NPM (National Palace Museum / 國立故宮博物院) (ed.) (2003). 福尔摩沙：十七世紀的臺灣・荷蘭與東亞. (*Ilha Formosa*: The Emergence of Taiwan on the World Scene in the 17th Century) Taipei: NPM. (In Chinese).

Okayama, Yoshiharu (岡山芳治) (2007). 'Trading conditions between Hirado and Western Europe' (平戶之西歐貿易狀況) in Wu Jian-yi (ed.) *Exhibition of Koxinga* (國姓爺：足跡文物特展). Tainan: Tainan City and the National Museum of History, 34–41 (in Japanese and Chinese).

Su, Chi-ming (蘇啓明) (2007). 'Zheng Chenggong's Maritime Supremacy' (鄭成功的海上霸權) in Tainan City Government / NMH (eds). *Exhibition of Koxinga*, 25–33. (In Chinese).

Tainan City Government / NMH (National Museum of History) (eds.) (2007). *Exhibition of Koxinga* (國姓爺：足跡文物特展). Tainan: Tainan City Government. (In Chinese).

TCCAB (Tainan City Cultural Affairs Bureau) (2011). *Sail with Koxinga: The Activities and Achievements of the 2011 Koxinga Cultural Festival* (成功啟航 - 2011鄭成功文化節活動成果專輯). Tainan: Tainan City Cultural Affairs Bureau (台南市文化局). (In Chinese).

Ts'ao, Yong-ho (曹永和) (2003). 導論：十七世紀作為東亞轉運站的臺灣 ('Taiwan as a Center of East Asian Maritime Traffic in the 17th Century'), in NPM, *Ilha Formosa*. Taipei: NPM, 13–32.

Wu, Micha (吳密察) (2005). 認識台灣歷史：鄭家時代 (*A History of Taiwan in Comics: The Koxinga Period*). Taipei: Third Nature Publishing Co.

Yu, Xinhe (余新河) (1994). 'Koxinga is an International Hero' (鄭成功是国际英雄), in *Fujian History Journal*, commemorative special issue, 42–51. (In Chinese).

Zhang, Zongzhi (张宗治) (ed.) (1985). *Koxinga Memorial* (郑成功纪念馆). Cultural Artefacts Publishing House (文物出版社). (In Chinese).

10

MANOEUVRING IN THE LINGUISTIC BORDERLAND

Southeast Asian migrant women's language strategies in Taiwan

Isabelle Cheng

Alien wives who speak foreign languages

Transnational marriage migration occurs when one spouse moves across state borders to be united with the other spouse in another state. Such migration is premised on the recognition of a citizen's right to enjoy a family life. Empirically, as part of the feminisation of migration in East Asia, marriage migration has taken the shape of women in Southeast Asia and China marrying men in better-off countries, such as Taiwan, South Korea, Japan, or Singapore (Yang and Lu 2010). Major originating states, such as Vietnam, Indonesia, the Philippines, Thailand, and Cambodia, are known for their rich ethnic diversity. However, the women's major destination states (excluding Singapore) are largely considered to be ethnically homogeneous states (Bélanger et al. 2010). Take Taiwan, for example: As of February 2020, 559,638 men and women residing in Taiwan have the status of local citizens' spouses; over 92% of these non-local spouses are women (NIA 2020a). With regard to origin, 63% of these non-local spouses are from Mainland China (excluding Hong Kong and Macao), 19% from Vietnam, 6% from Indonesia, and 2% from the Philippines, with the remaining 10% from other neighbouring areas and beyond (NIA 2020b). In other words, if Mandarin-speaking China is excluded, more than a quarter of migrant spouses in Taiwan are from multi-ethnic, multi-lingual, and middle-income countries in Southeast Asia.

Despite being inter-ethnic, transnational marriage migration defies the presumption that inter-ethnic unions will result in the fusion of the cultures of different ethnic groups. In the practice of marriage migration to Taiwan and other Asian Tigers, the opposite is true (Chen and Yu 2005). Their courtship is expected to be a 'fast track' in the sense that soon after the women's meeting with, and being chosen by, their suitors on trips to the women's countries organised by matchmakers, the women are married to them and embark on their migration on their own

(Wang and Chang 2002; see Tseng 2015 for a critique of commercial matchmaking). Their husbands return to Taiwan and await their reunion, while matchmakers continue to assist the women in applying for their spousal visa, which entitles them to reside in Taiwan. Matchmakers also include short-term Chinese-language orientation for the women as part of their services.[1] Such services give an impression that there is no need on the part of Taiwanese husbands and in-laws to commit themselves to communicating with the women in their own languages.

An obvious signifier of this lack of mutual understanding after the women's migration is the challenge of communicating with their in-laws in the private home. Stigmatised as underclass rural women of limited education, they are believed to be materialistic and to see their marriage as the means to rid themselves and their families of economic hardship (Hsia 2007). Likewise, their husbands (and, sometimes, in-laws as well) are also believed to be at the bottom of the socio-economic hierarchy and therefore less acculturated for civility or lacking resources to embrace globalisation in the form of cultural exchange (Cheng 2017; Keng 2016). This everyday challenge also extends to the women's contact with the general public outside of the home in the context of employment, motherhood, or exercising citizenship. These women encounter the challenge of the host society's under-appreciation of their cultural inheritance embedded, arguably, in the ethnic homogeneity of that society. Faced with these biases, how do migrant women negotiate their communication with their in-laws? Considering that their life course will evolve and they will acquire social roles performed outside of the home, e.g. as workers and citizens, how does their use of language become part of the process of their socio-economic integration?

Marginalised second-language (L2) speakers

Being an outsider in the receiving society, migrant women in transnational marriages are an obvious public policy target for assimilation. Through the lens of methodological nationalism (Wimmer and Glick-Schiller 2002), their biological reproduction is intertwined with their adoption of local language, since the latter is related to social reproduction in the form of child-rearing and motherhood duties (Bélanger 2007; Bélanger et al. 2010; Cheng 2013; Lan 2019). Seeing their use of language from the perspective of aiding children's academic performance (Chin and Yu 2009; Hsiao 2009; Chen 2011) is a case of methodological sexism (Dumitru 2014) since women's motherhood is evaluated instrumentally. Research interests in this regard (motherhood and early education) are legitimised by either verifying or rebuking popular discourses that frame 'mixed' children as lower achievers, due to the perceived incapability of their mothers (Keng 2016) and the absence of involvement of local fathers in their children's early development (Keng 2016; Hsiao 2009).

Migrant women's use of language is not only held responsible for their children's academic performance and personality development but also for their own wellbeing. Without stressing the equal responsibility of the host society in general and their husbands as well as in-laws in particular for investing in mutual understanding, scholarship also tends to consider that women's use of language is responsible for their suffering of gender-based violence (Williams and Yu 2006) or their weak integration into the host society (Liao and Wang 2013). Insufficient integration can be viewed as isolation, discrimination (Yang and Wang 2011), or a lower level of social support, which is correlated with depression (Lin and Hung 2007). Since immigrant minorities are conventionally regarded as less resourceful at maintaining their mental and physical health, marriage-migrant women are also found to be less capable of caring for themselves because a language barrier restricts their access to information and care (Yang et al. 2015; Huang and Yang 2018).

Thus, migrant women's use of language tends to be conceived as a quantifiable matter of personal endeavours and measurable results. That is, the higher the level of migrant women's proficiency in local languages, the better off they will be socially, economically, mentally, and physically. Employing a lineal progressive approach, this stream of research emphasises women's subjective and proactive engagement with local languages in order to receive the rewards of better socio-economic integration. Although agency is not absent from these research designs, it is conceived more as an end result of personal endeavours rather than being part of their interactions with their social environs. Some researchers have paid more attention to this interactional or relational agency and found that attending language orientation classes is utilised by some women as an escape from abuse (Wang 2007) and that language becomes a resource for collective action for improving their legal treatment (Hsia 2006, 2007, 2009). Critical of the lineal approach and aligning itself with the relational perspective, this chapter is aimed at exploring what migrant women do with their languages, including their own and those local languages spoken by the host society, for resisting their marginalisation and othering (e.g. Park 2017), rather than how they are measured by the host society for their linguistic performance as L2 speakers.

In sum, the literature reviewed above prioritises migrant women's experiences as L2 speakers without taking into account their identity as first-language (L1) speakers. The use of L1 and L2, the critical resources for their identity construction, is imagined as a trade-off rather than mutual constitution. When focusing on their L2 adoption, these studies are more concerned about the end result (how well they speak) rather than the process whereby the use of L2 is punctuated by the change of their life course and by their role playing inside and outside of the private home. To underline this dynamic relationship between these women and the fluid linguistic environment in their everyday life, this chapter proposes to see their use of L1 and L2 as operating in a 'linguistic borderland' where they switch between different languages in accordance with the role being played, such as being a wife, mother, daughter-in-law, worker, or citizen. The concept of the linguistic borderland sees their use of language as a strategy for drawing on resources available to them as well as reacting to the marginalisation imposed on them. This concept rejects the approach of assessing their level of proficiency in

L2 and using this assessment to measure their level of integration. Applying the linguistic borderland concept foregrounds the dynamism that highlights what they do with their languages rather than evaluating how well they speak the language. The concept of linguistic borderland also grasps their performance of the hybrid identity that is role-contingent and context-dependent shifting between being an L1 and L2 speaker.

Linguistic borderland

This chapter is aimed at emphasising the dynamic relationship between migrants and the languages spoken by them in their social surroundings that may include or exclude them. To achieve this purpose, this chapter delves into the theoretical potential offered by border studies and borderland studies. Scholarship in borderland studies has diversified from focusing on territory, local community, sovereignty, governance, and security to markets and globalisation with an emerging interest in introducing a cultural dimension (Brunet-Jailly 2010). An advantage of introducing culture into the study of border is to re-conceptualise borders as 'fluid, hybrid, multifragmented space where individuals negotiate linguistic, ethnic, and gender identities' (Pastor 2011: 186). Therefore, a contact with an outer group can be conceptualised as 'border-crossing' (Pastor 2011: 187), whereas 'borderland' is theorised as the resistance against and transcendence of the bifurcation of identity inherent within biracial individuals (Anzaldua 1987).

Inspired by this fluidity introduced to the originally territory-bound concept of border and borderland, this chapter proposes to situate migrants' use of language within a situational borderland. Surrounding an existing demarcation, border and borderland are concepts used together to refer to a state of affairs where people or places are separated from each other by a geographical, administrative, or perceptional line. Separated by, and constituted along, this line, a borderland is the social, geographical, or administrative space where people meet from both sides of the demarcation. A demarcation is premised on the existence of perceived and acknowledged sameness. Behind the line, sameness is believed to enhance mutual trust and reduce social confrontations. Therefore, maintaining the demarcation is conceived as a common interest since it ensures the stability of the perceived sameness. The maintenance of demarcation can be executed by an established political authority or by an endogenous social pressure that rewards acts or thoughts conforming to the sameness or punishes those which deviate from the sameness. When a demarcation is crossed or challenged, a borderland becomes a contact zone where convergence, integration, or confrontation takes place (in the form of multiple ethnicities in geographical borderlands, see Barwiński 2017), depending on the cause, process, and outcome of these transcending or transgressing acts or thoughts. When the strength of convergence, integration, or confrontation is beyond the processing capacity of the people behind the line, the demarcation may decay, be destroyed, or be absorbed until a replacement demarcation is brought into being.

A demarcation is effectively drawn between people who speak different languages (e.g. Dunlop 2013). As a tool for thinking, expression, and communication in the aural and written form, language is indispensable for social interactions. At an individual level, language is inseparable from personal identity. At a collective level, language is key to the maintenance of perceived sameness, which is integral to the construction of a collective identity. Thus, shifting from one language to another in order to engage in social or economic activities is to cross the demarcation and enter a linguistic borderland. In this linguistic borderland, multiple languages are spoken so that the acts and thoughts of their speakers can be facilitated. Depending on the roles played by the speakers and their interactions with each other, a linguistic borderland exists and evolves as a situational, contextual, or physical space where, as mentioned above, convergence, integration, or confrontation take place. How these outcomes unfold in everyday life is integral to the speakers' personal identity, the fluid performance of which is contingent on the situation or context. Thus the acts and thoughts taking place in the linguistic borderland are at the core of the construction of personal identity.

These interactions are also at the core of the politics of identity at a collective level. When the collectivity is a nation-state, the linguistic borderland poses a challenge to socio-political stability since its facilitation of the switch between languages harbours potential disruption to the perceived sameness amongst the people who belong to a specific language group. It is not surprising that the recognition of language and the subsequent endowment of the socio-political status of any languages (i.e. the official distinction between languages and dialects) is a contested public policy, regardless of whether it is a mono- or multi-lingual nation. Therefore, the intent of regulating the linguistic borderland is essential to nation-building, a project which may be founded upon assimilation, which prioritises sameness, or multiculturalism, which accommodates a degree of differences out of respect or practicality (Han 2011; Dowling et al. 2012).

In this light, migration becomes a challenge to the state's intention to regulate the linguistic border, since it brings speakers of different languages to cross the demarcation and mingle with the nation. When the demarcation is created by state borders that are safeguarded by sovereignty, they may be prevented from crossing if they do not meet the requirements for entering legally. Once they have entered, migrants and the host population are situated within the linguistic borderland whenever they interact. Whether in public or private places, their interactions are not free from the host state's intent to regulate (in the form of assimilation or multiculturalism) and the social pressure to maintain the sameness.

Such is the constraint encountered by marriage-migrant women from Southeast Asia who migrate alone to Taiwan after their marriage. This linguistic borderland is situated in the private home as well as in the public domain. In both spaces, this linguistic borderland is intersected by the biases of gender, class, and ethnicity; this intersection constitutes the power relation that disadvantages migrant women as the *inferior other*. As women who move out of their home country on their own to families in Taiwan, they are constantly acting in the linguistic borderland as wives, mothers, and daughters-in-law. As their life course evolves, they also acquire the roles of workers and citizens in the public domain. Disadvantaged by the power relation embedded in the linguistic borderland, they are under pressure from their in-laws and the host state, whose interest is to make them speak local languages so as to maintain the sameness. Negotiating this pressure on their choice of language, migrant women draw resources from their own cultural capital or come to terms with the restrictions on their freedom to manoeuvre. All these strategies demonstrate how they may exercise their agency in spite of the structural constraints. Their endeavours open a new window of opportunity for us to re-evaluate immigrants' cultural capital of bilingualism or multilingualism as well as to recognise the flux and fluidity of language use in their everyday encounters (Piller and Takahashi 2011).

Research method

Aiming at contextualising the richness and diversity of migrant women's everyday experiences, this research involved interviews with migrant women from Vietnam, the Philippines, and Indonesia. Those from Indonesia are of Chinese ancestry. The majority of interviews were conducted between 2009 and 2010 with additional interviews conducted between 2013 and 2019. I met most of the interviewees in the greater Taipei area (including Keelung) with a smaller number in Taichung, Tainan, Kaohsiung, Pingtung, and Penghu. The recruitment of interviewees was based on personal referrals given by migrants themselves or Taiwanese people who had regular contacts with migrants, including placement agencies, matchmakers, churches, and teachers who ran Chinese-language courses for migrant spouses' orientation. Unable to speak Vietnamese or Bahasa Indonesia, I interviewed Vietnamese and Indonesian women in Mandarin, whereas English was used for interviewing Filipino women, as requested by them.

This research is focused on the interviewees' shared experiences and engages with the internal diversity determined by age, socio-economic status, or cultural capital within each group. Including Tagalog and Visaya speakers, the Filipino group consists of 14 women whose commonality is their speaking English, a cultural capital obtained via college or university education. The Vietnamese interviewees (including four ethnic Chinese) include 28 women from north, central, and southern Vietnam whose education attainment varies from illiteracy in Vietnam to a postgraduate degree acquired in Taiwan. Reflecting the diversity of dialects spoken amongst ethnic Chinese in Indonesia, the 21 Indonesian Chinese interviewees spoke Hakka, Teochew, Hokkien, Foochow, or Cantonese, including two Mandarin speakers aged in their 50s and 60s. They attended non-state schools during childhood which used Mandarin as the medium for teaching. The growth of Indonesian identity amongst the younger generation of ethnic Chinese made some of them monolingual in Bahasa Indonesia as they ceased to speak the dialect(s) spoken by their parents' generation.

To conceal their identity while delineating interview results, all interviewees are referred to by pseudonyms reflecting their language strategies. English names are given to Filipino women and Vietnamese names are given to Vietnamese women. For those younger Indonesian Chinese who do not speak any Chinese dialect, they are given Indonesian names; for Chinese dialect speakers, the spellings of their Chinese names are composed according to the dialect spoken by them.

The following pages will give detailed accounts about how the interviewees manoeuvre in the linguistic borderland with the resources available to and restrictions on them. It has to be noted that the borderland itself has evolved since the early 1990s when these women established their families in Taiwan. This evolution is punctuated by two specific public policies, namely, the adoption of Chinese-language proficiency as one of the prerequisites for naturalisation eligibility in 2005 (Cheng 2013) and the implementation of the New Southbound Policy since 2016. The former underlines the state's attempt to enhance sameness, whereas the latter shows the tolerance for difference. The latter has seen a multitude of measures undertaken by the government to encourage the speaking of Southeast Asian languages amongst mixed children and the general public in the hope of deepening the socio-political relationship between Taiwan and Southeast Asia (Cheng et al. 2018; Lan 2019). However, in the 1990s when mixed children were growing up, they were discouraged from speaking their mother's language (Hsia 2019), as shown by the interviewees' personal accounts in the following pages. Thus, this chapter offers a retrospective critique of migrant women's struggle against such hegemonic power in their everyday life.

The Filipinos: There are also people who can't speak English

One of the most frequent comments given by Filipino women about their actions in the borderland is: 'It's difficult for us to adjust here because of language', as pointed out by Jo (the author's interview, 29 January 2010, Pingtung). In her late 40s and a mother of two school-age children, Jo had resided in Taiwan for 15 years at the time of the interview. As well as running a grocery shop, Jo was a caregiver at a hospital in Pingtung. Her comment resonated with Kelly, a former caregiver and now a spouse and activist in Taipei working at a migrant shelter. However, as mentioned by Kelly, a critical resource available to them is the English language, since their husbands are willing to communicate with them in English (the author's interview, 13 August 2019, Taipei).

English-speaking ability and college-level education are forms of cultural capital that Filipino women are widely known for in Taiwanese society. Searching 'Filipino workers' online reveals that placement agencies advertise English-speaking as Filipino workers' competitive advantage.[2] It has been argued that English-speaking supports Filipino migrant workers' self-esteem because 'They (Taiwanese employers) have more money but I speak better English' (Lan 2003). Grinning at this comment, Kelly also reminded me that stressing English-speaking was part of the Philippine government's 'propaganda', which lauded the Philippine nation for being 'global workers'. Associated with modernity (Del Rosario 2005), English-speaking marks the boundary between the educated and the uneducated in the Philippines. As pointed out by Andrea, a high school graduate from Cebu, 'In the Philippines there are *also* people who can't speak English because they didn't go to school' (the author's interview, 27 January 2010, Pingtung).

Speaking English is not only a matter of practicality and self-esteem but also aided the women's exercise of citizenship. If language is a barrier for other Southeast Asian women to access information about public affairs, locally produced English-language newspapers or TV programmes provide Filipino women with information. An illustrative case is 65-year-old Virginia. Virginia was the second oldest student in the evening Chinese class in Taipei where I conducted participant observation. Before migrating to Taiwan, Virginia was a primary school teacher and activist in Manila. She fought for pay rises for schoolteachers; one of the large-scale protests in which she participated resulted in the arrest of her colleagues. In Taiwan, she was a member of the Filipinos Married to Taiwanese Association (FMTA), an organisation founded by a Filipino marriage immigrant (Philippine Daily Inquirer 2009). As a citizen who had been living on the island for 18 years at the time of the interview, she made use of local English-language newspapers and maintained the habit of 'carefully analysing the different policies of political parties in order to find out which party serves the people better' (the author's interview, 18 May 2009, Taipei), a 'habit' that was also shared by Jennifer and Peony in Pingtung. When answering how they decided whom to vote for in the general election of 2008, Jennifer mentioned a local English-speaking TV channel as one of her sources of information and Peony pointed to an English-language newspaper sold at her shop. All three of them stressed that English-language sources of information were critical for their decision-making independently of their husbands' influence.

Despite the convenience and advantages of speaking English, it may reduce their incentive to adopt the Chinese language, which restricts their room for manoeuvre in the borderland. For those interviewees who went to the Chinese-language course in order to be eligible for naturalisation, speaking Chinese remained secondary in their daily lives. A lower level of Chinese proficiency can have an impact on the choice of entrepreneurship, such as the grocery shops ('*Sari Sari*' in Tagalog) run by Jo and Peony in Pintgung. Helping out at the *Sari Sari*, Jo's children were praised for speaking Tagalog by their Filipino customers and thus their speaking of Tagalog was accepted by their Taiwanese father. Unlike the bilingual shop signs of Vietnamese or Indonesian eateries (e.g. Mika 2008: 24), the signs at Jo's and Peony's shops did not show Chinese characters. Arguably, this is because, unlike Vietnamese or Indonesian cuisines, which have a wider market appeal, products sold at *Sari Sari* are less appealing or relevant to the daily consumption of Taiwanese buyers and thus there is less contact between Filipino shop owners and Taiwanese buyers.

Although English is universally associated with Western cultures, transnational mobility, and job competitiveness, in Taiwan it is strongly associated with *white*

Caucasian ethnicity (Lan 2011), which does not include the Filipinos. In the disadvantageous power relation between the discriminated-against Filipino women and their Taiwanese in-laws, the former's use of English is not appreciated. While Caucasian mothers or English-speaking American-born Chinese ('ABC') mothers are encouraged to speak English rather than Chinese to their children (interview with an ABC mother, April 2009, Taipei), Filipino women, such as Annabelle, were discouraged from speaking English (and Tagalog) because of their in-laws' fear of being excluded or bad-mouthed.

Thus, when the linguistic borderland is situated in the private home, there is a limit on how far English can be used for family life. As Kelly reflected upon her own transition, when she was a migrant worker she had no incentive to speak Chinese; after she got married, she had to communicate with her in-laws in Chinese, a transition that Hồ Minh Mai had also gone through from being a factory worker to a wife-mother. In practice, Filipino women developed a division of labour between English, Tagalog, and local languages. To communicate with families and to be employed outside of the home, they spoke a degree of Mandarin and Hoklo. For those who were housewives, lacking regular social contact with other people outside the home decreased their exposure to the local linguistic environment. It is common that Filipino mothers speak English to their children, who then reply in Mandarin or Hoklo. Peggy and Clare were keen to teach English to their children, but their children were not interested.

English-speaking, with a degree of comprehension of local languages, did not contribute to the intimacy between mothers and children. As part of their motherhood duties, they are responsible for assisting with the academic performance of their children and are required to communicate with the school. Mostly lacking Chinese reading comprehension, Filipino mothers sign their children's communication logbooks without sufficiently understanding the content (for logbooks, see Chen 2011). Thus, Annabelle told her daughter that the girl had to look after herself for her schoolwork because Annabelle could not offer much help. The linguistic limitations also constrained Annabelle's ability to transmit Filipino culture in full to her daughter, who needed Annabelle's help to complete a specific school assignment on this topic. When asked about whether they were inclined to speak either Tagalog or Visaya to their children, Filipino interviewees shrugged off the speaking of 'mother tongue' and were sympathetic, saying that their children had a heavy workload. Most of all, they felt there was no *practical* advantage in learning Tagalog. Although it was for their children's benefit if they spoke good English, it was up to their children whether or not they would want to learn English from their mothers.

The Vietnamese: I wish to sing a Vietnamese nursery rhyme to my baby

In contrast to Filipino workers' English proficiency as advertised by placement agencies, Vietnamese workers are promoted for their proximity to Chinese culture.[3] In popular discourse, this is somewhat attributed to the higher level of Chinese proficiency. On the whole, Vietnamese interviewees were able to enter the linguistic borderland with a higher level of proficiency in the Chinese language soon after their arrival. Hồ Minh Mai's husband argued that this was out of necessity, as there was no other alternative for Vietnamese wives to bridge the gap. He also argued that Vietnamese women speaking Hoklo was an indication of their wider social contacts gained either from running a family business or engaging in employment outside the home, particularly if their in-laws are not Hoklo speakers (the author's interview, 26 May 2009, Tainan). Another contributing factor to their Chinese proficiency is their enrolment in Chinese-language courses in order to be eligible for naturalisation.

Thus, entering the linguistic borderland for instrumental or pragmatic reasons (employment and naturalisation) is common amongst Filipino and Vietnamese women. However, for Trần Thi Loan, Chinese-speaking was a source of empowerment that enabled her to explore her own cultural heritage, realise her community service, and fulfil her responsibilities of motherhood. Loan was from Can Tho, one of the five poor Mekong Delta provinces where there was a high rate of marriage with Taiwanese men (Hugo and Nguyen 2007: 373–374). She dropped out in the second year of primary school and remained nearly illiterate in the Vietnamese language. Loan's husband was a police officer. He encouraged Loan to go to school rather than finding a job, although Loan was pressed by her mother for remittances (see Bélanger et al. 2011 for Vietnamese women's remittance). For six years, Loan attended evening classes which were provided for illiterate Taiwanese senior citizens. She earned the primary school certificate and secondary school diploma. At the time of interview, Loan was a teaching assistant for a *qigong* (氣功)[4] class at a community centre. At the beginning of the interview, I invited Loan to write down the name of her hometown in Vietnamese, hoping that this could be an ice-breaker. It took her a while. She apologised: 'I haven't used Vietnamese language for a long time. I've almost forgotten how to write. *I've become Taiwanese*'. Surprised by her reply, I asked her why and she explained:

> Little by little I began to prefer Taiwan because in Taiwan I can continue to learn and make progress. You see, I came from a backward country, I lived in the countryside. There was nothing to learn over there. There was no substance in people's daily conversation. I want to learn more, I don't mind earning little money. *I want to be able to speak properly.*

I asked what she would do if her daughter's schoolwork was to introduce Vietnamese culture, the same question I posed to Annabelle in Pingtung. Loan explained:

> I didn't really understand our national culture when I was in Vietnam because I wasn't educated. I wouldn't know how to present the Vietnamese culture. […] It's really regrettable that I didn't go to school over there but

there's nothing I could do about it. [...] After I came to Taiwan, I started to learn Chinese. *After I was able to speak Chinese, I became more confident in myself and I decided I should educate myself for Vietnamese.* My Mandarin is getting better, so is my Vietnamese. I have also practised *qigong* for five years. In the past, my mother always asked me for money, which was a great pressure on me. I suffered serious depression. When she fell ill, I went back to look after her because I didn't have money to pay her medical bills. I applied *qigong* to her, hoping that she would recover faster and it worked well. After that, I also applied it to my relatives. My mother was very pleased and never asked me for money again. I want to help Taiwanese and my fellow countrymen with this skill.

(the author's interview, 22 May 2009, Kaohsiung, emphasis added)

Deprived of primary education when growing up in Vietnam, Loan considered herself ignorant of the 'national culture' of Vietnam, the 'higher culture' gained from education (Gellner 2002: 35–38). She did not see everyday practices as an equivalent to 'national culture'. However, the Chinese proficiency gained via supplementary education in Taiwan and, more importantly, the confidence gained from speaking Chinese, empowered her to reacquaint herself with Vietnamese culture and, assisted by her *qigong* skills, to reach out to the public. As for helping with her daughter's schoolwork, at the time of the interview she was buying children's books from Vietnam to read to her daughter.

However, for other Vietnamese interviewees, in the linguistic borderland that is underlined by their weaker position in relation to their in-laws, speaking Chinese came in tandem with the latter's forbidding them to speak Vietnamese. Imagining that their Vietnamese daughters-in-law would be under 'bad' influences, some in-laws prevented them from reading Vietnamese-language material. Therefore, the Taiwanese editors of a locally produced Vietnamese-language newspaper decided to create bilingual headlines (Vietnamese–Chinese) in their newspaper to reduce the fear of mothers-in-law that their Vietnamese daughters-in-law might be misled by the content of their newspapers (the author's interview with the editors, 22 April 2009, Taipei).

If zero tolerance for speaking Vietnamese satisfied their in-laws' interest in reducing communications unintelligible to them, then the in-laws' advantage in the linguistic borderland was achieved at the expense of diminishing mother–child intimacy. A young mother of a 7-year-old boy, Phạm Thi Phuong married a man who was the youngest son of a farming family in the mountainous area in central Taiwan. I showed her my Vietnamese–Chinese phrasebook given to me by a Vietnamese woman in Chinshan on the east coast. She seemed to enjoy teaching me to say a few simple words in Vietnamese and my ice-breaking device reminded her of the visits of social workers, who also used a phrasebook to communicate with her. So I asked how she felt about speaking Vietnamese to her son. She responded by citing an incident. She was trying to comfort her crying baby son and wanted to sing a nursery rhyme to calm him down. She did not know any in Chinese but she could not sing a Vietnamese rhyme, either, because her in-laws had discouraged her from speaking Vietnamese. She could only cradle her son in her arms without a soothing melody (the author's interview, 21 March 2009, Taichung).

How Vietnamese interviewees manoeuvred in the borderland was partly affected by how they saw their children in relation to Taiwan. There were mothers like divorcee Nguyễn Khanh Van, who thought that their children were entirely Taiwanese because they were born in Taiwan and were fathered by Taiwanese men. Therefore, it made little sense for them to learn Vietnamese, except for knowing how to exchange pleasantries with their Vietnamese relatives (the author's interview, 14 April 2009, Taipei). There were also mothers like Ngô Thi Cuc, who saw her daughter as half Taiwanese and half Vietnamese. Her confidence in their daughter's mixed heritage was supported by her husband. Suffering poverty indicated by the minimal furnishing of their rented house in a rural area, her husband suggested his wife retain her Vietnamese nationality, and hoped that their daughter 'would remember she *is* Vietnamese', regardless of whether they resided in Taiwan or in Vietnam (the author's interview, 9 April 2009, Taichung).

The Indonesian Chinese: The people who once learned Mandarin

After the Republican revolution in China in 1912, in Indonesia, speaking Mandarin, the national language of the newly established Republic of China (ROC), and reading Chinese were regarded as respecting the cultural inheritance and authenticating the subjective Chinese identity amongst the Overseas Chinese community. However, after using Chinese as a teaching medium at non-state schools was banned in the 1960s (Murray 1964; FitzGerald 1973; Godley 1989), proficiency in speaking Mandarin and reading Chinese were largely lost in Indonesia. It is a given fact and a defining feature of their hybrid Chinese-ness (Handoko 2009). Before retiring in her early 40s, Le Fen Fen was a successful electronics engineer, having completed her university education in the 1980s in Taiwan. She found that most of her Indonesian Chinese friends who studied in Taiwan started with a low level of Chinese proficiency. For the younger interviewees born in the 1970s and 1980s, the Chinese language has become distant from their daily lives. Eighty per cent of the interviewees (aged between 22 and 52) neither spoke nor read Chinese before they came to Taiwan.

Thus, with the language barrier, Mandarin-speaking Taiwan is foreign to Indonesian Chinese as much as it is to Filipino and Vietnamese women. In the eyes of the government, Indonesian Chinese are indeed as foreign as Filipino and Vietnamese migrants. This is in spite of the fact that anecdotal information suggests that the majority of Indonesian wives in Taiwan are ethnic Chinese. For example, commercial matchmakers advertise their services specifically for arranging marriages with Indonesian Chinese (*yinni huaren*, 印尼華人).[5] However, in the National Immigration Agency's publicity promoting multiculturalism in Taiwan,

Indonesian spouses are presented as a *pribumi* (native Indonesian).[6] Thus, like their Filipino and Vietnamese counterparts, Indonesian Chinese are also under pressure to acquire proficiency in Chinese.

However, the interviewees acted in the linguistic borderland with the cultural capital they had gained before migrating to Taiwan. Choi Sook Yin and Ng Siew Day were two older interviewees who embraced speaking Mandarin instead of treating it as a pressure (see Cheng 2014 for the Chinese identity of Indonesian Chinese women in Taiwan). In her late 60s, Sook Yin was enthusiastic to learn Chinese, hoping to reaffirm her Chinese identity, a sentiment shared by Luu Mai Lan, a Vietnamese Chinese who grew up in a Cantonese-speaking family in Ho Chi Minh City. Sook Yin spoke Mandarin before she migrated to Taiwan, but she could not read. When asked why she attended Chinese-language classes for eight years, she recalled her childhood memories:

> Because I couldn't read! In Indonesia there was a school well-known for teaching the Chinese language. Unfortunately it was closed down by the government, so I couldn't go. I wanted to learn Chinese so I asked around where I could go [in Taipei]. Now I know how to use the phonetics system and look things up in the dictionary. I speak Hakka to my husband at home. If we spoke Mandarin, I'd speak better.
>
> *(the author's interview, 19 May 2009, Taipei)*

For those younger interviewees, they could draw resources from speaking a dialect, such as Hokkien, Teochew, or Hakka, that is more or less mutually intelligible with the Hoklo and Hakka spoken in Taiwan. For example, Hokkien and Teochew speakers may be able to communicate with Hoklo speakers and Hakka speakers may find each other in linguistic proximity. This eased their manoeuvring in the linguistic borderland. Nevertheless, to fulfil their duties of motherhood, they were expected to speak Mandarin. Wong Poh Min is a case in point (the author's interview, 6 June 2009, Penghu). Born in Kalimantan in 1980 to Teochew and Hakka parents, Poh Min spoke both dialects in addition to Bahasa Indonesia and had a secondary-level education. The mutual intelligibility between Poh Min's Teochew and her mother-in-law's Hoklo allowed them to communicate. However, when Poh Min's first child started going to school, her mother-in-law asked her to go to school with her child so that she could help the child study. She completed the primary school curriculum within three years. With this linguistic ability, Poh Min supervised her children's homework and signed their school logbooks. Since the logbooks were for communication between parents and teachers, checking and signing the logbook was publicly demonstrating her ability to fulfil the motherhood duties. This created a sense of fulfilment.

When the linguistic borderland was situated outside of the private home, Poh Min was also under pressure to speak Mandarin. She recalled an incident: When she sat down in a restaurant, she was given a menu and she twice asked the waitress to tell her what was offered on the menu. Her request was met with a cold reception: 'If you are *illiterate*, go to school and learn the language!' The waitress's comment reflected a widely held presumption that having an inability in the Chinese language was equated with being illiterate and *uneducated*. At the time of the interview, Poh Min worked as a receptionist at a hotel that required reading comprehension. Without it, she could not escape manual jobs such as washing dishes and cleaning, nor could she make her way around, make use of public transport, or travel independently. Most of all, being able to express herself in Mandarin enabled Poh Min to be received as a person of civility and good manners, a sense of achievement widely shared by other interviewees.

Without the initial ease facilitated by dialect speaking, Susani Halim was one of those interviewees who spoke Indonesian only. Thus, her experiences in manoeuvring in the linguistic borderlands in the private and public domains were similar to her Vietnamese counterparts, but she drew resources from her Christian belief that stabilised her marriage and later enabled her to exercise her citizenship in community affairs (the author's interview, 22 March 2009, Keelung). At the beginning of her marriage, Susani's husband Chiang Yi-cheng was not convinced that she could handle the challenges as a non-Mandarin speaker, in spite of Susani's university education and work experience in Jakarta. To 'protect' Susani from being tricked by unsavoury elements, he did not allow her to leave home on her own. Without a job, Susani became a homebound full-time mother. Susani did go out, though, to attend a Chinese-language course and with growing proficiency in Chinese she could better comprehend church services. Honouring his promise to Susani's Christian father, Yi-cheng went to a church with Susani, but they were under self-imposed segregation because of their low confidence. Their pastor acknowledged that it was also caused by exclusion, as local worshippers were reluctant to mingle with them. When their marriage deteriorated, Susani's father paid a visit from Jakarta and asked their pastor to give them counselling. Not until Susani suggested letting their only son play outside of the flat was she permitted to spend an hour every afternoon in the communal courtyard. There she met mothers from Thailand and Indonesia whom she gradually invited to their flat for language tuition delivered by the pastor. Described by themselves and by the pastor as 'coming out', opening their home to other migrant mothers transformed their marriage counselling into a platform for community participation.

Encouraged and assisted by the pastor, a community centre staffed by Susani was established and affiliated with the church. Receiving public funding, it assists migrant women and their mixed families. Susani later received professional training and became a government-contracted interpreter. Susani's voluntary civic participation extends her private motherly duty performed for her own family to other transnational families. As it did for other Vietnamese interviewees Hoàng Minh Suong, Ngô Xuân Phuong, Trinh Minh Ha, Hồ Minh Mai, Ly Van Trang, and Tiêu Nguyệt Ha (interviews, 2009–2019, Chinshan, Touliu, Pingtung, Tainan, Chiayi, Taipei), who were also interpreters for the government, her language ability broadened Susani's social contacts and connected her with law enforcement agencies, the local government, magistrates' courts, and high courts. This gives Susani (and those Vietnamese interviewees) a perspective as an interface between her fellow migrants and the host society. They transformed their home-bound caring duty into a motherhood-orientated exercise of citizenship (Lister 2002: 197).

Nevertheless, accent is an undercurrent that complicates migrant women's manoeuvring in the linguistic borderland (e.g. Park 2020). A case in point is Kalimantan-born Hoh Foong Lian (the author's interview, 29 January 2009, Pingtung). Born in 1971, Foong Lian attended a state school without access to a Chinese-language education. Foong Lian spoke Hakka at home and Indonesian outside of home. After finishing high school, she came to Taiwan as a factory worker in northern Taiwan where she learnt to speak Mandarin. After getting married and moving to southern Taiwan, she learnt to speak Hoklo because her parents-in-law did not speak Mandarin. Having no accent makes her well blended into the local community. This is in contrast to Susani's experience. Because of her Mandarin accent, at her service centre, inquirers often turned to her local friends for information until they were told that Susani was in charge of the centre. Susani used this recurring issue as a way to argue that their 'funny' accent allowed the locals to draw another line to separate migrant women from the mainstream society, a critique that was widely shared by Vietnamese interviewees.

Conclusion

This research was inspired by a unique interview with an Indonesian Chinese woman in Penghu. Introduced to me by her matchmaker, she was in her late 30s and came to meet me during her lunch break after finishing her dishwashing job at a restaurant. Tired, slow, and responding minimally to any questions, she sent an unspoken message that this interview in Mandarin was not something that she was willing or prepared to take part in. Realising that it was difficult to carry on given her reservation, I decided to ask her to teach me how to say a few words in Indonesian. My request seemed to change her from being a shy and quiet woman to someone who was cheerful and enjoyed the moment when she was emancipated from the restrictive Mandarin to freely express herself in her own language. In other words, spoken to by an academic researcher in the hegemonic Mandarin, she became a *muted* stranger to herself. Had I ended my interview without learning the Indonesian language from her, I would have concluded that she had a low level of linguistic integration and that she was alienated from her environment. I would have missed the opportunity to see how she was relaxed by her own language. In relation to me, she performed two contrasting self-identities in two languages.

Dedicated to this vivid performance of identity, my proposition of the linguistic borderland is to conceptualise how self-identity performed in different languages is role-contingent and context-dependent, a similar experience that is shared by the Filipino, Vietnamese, and Indonesian Chinese women discussed in this chapter. As shown in this chapter, migrant women's use of language has to be understood in fluid situations and contexts contingent on the roles played by them. The *relational* linguistic borderland emerged from their everyday encounters with families, neighbours, employers, colleagues, and strangers. Cultural fusion between the migrant women and their families did not take place before their marriage. It was the migrant women, the weaker party in the linguistic borderland, rather than their in-laws, that were required to enter the borderland where cultural fusion might take root.

As shown in the findings, migrant women drew from their cultural capital, such as speaking English or a Chinese dialect, to create the room for them to manoeuvre in the borderland. For the Filipino women, this was speaking English, which upheld their self-esteem, was convenient for communicating with their husbands and enabled their exercise of citizenship, an indication of their political integration. Nevertheless, in spite of being the preferred foreign language that is associated with Western culture, transnational mobility, and job competitiveness, English did not give them the advantage enjoyed by migrant workers in their relationships with in-laws and children. In the private domain, they needed Chinese proficiency to fulfil their motherhood duties.

Compared to their Filipino and Indonesian Chinese counterparts, Vietnamese interviewees had no prior cultural capital to assist their manoeuvres in the linguistic borderland. It is obvious that the expectation of speaking Chinese could be met but at the expense of depriving a mother of her intimacy with her child. On the other hand, Chinese proficiency, including speaking Mandarin, Hoklo, or Hakka, was correlated with their employment outside of the home. Speaking Chinese can be a critical resource leading to community service and exercise of citizenship, a route that was also identical with that of Indonesian Chinese interviewees.

For the Indonesian Chinese interviewees, although they were noted by matchmakers as ethnic Chinese, their Chinese-ness has been overlooked by the government. Thus, their experiences in the linguistic borderland inside and outside of the home are mostly similar to those of their Filipino and Vietnamese counterparts, including the exclusion caused by accents. Nevertheless, for those who retained Mandarin or a dialect, there was greater room for manoeuvre in the borderland, which could reduce the initial difficulty of communication.

To conclude, the concept of the 'linguistic borderland' is applied by this chapter in order to underline migrant women's fluid identity, and the agency derived from their roles in relation to the people in their social surroundings. Their use of language is essential to this relational and fluid identity shifting between being an L1 and L2 speaker. Their shifting between the languages is their entry to, or retreat from, the linguistic borderland that is found in their private home, at their children's school, or in their community centre. This linguistic borderland is also found in their relationship with their husbands, in-laws, children, children's teachers, customers, clients, as well as when they were reading English-language newspapers or reading children's books in the Vietnamese language. In the linguistic borderland, they encountered the pressure of conforming to the sameness and assimilating into Taiwanese identity is the interest held by Taiwanese husbands, in-laws, and the state. In response, as L1 or L2 speakers, they were empowered or discriminated when they acted as a mother, wife, daughter-in-law, worker, or citizen. Thus, instead of seeing their identity construction as a result of the trade-off between two (or more) languages, this chapter foregrounded what they did with their languages and demonstrated how their contextual identity interacted with the hegemonic pressure of assimilation.

In contemporary Taiwanese society, multiculturalism as a concept for respect for diversity in relation to marriage-migrant women is mostly visualised as an event where women catwalk their colourful costume or cook their foreign cuisine. Unsatisfied with this gaze upon migrant women for their exoticness, this chapter aligned itself with the endeavours of theorising 'everyday multiculturalism' (Wise and Velayutham 2009). The findings presented in this chapter may deepen our understanding of cultural encounters and the performance of identity in the everyday, or even mundane, setting in a linguistic context. As a relational concept that takes into account administrative and geographical connotations, the linguistic borderland and its application to the study of identity may have the potential to reach a balance between the postmodernist's inclination to deterritorialise personal identity and the traditionalist's stress on structural constraints set by the nation-state (Wilson and Donnan 1998: 1–2).

Notes

1 See advertisement under the heading 'travel cost' at http://loveugroup.org/profile-costs .php (visited on 5 April 2020).
2 See advertisement about Filipino workers at mingfa.tw/kde/Website/b10/07.html (visited on 5 April 2020).
3 See advertisement about Vietnamese workers at mingfa.tw/kde/Website/b10/07.html (visited on 5 April 2020).
4 Rooted in Chinese philosophy and medicine, *qigong* is a physical and mental training that coordinates body-posture and movement, breathing, and meditation that is believed to improve practitioners' physical and mental health.
5 See advertisement at vnbetw.com, ntl-marry.com/c05.shtml and loveugroup.org/products.php?cid=8. (visited on 5 April 2020).
6 See the image at immigration.gov.tw/5385/7344/70395/1432 (visited on 5 April 2020).

References

English references

Anzaldúa, G. (1987) *Borderlands/la frontera*, Vol. 3. San Francisco: Aunt Lute Books.
Barwiński, M. (2017) 'Borderland of nations, religions and cultures – The case of Podlasie', *European Spatial Research and Policy*, 24(2): 111–125.
Bélanger, D. (2007) 'The house and the classroom: Vietnamese immigrant spouses in South Korea and Taiwan', *Population and Society*, 3(1): 39–59.
Bélanger, D., Lee, H.K. and Wang, H.Z. (2010). 'Ethnic diversity and statistics in East Asia: "Foreign brides" surveys in Taiwan and South Korea', *Ethnic and Racial Studies*, 33(6): 1108–1130.

Bélanger, D., Linh, T.G. and Duong, L.B. (2011) 'Marriage migrants as emigrants: Remittances of marriage migrant women from Vietnam to their natal families', *Asian Population Studies*, 7(2): 89–105.

Brunet-Jailly, E. (2010) 'The state of borders and borderlands studies 2009: A historical view and a view from the Journal of Borderlands Studies', *Eurasia Border Review*, 1(1): 1–15.

Chen, E.C. (2011) 'Taiwanese-Vietnamese transnational marriage families in Taiwan: Perspectives from Vietnamese immigrant mothers and Taiwanese teachers'. Doctoral dissertation, University of Illinois at Urbana-Champaign.

Cheng, I. (2013) 'Making foreign women the mother of our nation: The excluding and assimilating immigrant wives from outside', *Asian Ethnicity*, 14(2): 157–179.

Cheng, I. (2014) 'Home-going or home-making? The citizenship legislation and Chinese identity of Indonesian Chinese women in Taiwan', in Kuei-fen Chiu, Dafydd Fell and Ping Lin (eds.) *Migration to and from Taiwan*. Abingdon: Routledge, pp. 135–159.

Cheng, I. (2017) 'Report: Invisible partner: The immobile husbands in the cross-border marriage', *Monumenta Taiwanica* 16: 109–112.

Cheng, I., Momesso, L. and Fell, D. (2018) 'Asset or liability: Transnational links and political participation of foreign-born citizens in Taiwan?', *International Migration*, 57(4): 202–217.

Chin, J. and Yu, S. (2009) 'School adjustment among children of immigrant mothers in Taiwan', *Social Behavior and Personality*, 36(8): 1141–1150.

Del Rosario, T.C. (2005) 'Bridal diaspora: Migration and marriage among Filipino women', *Indian Journal of Gender Studies*, 12(2–3): 253–273.

Dowling, J.A., Ellison, C.G. and Leal, D.L. (2012) 'Who doesn't value English? Debunking myths about Mexican immigrants' attitudes toward the English language', *Social Science Quarterly*, 93(2): 356–378.

Dumitru, S. (2014) 'From "brain drain" to "care drain": Women's labor migration and methodological sexism', *Women's Studies International Forum*, 47: 203–212.

Dunlop, C.T. (2013) 'Mapping a new kind of European boundary: The language border between modern France and Germany', *Imago Mundi*, 65(2): 253–267.

FitzGerald, C.P. (1973) *China and Southeast Asia Since 1945*. London: Longman Group Ltd.

Gellner, Ernest (2002) *Nations and Nationalism*. Oxford: Blackwell.

Godley, Michael R. (1989) 'The sojourners: Returned Overseas Chinese in the People's Republic of China', *Pacific Affairs*, 62(3): 330–352.

Han, H. (2011) 'Social inclusion through multilingual ideologies, policies and practices: A case study of a minority church', *International Journal of Bilingual Education and Bilingualism*, 14(4): 383–398.

Handoko, F. (2009) 'Education, language use and shifting identities among ethnic Chinese in Indonesia', *Chinese Southern Diaspora Studies*, 3: 183–192.

Hsia, H.C. (2006) 'Empowering "foreign brides" and community through praxis-oriented research', *Societies Without Borders*, 1(1): 89–108.

Hsia, H.C. (2007) 'Imaged and imagined threat to the nation: The media construction of the 'foreign brides' phenomenon' as social problems in Taiwan', *Inter-Asia Cultural Studies*, 8(1): 55–85.

Hsia, H.C. (2009) 'Foreign brides, multiple citizenship and the immigrant movement in Taiwan', *Asian and Pacific Migration Journal*, 18(1): 17–46.

Hsia, H.C. (2019) 'A political and economic analysis of the shifting gaze on the children of Southeast Asian marriage migrants in Taiwan'. Paper presented at the Conference on Marriage Migration, Family and Citizenship in Asia at the National University of Singapore, Singapore, 31 January–1 February 2019.

Hsiao, Y.-J. (2009) 'A study of childrearing, school strategies, and government policies that affect preschool children of immigrant mothers in southern Taiwan'. Doctoral dissertation, Spalding University.

Huang, S.S. and Yang, H.J. (2018) 'Is there a healthy immigrant effect among women through transnational marriage? Results from immigrant women from Southeast Asian countries in Taiwan', *Journal of Immigrant and Minority Health*, 20(1): 178–187.

Hugo, G. and Nguyen, T.H.X. (2007) 'Marriage migration between Vietnam and Taiwan: A view from Vietnam', in I. Attane and C.Z. Guilmoto (eds.) *Watering the Neighbour's Garden: The Growing Demographic Female Deficit in Asia*. Paris: Committee for International Cooperation in National Research in Demography (CIRED), pp. 365–392.

Keng, K.-Y. (2016) 'School performance of second generation Southeast Asian Taiwanese stigmatised and undiscovered potentials in globalisation'. Doctoral dissertation, University of Hawaii.

Lan, P.C. (2003) '"They have more money but I speak better English!" Transnational encounters between Filipina domestics and Taiwanese employers', *Identities: Global Studies in Culture and Power*, 10(2): 133–161.

Lan, P.C. (2011) 'White privilege, language capital and cultural ghettoisation: Western high-skilled migrants in Taiwan', *Journal of Ethnic and Migration Studies*, 37(10): 1669–1693.

Lan, P.C. (2019) 'From reproductive assimilation to neoliberal multiculturalism: Framing and regulating immigrant mothers and children in Taiwan', *Journal of Intercultural Studies*, 40(3): 318–333.

Liao, P.-C. and Wang, Y.-H. (2013) 'Growing up in Taiwan: Cultural adjustment and challenges for children of foreign brides', *Journal of Diversity Management*, 8(1): 15–22.

Lin, L.-H. and Hung, C.H. (2007) 'Vietnamese women immigrants' life adaptation, social support, and depression', *The Journal of Nursing Research*, 15(4): 243–254.

Lister, Rush (2002) 'Sexual citizenship', in Engin F. Isin and Bryan S. Turner (eds.) *Handbook of Citizenship Studies*. London: Sage Publications, pp. 191–207.

Mika, Okushima 奥島美夏 (2008) 序説 インドネシア・ベトナム女性の海外進出と華人文化圏における位置づけ (Introduction: Increasing numbers of Indonesian and Vietnamese women in East Asia and their status in Chinese society) (in Japanese). 異文化コミュニケーション研究 20: 21–42.

Murray, Douglas P. (1964) 'Chinese education in Southeast Asia', *The China Quarterly*, 20: 67–95.

Park, M.Y. (2017) 'Resisting linguistic and ethnic marginalization: Voices of Southeast Asian marriage-migrant women in Korea', *Language and Intercultural Communication*, 17(2): 118–134.

Park, M.Y. (2020) '"I want to learn Seoul speech!": Language ideologies and practices among rural marriage-migrants in South Korea', *International Journal of Bilingual Education and Bilingualism*, 23(2): 227–240.

Pastor, A.M.R. (2011) 'Crossing language and identity as a critical border ethnographer in Southern California', *Journal of Language, Identity & Education*, 10(3): 186–205.

Philippine Daily Inquirer (2009) 'Filipina for Filipinas in Taiwan', 24 February, retrieved 5 April 2020 from https://www.coolloud.org.tw/node/36022.

Piller, I. and Takahashi, K. (2011) 'Linguistic diversity and social inclusion', *International Journal of Bilingual Education and Bilingualism*, 14(4): 371–381.

Tseng, H.-H. (2015) 'Gender and power dynamics in transnational marriage brokerage: The ban on commercial matchmaking in Taiwan reconsidered', *Cross-Currents: East Asian History and Culture Review*, 4(2): 519–545.

Wang, H.Z. (2007) 'Hidden spaces of resistance of the subordinated: Case studies from Vietnamese female migrant partners in Taiwan', *International Migration Review*, 41(3): 706–727.

Wang, H.-Z. and Chang, S.-M. (2002) 'The commodification of international marriages: Cross-border marriage business in Taiwan and Vietnam', *International Migration*, 40(6): 93–116.

Williams, L. and Yu, M.K. (2006) 'Domestic violence in cross-border marriage. A case study from Taiwan', *International Journal of Migration, Health and Social Care*, 2(3/4): 58–69.

Wilson, T.M., & Donnan, H. (eds.) (1998) *Border Identities: Nation and State at International Frontiers*. Cambridge: Cambridge University Press.

Wimmer, A. and Glick-Schiller, N. (2002) 'Methodological nationalism and beyond: Nation-state building, migration and the social sciences', *Global Networks*, 2(4): 301–334.

Wise, A. and Velayutham, S. (eds) (2009) *Everyday Multiculturalism*. Basingstoke: Palgrave Macmillan.

Yang, W.S. and Lu, M.C.W. (eds.) (2010) *Asian Cross-Border Marriage Migration: Demographic Patterns and Social Issues*, Vol. 2. Amsterdam: Amsterdam University Press.

Yang, Y.M. and Wang, H.H. (2011) 'Cross-cultural comparisons of health-related quality of life between Taiwanese women and transnational marriage Vietnamese women in Taiwan', *Journal of Nursing Research*, 19(1): 44–52.

Yang, Y.M., Wang, H.H., Lee, F.H., Lin, M.L. and Lin, P.C. (2015) 'Health empowerment among immigrant women in transnational marriages in Taiwan', *Journal of Nursing Scholarship*, 47(2): 135–142.

Chinese references

Chen Chih-jou Jay 陳志柔 and Yu, Te-lin 于德林 (2005) 台灣民眾對外來配偶移民政策的態度 (Public attitudes towards Taiwan's immigration policies), 台灣社會學 (*Taiwanese Sociology*), 10: 95–148.

NIA (National Immigration Agency) (2020a) 外籍配偶人數與大陸(含港澳)配偶人數按證件分 (Numbers of foreign and mainland (including Hong Kong and Macao) spouses by legal status), retrieved 4 April 2020 from https://www.immigration.gov.tw/5382/5385/7344/7350/8887/?alias=settledown.

NIA (2020b) 新住民打造多元文化社會 (New immigrants building a multicultural society), retrieved 4 April 2020 from https://www.immigration.gov.tw/5385/7344/70395/143257/.

INDEX